S0-BSM-144

CISTERCIAN STUDIES SERIES: NUMBER ONE HUNDRED ELEVEN

Bede the Venerable

HOMILIES ON THE GOSPELS

Book Two

CISTERCIAN STUDIES SERIES: NUMBER ONE HUNDRED ELEVEN

Bede the Venerable

HOMILIES ON THE GOSPELS

Book Two
Lent to The Dedication of the Church

Translated by
Lawrence T. Martin
and
David Hurst OSB

Cistercian Publications
Kalamazoo, Michigan
1991

© Translation copyrighted, Cistercian Publications 1991.

A translation made from the critical edition of Dom David Hurst OSB, *Bedae Homiliae evangelii.* Corpus Christianorum, 122. Turnhout: Brepols, 1955.

The work of Cistercian Publications is made possible in part by support from Western Michigan University to the Institute of Cistercian Studies.

Available in Britain and Europe from
Cassell / Mowbray
Villiers House   41 / 47 Strand
London WC2N 5JE

Available elsewhere from the publisher
Cistercian Publicatons (Distribution)
Saint Joseph's Abbey
Spencer, Massachusetts 01562

Library of Congress Cataloguing in Publication Data

Bede, the Venerable, Saint, 673-735
    [Homiliae evangelii. English]
    Homilies on the Gospels / Bede the Venerable: translated by Lawrence T. Martin and David Hurst
    p. cm. — (Cistercian studies series: no. 110)
    Translations of: Bedae homiliae evangelii.
    Contents: bk. 1. Advent to Lent — bk. 2. Lent to the Dedication of the Church.
    ISBN 0-87907-610-0 (bk. 1). — ISBN 0-87907-710-7 (bk. 1 pbk.).
    ISBN 0-87907-711-5 (bk. 2). — ISBN 0-87907-911-8 (bk. 2 pbk.).
    1. Bible. N.T. Gospels—Sermons. 2. Church year sermons—Early works to 1800. 3 Occasional sermons—Early works to 1800. 4 Sermons, English—Translations from Latin—Early works to 1800. 5 Sermons, Latin—Translation into English—Early works to 1800. I. Martin, Lawrence T., 1942- . II. Hurst, David, OSB. III. Title. IV. Series. BX1756.B37H66 1990
252'.6—dc90   89-39171
                                                   CIP

Typography by Ideas In Graphics, Grand Rapids, MI
Printed in the United States of America.

The editors of Cistercian Publications express their deep appreciation to John Leinenweber, Hermitage of the Dayspring, Kent, Connecticut, and to Professor Gerald Bonner, Emeritus Reader in Theology at the University of Durham, for their help in preparing the manuscript for publication.

❧

The author expresses his appreciation to Sonia Dial for her great help in typing the manuscript and creating the indices.

❧

The preparation of this volume was made possible in part by a grant from the Division of Research Programs of the National Endowment for the Humanities, an independent federal agency.

contents

aBBReViatioNs

EDITIONS CITED

CC   *Corpus Christianorum*

CSEL   *Corpus Scriptorum Ecclesiasticorum Latinorum*

Glare   P. G. W. Glare, ed., *Oxford Latin Dictionary*

GCS   *Die Griechischen Christlichen Schriftsteller der ersten Jahrhunderte*

HBS   *Henry Bradshaw Society for Editing Rare Liturgical Texts*

LXX   The Septuagint

Niermeyer   J. F. Niermeyer, *Mediae Latinitatis Lexicon Minus*

PG   *Patrologiae cursus completus,* Series graeca

PL   *Patrologiae cursus completus,* Series latina

RED   *Rerum ecclesiarum documenta*

TU	*Texte und Untersuchungen zur Geschichte der altchristlichen Literatur*
Vet. Lat.	The Old Latin translation of the Scriptures
Vulg.	The Vulgate

Scriptural citations have been given according to the enumeration and nomenclature of *The Jerusalem Bible*. Psalm citations are given by Hebrew enumeration with Vulgate enumeration in parentheses.

AUTHORS AND WORKS CITED

Adamnan.	Adamnanus, Priest of Iona (d. 704)
De loc. sanc.	*On the Holy Places*
Ambr.	Ambrose, Bishop of Milan (340–397)
Expos. evang. sec. Luc.	*Commentary on the Gospel according to Luke*
Aug.	Augustine, Bishop of Hippo (354–430)
Ad Gal.	*Commentary on the Epistle to the Galatians*
Contra Faust.	*Against Faustus*
Contra Iul.	*Against Julian*
Contra litt. Pet.	*Answer to Petilian*
De agone christ.	*The Christian Combat*
De civ. Dei	*The City of God*

De cons. evang.	*Harmony on the Gospels*
De corrept. et gratia	*On Rebuke and Grace*
De divers. quaest.	*On Eighty-three Different Questions*
De Gen. ad litt.	*Literal Commentary on Genesis*
De Gen. contra Manich.	*Genesis against the Manichaeans*
De nupt. et concup.	*On Marriage and Concupiscence*
De trin.	*On the Trinity*
Ennar. in Ps.	*Commentary on the Psalms*
Ep.	*Letters*
Quaest. ad Simpl.	*Various Questions for Simplicianus*
Retract.	*Retractations*
Serm.	*Sermons* (followed by "Morin" = those additional sermons of Augustine edited by G. Morin in *Miscellanea Agostiniana*)
Serm. dom. in monte	*On our Lord's Sermon on the Mount*
Tract. in Ioh.	*Commentary on the Gospel according to John*

Bede	Bede the Venerable (673–735)
De loc. sanc.	*On the Holy Places*
De tempor.	*On times*
De temp. rat.	*On the System of Time*
Ex. Act. Ap.	*Exposition on the Acts of the Apostles*
HA	*History of the Abbots*
Hom.	*Homilies on the Gospels*
In epist. vii cath.	*Commentary on the Catholic Epistles*
In Luc.	*Commentary on the Gospel according to Luke*
In Marc.	*Commentary on the Gospel according to Mark*
Bened.	Benedict, abbot of Monte Cassino (480–544)
Reg.	*Rule for Monks*
Cyprian	Cyprian, Bishop of Carthage (d. 258)
De unitate	*The Unity of the Catholic Church*
Eusebius/Rufinus	Eusebius, Bishop of Caesarea (264–340)
Hist. eccl.	*Church History* (in the Latin translation of Rufinus of Aquileia [345–410])

Greg.	Gregory the Great, Bishop of Rome (540–604)
Dial.	*Dialogues*
Hom. de nat.	*Homily on Christmas*
Hom. in evang.	*Homilies on the Gospels*
Hom. in Ezech.	*Homilies on Ezechiel*
Moral.	*Morals, Commentary on Job*
Gregory of Nyssa	Gregory, Bishop of Nyssa (d. 394)
De vita Moysis	*The Life of Moses*
Horace	Quintus Horatius Flaccus (BC 65–8)
Ep.	*Letters*
Isid.	Isidore, Bishop of Seville (c. 560–636)
Etymol.	*Etymologies*
Jer.	Jerome, monk (340–420)
Adv. Helv.	*Against Helvidius*
Adv. Iov.	*Against Jovinian*
De vir. ill.	*On Famous Men*
Ep.	*Letters*
Hom. de nat.	*Homily on Christmas*
In Dan.	*Commentary on Daniel*
In Ezech.	*Commentary on Ezechiel*

In Matth.	*Commentary on the Gospel according to Matthew*
Nom.	*Interpretation of Hebrew Names*
Quaest. Hebr.	*Hebrew Questions*
Sit.	*Book of Places*
Joseph.	Flavius Josephus, Jewish historian (c. 38-c. 100)
Ant. Iud.	*Antiquities of the Jews*
Leo	Leo the Great, Bishop of Rome (d. 461)
Serm.	*Sermons*
Pliny	Pliny the Elder (AD 23-79)
Nat. hist.	*Natural History*
Quoduultdeus	Quodvultdeus, Bishop of Carthage (d. c. 453)
Sermo de symbolo	*Sermon on the Creed*

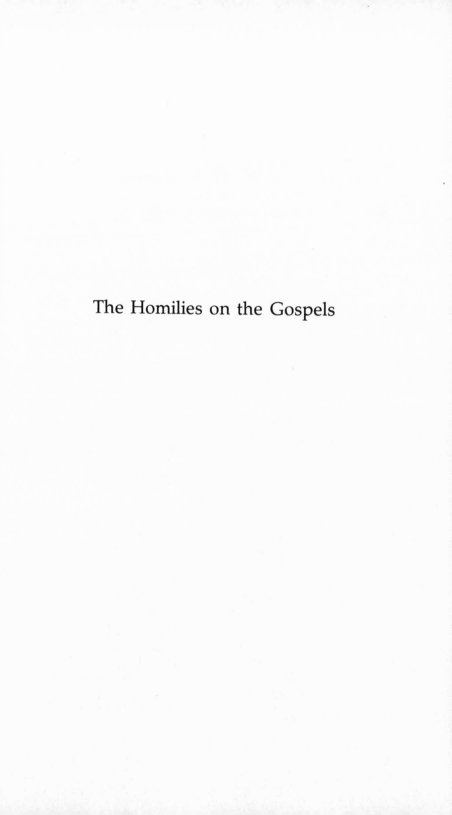

The Homilies on the Gospels

scriptural homily texts

Matthew 14:1–12	Homily II.23
Matthew 20:20–23	Homily II.21
Matthew 21:1–9	Homily II.3
Matthew 28:1–10	Homily II.7
Matthew 28:16–20	Homily II.8
Mark 7:31–37	Homily II.6
Luke 1:5–17	Homily II.19
Luke 1:57–68	Homily II.20
Luke 6:43–48	Homily II.25
Luke 11:9–13	Homily II.14
Luke 24:1–9	Homily II.10
Luke 24:36–47	Homily II.9
Luke 24:44–53	Homily II.15
John 2:12–22	Homily II.1
John 3:1–16	Homily II.18
John 6:1–4	Homily II.2
John 10:22–30	Homily II.24
John 11:55–12:11	Homily II.4
John 13:1–17	Homily II.5
John 14:15–21	Homily II.17
John 15:26–16:4	Homily II.16
John 16:5–15	Homily II.11
John 16:16–22	Homily II.13
John 16:23–30	Homily II.12
John 21:15–19	Homily II.22

homily II.1

John 2:12–22   *In Lent*

I t tends to disturb some people that in the opening portion of this gospel reading it is said that when our Lord
went down to Capernaum, not only his mother and his
disciples followed him, but also his brothers. There have
been heretics who supposed that Joseph, the husband of
the blessed virgin Mary, begot of another wife those whom
the scriptures call the Lord's brothers. Others, with greater
lack of faith, have supposed that he begot these of Mary
herself after our Lord's birth. But we, dearly beloved
brothers, without any hesitation or questioning must be
aware and confess that not only the blessed Mother of God,
but also Joseph, the most blessed witness and guardian of
her chastity, always remained wholly aloof from the con-
jugal act; and further, that those who after the customary
manner of the scriptures are called our Savior's brothers
or sisters were not their children but their relatives.
Abraham spoke to Lot in the following way, *'I beseech you,
let there be no wrangling between you and me, and your shepherds and mine; for we are brothers'.*[1] Laban [said] to Jacob,
'Because you are my brother, why should you have to serve me

1. Gn 13:8

1

for nothing'.[2] It is a fact that Lot was the son of Haran, Abraham's brother,[3] and Jacob the son of Rebekah, Laban's sister;[4] but on account of their kinship they were called brothers. Because of this most common practice in the holy scriptures, we should, as I have said, understand that the relatives of Mary and Joseph are called our Lord's brothers.[5]

As to the fact that it was when the Passover was at hand that Jesus was going up to Jerusalem, this provides us with an example of the vigilance of mind with which we ought to be subject to the Lord's injunctions. He, when he appeared as a weak human being, kept the same decrees which he established by the authority of his divinity. Lest his servants should suppose that they could avoid scourges or receive rewards without [offering] numerous sacrifices of their prayers and good deeds, even he, the Son of God, went up with his servants to worship and offer sacrifices.

But let us see what he found them doing there when he arrived at Jerusalem, and what he himself did in the same place: *And he found in the temple those who were selling sheep and oxen and doves, and money-changers sitting there. And when he had made a kind of whip out of cords, he drove them all out of the temple, the sheep also and the oxen; and he scattered the money, and overturned the tables of the money-changers.* Oxen and sheep and doves were being purchased for this purpose, that they might be offered in the temple; the money-changers were sitting at their tables for this purpose, that between the buyers and sellers of the sacrificial offerings there might be a ready exchange of money. It seems, then, that since these things were being bought for the purpose of offering them to the Lord in the temple, they were being lawfully sold in the temple. But our Lord was unwilling that anything having to do with earthly trade be practiced in his house, not even what might be considered acceptable. He scattered the fraudulent traders, and drove them all out, together with the things that had to do with the carrying on of trade:[6]

2. Gn 29:15   3. Gn 11:26, 31   4. Gn 25: 20, 26
5. Aug., *Tract. in Ioh.* 10, 2 (*CC* 36:101, 18/27); Bede, *Hom.* I.5 (*CC* 122:35, 106/15); Jer., *Adv. Helv.* 14, 19 (*PL* 23:197/98, 203).
6. Aug., *Tract. in Ioh.* 10, 4 (*CC* 36: 102, 14/25)

What, my brothers, do you suppose our Lord would do if he should discover people involved in disputes, wasting time gossiping, indulging in unrestrained laughter, or engaged in any other sort of wicked actions, since, when he saw persons in the temple buying the sacrificial offerings which were to be made to him, he was prompt in getting rid of them? I have said this with reference to those who enter a church, and not only disregard their intention to pray, but also increase the things for which they should have been praying [for forgiveness]; moreover, they convict themselves of this kind of foolish behavior by wrangling and [acts of] hatred, and even by disparaging others. They pile sins upon sins, weaving, as it were, a very long rope by their heedless addition. They are not afraid of being condemned for this at the examination of the strict Judge.

We read in the holy gospels that our Lord twice cast out traders of this sort when he found them in the temple: now, that is in the third year before his passion (as we recognize from the writings of this evangelist which follow); and in the year that he suffered, when, five days before the Passover, he came to Jerusalem seated upon a donkey.[7] But everyone of good sense understands that he does this same thing in the temple of holy Church by the examination [made at the time of] his daily visitation. These things should cause [us] great perturbation, beloved; we should dread them exceedingly with well-deserved fear, and carefully avoid them with painstaking diligence, lest he come unexpectedly and find something evil in us, as a result of which we should rightly be scourged and cast out of the Church.[8] This we should observe most of all in that place which is specially called *'a house of prayer,'*[9] lest we do anything unsuitable there, and hear with the Corinthians from the Apostle, *Do you not have houses* for doing or speaking about temporal matters, *or do you despise the Church of God?*[10] And lest with the Jews we hear from the prophet, *My beloved has committed many evil deeds in my house.*[11]

---

7. Mt 21:12-13; Mk 11:15-17; Lk 19:45-46
8. Jer., *In Matth.* 21, 15 (CC 77:188, 1350/56)
9. Mt 21:13; Is 56:7   10. 1 Co 11:22   11. Jr 11:15

We should rejoice that we have become the temple of God by our baptism, according to the testimony of the Apostle, *For the temple of God, which you are, is holy.*[12] [And we should rejoice] that we are the city of the great king, of which is sung, *Its foundations are on the holy mountains*[13]: the foundations of the Church are on the solid ground of the faith of the apostles and prophets. But it should cause us no less trembling that the Apostle said, *If anyone dishonors the temple of God, God will blot him out;*[14] and the righteous Judge himself said, *I will blot out from the city of the Lord all who work iniquity.*[15]

We should rejoice that the solemnity of the Passover is being celebrated in us when we attempt to pass from vices to virtues. The word Passover[16] means passing over.[17] We should rejoice that the Lord deigns to visit our hearts, namely his city, and that he deigns to illumine this Passover of our good actions by his benevolent presence; but we should have plenty of fear of his finding us doing something in his city other than what he himself loves, and revealing himself to us as a very strict requiter, which we will not love; [we should fear] that he may discover us to be money-changers in his temple, and sellers of oxen, sheep and doves, and so condemn us.

Oxen represent teaching about heavenly life, sheep the works of undefiled piety, and doves the gifts of the Holy Spirit. It is with the help of oxen that we usually plow a field: the field is the [human] heart, carefully cultivated by the Lord's heavenly teaching and properly prepared to receive the seeds of the word of God. Innocent sheep furnish their fleece for the clothing of human beings. The Spirit descended upon our Lord in the appearance of a dove.[18] But those persons sell oxen who impart the word of the gospel to their hearers, not out of divine love, but with a view to earthly gain: the Apostle censures such as these [by

---

12. 1 Co 3:17   13. Ps 87:1 (86:1)   14. 1 Co 3:17

15. Ps 101:8 (100:8)   16. *pascha*

17. Aug. *Tract. in Ioh.* 55, 1 (CC 36: 463, 11/12); Bede, *Hom.* II.5 (CC 122: 214, 7/16)

18. Lk 3:22

saying] that *they proclaim Christ not sincerely.*[19] They sell sheep
who carry out the works of piety for the sake of human
praise: of them our Lord says that *'they have received their
reward'.*[20] They sell doves who give the grace of the Spirit
they have received not without recompense, as has been
commanded,[21] but for pay; who bestow the imposition of
hands by which the Spirit is received, albeit not for mone-
tary gain but [to gain] the favor of the public, who confer
sacred orders, not on the merit of the [ordinand's life] but
as a personal favor.[22] They change money in the temple who
perform their service in the Church not pretending that they
are doing it for heavenly reasons but clearly for earthly pur-
poses, seeking their own [advantage] and not that of Jesus
Christ.[23]

Our Lord shows what reward awaits hypocritical workers
of this sort when he made a scourge of cords and drove them
all out of the temple. They are cast out as sharers of the
inheritance of the saints[24] if, after they are chosen to be
among the saints, they either perform good acts deceitfully
or evil acts openly. He also drives out the sheep and oxen
when he shows both the life and teaching of such persons
deserves condemnation. The cords with which he expelled
the wicked persons from the temple by scourging them are
the progressive development of [their] evil actions, which
provide material to the strict Judge for condemning those
who are to be rejected. So it is that Isaiah says, *Woe to those
who spin out iniquity in cords of vanity;*[25] and Solomon says
in the book of Proverbs, *Iniquitous deeds entrap a wicked person, and he is bound by the cords of his sins.*[26] The person who
heaps sins upon sins, for which he will be condemned more
severely, is like one lengthening the cords with which he
can be bound and scourged, adding to them little by little.
[Jesus] also scattered the money of the money-changers
whom he had expelled and whose tables he had overturned:

19. Ph 1:17   20. Mt 6:5   21. Mt 10:8
22. Aug., *Tract. in Ioh.* 10, 5-6 (CC 36: 103, 1 - 104, 33); Greg., *Hom. in
    evang.* 1, 4, 4; 1, 17, 13 (*PL* 76: 1091B-D, 1145B-C)
23. Ph 2:1   24. Col 1:12   25. Is 5:18
26. Pr 5:22

when the damned are condemned in the end, he will even take away the form[27] of those things they have loved, according to what is written, *And the world and its concupiscence will pass away.*[28]

And he said to those who were selling doves, 'Remove these things from here; do not make my Father's house a house of trade'. He ordered that the selling of doves be removed from the temple because one who has received the grace of the Spirit freely ought to give it freely.[29] Hence Simon the magician, who wished to buy this [grace] for money in order to sell it for a higher price, heard, *'Your money [go] with you to perdition; may you have no part or lot in this utterance'.*[30] We should note that not only those who look for compensation in money or praise or even honor when they confer sacred orders are sellers of doves, and make the house of God the house of trade, but also those who exercise their rank or spiritual grace in the Church (which the Lord has lavished upon them) not with a simple intention, but for the sake of some kind of human recompense, contrary to that [saying] of the apostle Peter, *One who speaks,* [let it be] *like the words of God; one who serves,* [let it be] *as from the strength that God provides, that in all things God may be honored through Jesus Christ.*[31]

Therefore let all such people remove these [disorders] from their actions in order not to make the house of God a house of trade, if they wish not to be removed from the Church when the Lord comes. And we should not pass over the fact that Scripture carefully sets before us both natures of our Saviour, the human and the divine. That we may understand that he is the true Son of God, let us hear what he himself says, *Do not make my Father's house a house of trade.* One who names the temple the house of his Father is openly showing that he is the Son of God the Father. And on the other hand, so that he may be identified as a true son of man, let us recall that at the beginning of this reading, as he was going down to Capernaum, he was shown to have had his mother as a companion.

27. *figuram*, 1 Co 7:31   28. 1 Jn 2:17   29. Mt 10:8
30. Ac 8:18-21; Ambr. *Expos. evang. sec. Luc.* 9, 19 (CC 14: 338, 175/79)
31. 1 P 4:11

There follows: *His disciples remembered that it had been written, 'The zeal for your house has consumed me'.* Our Savior drove out the wicked from the temple because of zeal for his Father's house. Let us also be zealous, dearly beloved brothers, for the house of God. As far as we can, let us devote ourselves [to seeing to it] that nothing evil be done there. If we see a brother who belongs to the house of God swollen up with pride, given to calumny, a slave to drunkenness, enfeebled because of self-indulgence, wild with fury, or enslaved by any other vice, let us strive, as far as our capacity suffices, to reprimand [such a one] and to correct his perversity and corruption. And if are unable to accomplish any correction in such cases, let us do [what we can], with all our might, to bear [with this kind of behavior], not without the most painful sorrow of mind. Let us see to it especially that nothing unsuitable, nothing that would stand in the way of our own or our brothers' prayers, should happen where the body of the Lord is consecrated, and where there can be no doubt that a retinue of angels is always present.

There follows: *The Jews answered and said to him, 'What sign do you show us for doing these things'? Jesus answered and said to them, 'Destroy this temple, and within three days I will raise it up'.* The evangelist later on[32] makes clear of which temple he was speaking, namely the temple of his body, which was put to death by them at his passion, but which he raised up from death after three days. Since they were asking a sign from our Lord as to why he cast out of the temple the customary businesses, he answered that with perfect justice he banished the wicked from the temple, since the temple represented the temple of his body, in which there was no stain of any kind of sin. It was not without reason, typologically speaking, that he cleansed the temple of wickedness, since by the power of his divine majesty he would be able to raise from the dead the true temple of God after it had been put to death by human beings.

32. Jn 2:21

The Jews said, 'This temple was built in forty-six years, and you will raise it up in three days'? They answered as they understood. But lest we too should perceive our Lord's spiritual word in a carnal way, the evangelist subsequently explained what temple it was of which he was speaking. As for their stating that the temple was built in forty-six years, they meant not its first but its second building. For Solomon, the first [builder], finished the temple very rapidly[33] within seven years, during [a time of] great peace in his kingdom.[34] It was destroyed by the Chaldeans,[35] but after seventy years it began to be rebuilt, at the bidding of Cyrus the Persian, when the captivity was lightened.[36] But the descendants of those who were deported were unable to finish the work, which they were doing under the rulers Zerubbabel and Jeshua, before forty-six years [had passed], on account of the resistance of the neighboring nations.[37]

This number [forty-six] of years is also most apt for the perfecting of our Lord's [physical] body. Writers on natural history tell us that the form of the human body is completed within this number of days. During the first six days after conception it has a likeness to milk; during the following nine days it is changed into blood; next, in twelve [days] it becomes solid; during the remaining eighteen [days] it is formed into the perfect features of all its members; and after this, during the time remaining until birth, it increases in size. Six plus nine plus twelve plus eighteen make forty-five. If to this we add one, that is the day on which the body, divided into its separate members, begins to grow, we find the same number of days in the building up of our Lord's body as there were [years] in the construction of the temple.[38]

And because that temple made by [human] hands[39] prefigured our Lord's most sacred body, which he took

33. var.: 'very becomingly'
34. 1 K 6:38; Joseph., *Ant. Iud.* 8, 4; Bede, *Hom.* II.24 (*CC* 122: 363, 181/202)
35. 2 K 25:9   36. Ezr 1:1-3   37. Ezr 4:1-24
38. Aug., *De Divers. Quaest.* 56 (*CC* 44A: 95, 1 - 96, 23); Bede, *Hom.* II.24 (*CC* 122: 365, 264/69)
39. Heb 9:11; Ac 7:48

from the Virgin (as we learn from this place) [and] in like manner pointed to his body which is the Church,[40] and to the body and soul of each one of the faithful (as we find in quite a few places in the scriptures)[41] I would like to record some details concerning the construction of the temple itself, from which this fraternal gathering may recognize how everything that is written about it is applicable to Christ's Church. The temple stood facing east[42] with its door toward the rising [sun], so that as soon as it rose it could bathe the whole of the interior with its radiance. Holy Church directs the entire concentration of her mind to the grace of him concerning whom Zechariah said, *The Orient from on high has visited us, to enlighten those who sit in darkness and in the shadow of death;*[43] and mindful always of [God's] promise, in which he says, *Open your mouth wide, and I will fill it,*[44] [the Church] happily answers, *I opened my mouth and panted,*[45] *because I desired your commands,*[46] which is to say, 'I opened the devotion of my heart and merited to drink in the light of your Spirit, for I learned to desire nothing else in the world than the observance of your commands'.

The exterior [of the temple] appeared to be built of white stone; inside, the ceiling panels, the walls, the floor, beams, doors and all the furnishings were covered with pure gold.[47] The Church reveals to everyone, outwardly, the firmness of perfect action, but only those who by reverent consideration have learned to come inside understand by how many virtues of the soul it is superior interiorly, and with what a great light of charity it shines when these [are regarded] individually.

Plates of gold were secured to planks of cedar or fir, or at any rate to [the wooden sections] made of olive wood,[48] which are all excellent [kinds of] wood. The luster of the

40. Eph 1:22-23; 5:23; Col 1:18, 24
41. Rm 12:5; 1 Co 6:15, 12:27; Eph 5:29-30
42. Josephus, *Ant. Iud.* 8, 3, 2
43. Lk 1:78-79
44. Ps 81:10 (80:11)
45. *adtraxi spiritum*
46. Ps 119:131 (118:131)
47. Josephus, *Ant. Iud.* 8, 3, 2-3; 1 K 6:20-22, 30; 2 Ch 4:7-22
48. 1 K 5:8, 10; 6:9-10, 15, 33-34

Lord's love is impressed upon the hearts of believers by the remembrance of his most sacred passion, which was consummated on the precious wood of the cross, so that [the luster] may not fade away.

The temple was divided by a veil[49] [hung across] the wall in the center [of the building], and the outer [section of this part of the] building was called the sanctuary; the inner [section], where the Ark of the Covenant was placed was called the Holy of Holies. The Church is in part on pilgrimage on earth, [away from] the Lord, and in part she reigns with the Lord in heaven. The wall [across the] center is understood [as indicating] heaven, and the Ark of the Covenant [as indicating] the Lord, who alone is conscious of the Father's hidden mysteries and has passed into the inner reaches of heaven.

The way to the upper and third [parts of the] building was made through the innermost part of the southern wall, as if by an invisible entrance, so that only its beginning might be evident from the eastern corner of the beforementioned [southern] wall. Only he who could climb [it] knew the progress of this ascent, of which Scripture recalls: *The door in the center of the side was on the right* [i.e., southern] *part of the house, and they ascended by a circular stairway to the middle room and from the middle* [room] *to the third.*[50] When our Lord was suffering on the cross, *One of the soldiers opened his side with a lance, and immediately there came forth blood and water.*[51] This [prefigured] the water of baptism by which we are cleansed [from sin], and the blood of the Lord's chalice by which we are sanctified.[52] Through these holy mysteries of his side, as a consequence of our invisible faith, we ascend from the present life of the Church, in her pilgrimage on earth, to the life of heavenly blessedness, which the souls of the righteous enjoy once they have laid aside their bodies. When we have recovered our [earthly] bodies at the [general] resurrection, we will pass over from that life even to the supreme glory of eternal bliss, with our faith in our Lord's passion leading the way. It is undoubtedly of this

49. Ex 26:31-33; 1 K 6:16, 19   50. 1 K 6:8   51. Jn 19:34
52. Aug., *Tract in Ioh.* 9, 10; 120, 2 (CC 36: 96, 34/36; 661, 6/12)

glory that Isaiah says, *In their own land they will come into possession of a double portion, undying happiness will be theirs,* [53] that is, they will receive the eternal joys of an immortal body and a happy soul together in the land of the living, which is the only land of the saints. The lowest [part of the] building signifies the present way of life of the saints; the middle [part signifies] the repose of souls which is acquired after this [present] life; and the top [part signifies] the glory of the [final] resurrection, which will never be changed and will last for ever. The door in the center of the side, which was situated in the right [i.e., southern] part of the building, and which opened up the way to the upper parts, [represents] our faith in the passion of Christ, from whose pierced right side [while he was hanging] on the cross there flowed forth the sacraments, by receiving which we will be able to ascend to the joys of heavenly life.

The building of the first temple was completed in seven years, and the solemn ceremony of its dedication followed in the eighth year. The Church does not cease to receive a spiritual increase of its members throughout the entire present age (which progresses through a course of seven days), and also in the period of the future resurrection, when it will enter into the eternal feast of its dedication with the king of peace. Because our Lord rose from the dead on the eighth day, that is, after the seventh day, the sabbath, this number also rightly points to the future joys of our own resurrection.

Let this brief recounting of a few out of the many details of the building of the temple suffice, so that it may appear more clearly how all [the details] shine brightly with spiritual understanding. But as I am about to conclude my sermon, let me return to our Lord's words wherein he said to the Jews who were seeking a sign, *'Destroy this temple, and within three days I will raise it up.'* Let us give thanks for his mercy in imparting clearly to us who now believe in him [the meaning of] the mystery of his passion and his being raised from the dead, which he proposed at the close of his discourse

---

53. Is 61:7

to the unbelievers who were tempting him. The time is now near when we desire to celebrate the yearly solemnity of the destruction of the venerable temple, brought about by those who lacked faith, and also [the solemnity of] his being raised, which he himself manifested in a marvelous way on the third day as he had promised. Let us then cleanse the temples of our bodies and hearts, so that the Spirit of God may deign to dwell in us; and, as the Apostle advises, having cast aside the works of darkness, *let us put on the armor of light; let us walk honorably as in the daylight, not with revelry and drunkenness, not with debauchery and licentiousness, not with quarreling and jealousy, but let us put on our Lord Jesus Christ,*[54] who lives and reigns with the Father in the unity of the Holy Spirit, God before all ages of ages. Amen.

54. Rm 13:12-13

homily II.2

John 6:1-14   *In Lent*

Those who read or listen to the signs and miracles of our Lord and Savior properly do not receive them in such a way that they pay attention to what in them produces outward astonishment, but instead they consider what they themselves ought to be doing inwardly, following the example of these [signs], and what mystical truths they ought to be pondering in these [stories]. For behold, as the Passover, the Jews' festival day, was drawing near, our Lord provided encouragement for the multitude that was following him by his words of salvation, together with the help of his cures. As another evangelist wrote, *He spoke to them about the kingdom of God, and healed those who were in need of being cured;*[1] and when his [acts of] teaching and healing were completed, he refreshed them most abundantly from a small amount of food.

We too, dearly beloved brothers, together with the large group of our brothers gathered around us, should wholeheartedly follow our Lord's example in this action, as Easter, the festival day of our redemption, draws near. We should contemplate most diligently by what course of actions he

---

1. Lk 9:11 ff.

walked, so that we may deserve to follow in his footsteps. *For one who says that he abides in Him ought himself also to walk as he walked.*[2] By frequent hearing of his word we should eliminate whatever harmful ignorance we detect in ourselves; we should beg to be corrected[3] by the favor of his wonted benevolence from whatever seductive vice (which is a kind of spiritual illness) that we sense is ravaging us inwardly. If we perceive that we are hungry for the delightfulness of the heavenly life, we should plead for his grace, that he may see fit to satisfy us with the gifts of necessary compunction[4] and other spiritual virtues, so that at the most sacred time of his resurrection, being fittingly adorned internally and externally, we may partake of the sacraments of our salvation with a body and a heart that are pure. But having said this much by way of brief introduction, I would like to examine more diligently the whole sequence of this sacred reading and to indicate[5] to you dear ones whatever mystical [meaning] I am capable of pointing out in it.

Jesus went across the sea of Galilee, which is [also known as] *the sea of Tiberias.* I should say first of all that, according to the historical sense, the sea of Galilee, which is described by different names to correspond with the diversity of its outlying regions, is called the sea of Tiberias only in the location where, as they say, it provides the city of Tiberias on its western edge with salubrious hot springs. Once the river Jordan flows into it, it extends for eighteen miles in length and five in width.[6] [1*] Mystically speaking, this sea signifies the troubled and disordered swirling waters of this world, in which any perverse people who are unrighteously pleased are, as it were, like fish pulled down into the depths, not directing their mind to heavenly joys . Hence it is appropriate that this sea is given the name 'of Galilee,' that is, 'a whirlpool,'[7] for undoubtedly love of this transitory

---

2. 1 Jn 2:6
3. 'corrected' = *emendari*; var.: 'cleansed' = *emundari*.
4. Some MSS add: 'with his sweetness as with a feast of faith, hope and love'.
5. 'indicate' = *indicare*; var.: 'search out' = *indagare*.
6. Plin., *Nat. Hist.* 5, 15, 71
7. *rota*; literally "a wheel". This is from Jer., *Nom.* (CC 72:146, 12)

world sends hearts whirling, as it were, round and round; it does not allow them to be raised up to the desire for everlasting life. The psalmist says of such as these, *The wicked walk round in circles.*[8]

A very large multitude went and followed Jesus across the sea of Galilee in order to receive from him the most important heavenly gifts of teaching, healing and refreshment. Before our Lord appeared in the flesh, only the Jewish nation followed him by believing [in him]. But afterward, when through the divinely-arranged plan of his incarnation he drew near, trod upon and passed over the waves of this corruptible life, soon a very great multitude of believing nations followed him, desiring to be spiritually instructed, healed and satisfied, and entreating with the psalmist, *O Lord, it is to you that I have fled for refuge, teach me to do your will;*[9] *Have mercy on me, Lord, for I am weak; heal me, Lord, for all my bones are wracked* [with pain];[10] and again, trusting completely that he would receive from him the nourishment of everlasting life, [the psalmist] said, *The Lord feeds me, and there is nothing I shall lack; he has placed me there in a place of green pastures.*[11]

But as for the fact that Jesus went up onto a mountain, where he sat down with his disciples, but when the multitude came to him he descended, and gave refreshment on lower ground to those whom he had cured just a little while before, let us by no means believe that this was done without a reason. Let us rather believe that our Lord, to signify mystically that he distributed his teaching and spiritual gifts in conformity with the capacity of those who received them, entrusted his more simple sacramental [mysteries] to those whose minds were still weak and childlike in spirit, and imparted the more secret hidden mysteries of his majesty to those who had greater understanding and were more perfect in grasping [what was being revealed]. [To these] he suggested a stricter form of devout life, and he promised [them] greater gifts of heavenly rewards.

Accordingly, to one inquiring as to what he should do to possess eternal life,[12] as to one still below, [Jesus] laid

8. Ps 12:8 (11:9)   9. Ps 143:9-10 (142:9-10)   10. Ps 6:2 (6:3)
11. Ps 23:1-2 (22:1-2)   12. Lk 18:18

out the general gifts of his bounty, saying, '*You shall not kill, you shall not commit adultery, you shall not steal, you shall not bear false witness, honor your father and mother*'.[13] Later, when he was seeking more, and longing, so to speak, to ascend the mountain of the virtues, [Jesus] said, '*If you wish to be perfect, go, sell all that you have and give* [it] *to the poor, and you shall have your treasure in heaven; and come, follow me*'.[14] Our Lord not only displayed this [sort] of discerning guidance when he was teaching alone in the flesh, but now too he does not cease to display [it] [as he teaches] through the ministers of his word. Hence he bears witness concerning these [ministers], in the person of one good servant, that they ought to give their fellow-servants their portion of grain at the [proper] time;[15] they ought, that is, to provide the banquet of the word at the appropriate time and in due measure, in accord with the ability of those who are listening.

As to the fact that it was as the Passover was drawing near that our Lord taught, healed and refreshed the crowd, we can interpret this mystically thus—that 'Passover' means 'passing over'.[16] For all those whom the Lord reclaims by the inward sweetness of his favors he unquestionably prepares a salutary 'passing over,' namely that they may transcend the lustful concupiscences of the flesh by the loftiness of their minds, and that they may, by heavenly hope and love, tread under foot the degrading desires of the world, favorable and unfavorable equally. And although they may not yet be capable of reaching a higher condition of soul or body, because this is promised for the future, nevertheless, whatever the carnal look at and [desire] to embrace as lofty, they may scorn as nothing in comparison with eternal [goods]. This is in accordance with the example of the one who, seeing a *wicked person exalted and lifted above the cedars of Lebanon*, passed by, and by contemplating temporal things saw that it was as if he did not exist,[17] since he foresaw that he would soon be taken away.

13. Lk 18:20   14. Mt 19:21; Lk 18:22   15. Lk 12:42
16. Bede, *Hom.* II.1 (CC 122: 186, 80); *Hom.* II.5 (214: 7/16)
17. Ps 37:35-36 (36:35-36)

As for its being mentioned that Jesus lifted up his eyes and saw the multitude coming toward him, this is an indication of the divine benevolence, for he is wont to come by the grace of heavenly mercy to meet all those seeking to come to him. And lest they be able to go astray in their search, he is accustomed to open up the light of his Spirit to those hurrying [to him]. Now the Apocalypse of John bears witness that the eyes of Jesus mystically designate the gifts of his Spirit. [John] says, speaking figuratively of [Jesus], *And I saw a Lamb standing as though it had been killed, with seven horns and seven eyes, which are the seven Spirits of God sent forth into all the earth.* [18]

As to our Lord's asking Philip, in order to test him, *'Where shall we buy bread that these may eat?,'* this he doubtless did by his provident dispensation, not to learn something that he did not know, but so that Philip might recognize the sluggishness of his faith. His master knew of this, but he did not. Having been tested, he can recognize [the truth], and, the miracle done, he can amend. For he ought not to have doubted that with the presence of the Creator of [all] things, who brings forth bread from the earth and gladdens the hearts of human beings with wine, [19] bread [which could be bought for] a few denarii was sufficient for a crowd of several thousands, so that all might receive what was sufficient and go away satisfied.

The five loaves of bread with which he satisfied the multitude of people are the five books of Moses. [2*] If they are opened up by spiritual understanding, and then multiplied by [penetration of] their deeper meaning, they daily refresh the hearts of the believers who hear them. It is appropriate that they are reported to have been made of barley, because of the stricter ordinances of the law, and the thicker outer husks of its literal [interpretation] which, as it were, cover the inner pith of its spiritual sense. [20]

The two fishes which he added not inappropriately signify the writings of the psalmists and prophets. One [of these] by chanting, and the other by talking, to those who

18. Rv 5:6   19. Ps 104:14-15 (103:14-15)
20. Aug., *Tract in Ioh.* 24, 5 (CC 36: 246, 1/8)

listen, tell of the future sacramental [mysteries] of Christ and the Church. And it is also appropriate that it was animals that live in the water that prefigured the heralds of that age in which faithful people could in no way live without the water of baptism.

The boy who had the five loaves and two fishes, who did not distribute them to the hungry crowd but brought them to our Lord for him to distribute, is the Jewish people. They were childlike [in their understanding] of the literal sense, and they kept the words of the scriptures shut up within themselves. Nevertheless, our Lord, on his appearance in the flesh, took them and showed what usefulness and sweetness they had in them. By the manifold grace of the Spirit he disclosed how matters that seemed insignificant and unworthy of attention might be fruitful, and he handed these things over to be administered to all nations by the apostles and their successors.

Hence it is appropriate that the other evangelists relate how our Lord administered the loaves and fishes to his disciples, and the disciples then administered them to the crowd.[21] Although the mystery of human salvation received its start by being declared by our Lord, it was confirmed in us by those who heard it [from him]. He broke up the five loaves and two fishes, and distributed them to his disciples, when he opened their minds to understand everything that had been written about him in the law of Moses and in the prophets and the psalms.[22] The disciples set them before the crowd when *they preached everywhere, our Lord working with them, and strengthening their utterance by the signs that followed it.*[23]

The grass on which the crowd reclined while it was being refreshed is understood [as indicating] bodily concupiscence, which everyone who desires to be satisfied with spiritual nourishment ought to tread under foot and repress. *For all flesh is* [as] *grass, and all its glory like the bloom of grass.*[24]

Let all who long to be refreshed by the sweetness of the living bread, all who love to be renewed by the banquet

---

21. Mt 14:19; Mk 6:41; Lk 9:16   22. Lk 24:44-45
23. Mk 16:20   24. Is 40:6; 1 P 1:24

of heavenly grace, sit down upon the grass, let them trample upon the bloom of the grass. Let them chastise the body and subject it to slavery,[25] let them repress the pleasures of the flesh, let them restrain the changeable [urgings] of self-indulgence. Let them beware lest they faint away through [being dragged down] by a degrading [return] to their former self.

The five thousand men who ate suggest the perfection of those who are refreshed with the word of life. By the word 'men' scripture customarily indicates all those more perfect ones whom no feminine softness corrupts, the sort of people the Apostle longs for those to be whom he tells, *Be watchful, stand* [firm] *in faith, act manfully and take courage.*[26] The number one thousand, beyond which no calculation of ours extends, ordinarily indicates the fullness of the things which are being treated of; by the number five the well-known senses of our body are represented, namely, sight, hearing, taste, smell and touch. Individuals from among [these five thousand] who attempt to act manfully and take courage by living soberly and righteously and piously,[27] so that they may deserve to be renewed by the sweetness of heavenly wisdom, are those indicated by the five thousand men whom our Lord satisfied by this mystical banquet.

Nor must we overlook the fact that as he was on the point of refreshing the multitude, he gave thanks. He gave thanks in order to teach us always to give thanks for the favors we have received from heaven, and in order to impress [upon us] how much he himself gives thanks for our progress, how much he himself rejoices at our spiritual refreshment. For do you indeed wish to know, brothers, how much he rejoices with us at our salvation? The evangelist Luke tells how, after he gave his disciples the power of treading upon all might of the enemy, he indicated that their names were written in heaven, and [Luke] then concludes, *At that hour he exulted in the Holy Spirit and said, 'I give praise to you, Father, Lord of heaven and earth, that you have kept these things secret from the wise and prudent and have revealed them to little ones'.*[28]

25. 1 Co 9:27   26. 1 Co 16:13   27. Tt 2:12   28. Lk 10:19-21

It is therefore apparent that he rejoices with the faithful
at their salvation and life, since he praises the Father with
them by giving [him] thanks for revealing these secrets to
the humble of spirit after keeping them secret from the
proud.

But as for his ordering the disciples, after the crowd had
been satisfied, to gather up whatever fragments were left
over, so that they might not perish, this unquestionably signifies that there are many hidden mysteries of the divine
tidings that the minds of ordinary people do not grasp.[3*]
There are some that those less learned are unable to assimi-
late on their own, but which they are able to understand
once they are explained by teachers. Those more able, then,
should, by probing them more diligently, gather these
[mysteries] up, and, by their speaking or writing, make
them a guide for the less [learned], so that the nourishment
of the word may not perish because of their inertia and be
kept from the people [by those] who, through God's gift,
know how to gather these [mysteries] up by interpreting
[them].

They gathered [the fragments] *up, and filled twelve baskets
with the fragments.* Because the height of anything's perfection is customarily indicated by the number twelve, the complete concurrence of spiritual teachers is correctly
represented by the twelve baskets full of fragments. They
are ordered both to gather up by meditating [on them] the
obscure points of the scriptures which the crowd is unable
[to understand] on its own, and to preserve the results of
their meditation and [the Lord's] commandments in their
writings for their own use as well as that of the crowds.
This is what the apostles themselves and the evangelists
did, by including quite a number of mystical sayings of the
law and the prophets in their works, with the addition of
their own interpretation. This is what a large number of their
followers, guides of the Church throughout the entire world,
have done by scrutinizing complete books of both testa-
ments of the scriptures in very diligent explanations, and
although they have been despised by men, yet they have
been fecund with the bread of heavenly grace. Menial work

is customarily performed with baskets. Hence the psalmist says of the [Jewish] people who labored in Egypt with clay and bricks,[29] *Their hands performed their labor with baskets.*[30]

When those men had seen the sign which [Jesus] had done, they said, *'This is truly the prophet who is to come into the world'.* Rightly did they say, *'This is truly the prophet,'* [calling] our Lord the great prophet, the herald of the great salvation soon to come about for the world. He also saw fit to call himself a prophet when he said, *'For it cannot be that a prophet should perish outside Jerusalem'.*[31] But they had not yet reached the point of having full faith, since they did not know how to speak of him as the Lord. Therefore, on seeing the sign that Jesus had wrought, they said, *'This is truly the prophet who is to come into the world'.*

We have a more certain recognition of the truth and of faith. On seeing the world which Jesus has made, and the signs with which he has filled it, we should say that he is truly the Mediator between God and human beings,[32] who fills the world with his divinity,[33] *and the world was made by him;*[34] that he came among his own [creation],[35] to seek out and save the human race which was lost,[36] and to renew the world which he had made; that he is in the world by his divine presence with his faithful ones *for all days, even to the consummation of the world;*[37] that at the consummation of the world he will come into the world in his humanity to render to each individual in accord with his works,[38] casting the wicked and sinners into eternal fire,[39] but bringing the righteous into eternal life,[40] in which he lives and reigns with the Father in the unity of the Holy Spirit throughout all ages of ages. Amen.

---

29. Ex 1:14
30. Ps 81:6 (80:7)
31. Lk 13:33
32. 1 Tm 2:5
33. var.: 'was in the world'
34. Jn 1:10
35. Jn 1:11
36. Mt 18:11; Lk 19:10
37. Mt 28:20
38. Mt 16:27; Rm 2:6
39. Mt 25:41
40. Mt 25:34

NOTES

1. Pliny gives the dimensions of the sea of Galilee, or Tiberias, as sixteen miles long and six miles wide. The measurement in Bede may be attributable to the error of copyists, who in various manuscripts frequently misread the roman numerals which are used. At the present time we cannot be certain of the text of Pliny Bede might have used.
2. These are the first five books in the Old Testament—Genesis, Exodus, Leviticus, Numbers and Deuteronomy—known collectively as the Penteteuch or Torah, and traditionally believed to have been composed by Moses himself.
3. Bede here plays upon the double meaning of *colligere*, to 'gather up' the fragments, but to 'think about' the hidden mysteries of the divine tidings. In the following paragraph he makes this figurative meaning explicit in 'They are ordered both to gather up by meditating [on them] *(colligere et meditata)* the obscure points of the scriptures...'

homily⁻ ii.3

he Mediator between God and men, the man Christ Jesus,[1] who had come down to earth from heaven in order to suffer for the salvation of the human race, as the hour of his passion was drawing near, willed to draw near the place of his passion. Even by this it was to become apparent that he would not be suffering unwillingly but of his own volition. He willed to come [riding] upon a donkey, and be called 'king' and praised by the crowd, so that everyone, guided again by this, might recognize that he was the Christ whom once upon a time the promise of the prophecy[2] had designated the one who would come in this manner. He willed to come five days before the Passover, as we have learned from the gospel of John,[3] that by this again he might show that he was the stainless lamb who would take away the sins of the world.[4]

It was commanded that the paschal lamb, by whose immolation[5] the people of Israel were freed from slavery in Egypt, should be selected five days before the [feast of] Passover, that is, on the tenth [day of the lunar] month,[6] and immolated on the fourteeth [day of the lunar] month[7]

1. 1 Tm 2:5   2. Zc 9:9   3. Jn 12:12   4. Jn 1:29
5. var.: 'blood'   6. Ex 12:3   7. Ex 12:18

23

at sundown. This signified the one who was going to redeem us by his blood, since five days before the [feast of] Passover (that is, today), accompanied by the great joy and praise of people going ahead and following, he came into God's temple, and he was there teaching daily. At last, after five days, having observed up to that point the sacraments of the old Passover, he brought them to perfection, and he handed over the new sacraments to his disciples to be observed henceforth.[8] [Then], having gone out to the Mount of Olives, he was seized by the Jews[9] and crucified [the next] morning.[10] He redeemed us from the sway of the devil on that very day when the ancient people of the Hebrews cast aside the yoke of slavery under the Egyptians by the immolation of a lamb.

Our Lord, the counterpart of the paschal lamb, five days before he entered upon his suffering, came to the place of his passion, to teach that he was the one concerning whom Isaiah had predicted, *Like a sheep he was led to the slaughter, and like a lamb he became silent before his shearers and opened not his mouth;*[11] and a little before that, *But he was wounded for our iniquities, and by his stripes we were healed.*[12] But the hearts of the envious leaders [of the Jews] preferred to persecute him in everything that he providentially carried out rather than to believe in him. The wretched men strove mightily to hand over to death the author of life rather than to be themselves brought to life by him. Let us, avoiding the blindness of these faithless ones, follow the example rather of those who faithfully praised our Lord, and let us investigate thoroughly his mystical path by our mystical interpretation, as is proper.

The donkey and its foal on which he sat when he came to Jerusalem represent those with a guileless heart from among each of the two peoples, namely the Jews and the gentiles. Directing them and restraining them from harmful freedom of action by his rule, he leads them to the vision

---

8. Lk 22:14-20   9. Lk 22:39-54   10. Mk 15:25
11. Is 53:7   12. Is 53:5

of heavenly peace.[13] (Jerusalem is interpreted 'vision of peace'.)[14]

And it is appropriate that, when our Lord had come to the Mount of Olives, he sent [on ahead] the disciples to bring these animals [to him], for we come to him not by our own merits but by the bestowal of his grace alone, as John bears witness, saying, *And in this is charity, not as if we loved God, but that he loved us.*[15] The Mount of Olives suggests the eminence of our Lord's love, with which he has mercifully deigned to illumine and save us, not only because it is a property of oil to provide light and comfort for our labors and sorrows,[16] but also because it tends to float on top of[1*] other liquids with which it is mixed. The Apostle, when about to speak of charity, says, *I will show you a still more excellent way.*[17]

On coming to the Mount of Olives, then, our Lord ordered that donkeys be brought for him, on which he might make for Jerusalem, figuratively signifying what he clearly said elsewhere, that *God so loved the world that he gave his only-begotten Son, that everyone who believes in him may not perish but may have eternal life.*[18] He sent [on ahead] two of his disciples, to bring these beasts of burden to him, in order to signify that preachers were appointed for both peoples, namely the circumcision and the uncircumcision.[19] He sent two in order that he might warn these preachers to be perfect in their teaching as well as in their actions, lest being unlearned they might mingle words of error with the truth, or by living perversely they might deny what they had properly taught.

[Jesus] said, *'You will find the donkey tied up, and its foal with it; loose it and bring it to me'.* Other evangelists testify that the foal also was tied up.[20] Each of the two peoples, [Jews and gentiles], was bound by the ropes of its sins, and needed a divine loosing. The former [was tied] by not observing[21]

---

13. Greg., *Hom. in Ezech.* 2, 5, 2 (CC 142: 275, 33 - 276, 37)
14. Jer., *Nom.* (CC 72: 121, 9/10)   15. 1 Jn 4:10
16. Jer., *In Matth.* 21, 1 (CC 77: 182, 1177/78)
17. 1 Co 12:31   18. Jn 3:16
19. Jer., *In Matth.* 21, 5 (CC 77: 183, 1203/1206)
20. Mk 11:2-4, Lk 19:30   21. var.: 'by making bad use of'

the law which it had received, the latter by never receiving
a law which it might keep.[22] Hence the Apostle does well
to say that *there is no distinction, for all have sinned and need
the glory of God, being justified freely by his grace.*[23] It is appropriate that the other three evangelists, since they wrote
for [pagan] nations, report that only the foal was brought
to our Lord.[24] The evangelist Matthew, however, since he
wrote his gospel for the Hebrew people and in the Hebrew
language,[25] mentions the donkey too, doubtless by a
providential dispensation, so that both [groups] could mystically teach that those whose salvation they sought by their
writing were indicated by our Lord as destined for salvation.

[Jesus] said, *'And if anyone says anything to you, say that
the Lord has need of these, and right away he will let them go'.*
Teachers are commanded that if any adversity stands in their
way,[26] if anyone prevents sinners from being loosed from
the devil's snares and brought to the Lord by their confession of faith, not only should they not desist from their
preaching, but they should constantly suggest that the Lord
has need of such as these for the building of his Church.
For although persecutors may be full of rage and cruel, they
cannot oppose the salvation of those whom the Lord knows,
because those whom he has foreordained to eternal life[27]
belong to him. Joined to this fact is the testimony of the
prophet,[28] so that it may be apparent that the Lord fulfilled
everything that had been written of him; but the Scribes
and Pharisees, blinded by envy, were unable to understand
what they read.

*Say to the daughter of Zion, 'Behold, your king will come to
you, gentle, and sitting upon a donkey, and its foal, the offspring
of a beast of burden'.* The daughter of Zion is the Church of
the faithful, associated with the heavenly Jerusalem, which
is the mother of us all,[29] of which there then existed no small
group among the people of Israel. They had a king who

22. Aug., *Tract in Ioh.* 51, 5 (CC 36: 441, 5/24)
23. Rm 3:22-24   24. Mk 11:7; Lk 19:32-35; Jn 12:14-15
25 Jer., *In Matth.* Praef. (CC 77: 2, 27/28)
26. Some MSS add: 'if anyone speaks against the word of truth'
27. Ac 13:48   28. Zc 9:9, which Mt quotes just below
29. Ga 4:26

was gentle, for it was not [God's] wont to give an earthly kingdom to the merciless, but a heavenly kingdom to the gentle, as [Christ] said, *'Learn of me, for I am meek and humble of heart, and you will find rest for your souls'.*[30] Of these the psalmist said, *The gentle shall possess the earth, and shall delight in an abundance of peace.*[31] A gentle king bestowed a land of peace upon the gentle, that is,[32] upon those who are humble of heart— those people whom once a wicked king, that is, the devil, by the wound of pride, spread out over a land of war and tribulations. [The prophet] had said, *Sitting upon a donkey, and its foal, the offspring of a beast of burden,* for he rested in the hearts of the humble and quiet and those who trembled at his word,[33] whether of those in the synagogue who knew how to bear the yoke of his law, or of those who were for a long time unbridled in their gentile freedom, but had been converted to the grace of faith and truth at the urging of the synagogue.

Bringing forward the donkey and its foal, the disciples placed their garments upon them and made our Lord sit thereon. The garments of the disciples are the works of righteousness, as the psalmist testifies when he says, *Your priests will clothe themselves with righteousness.*[34] The donkeys which the disciples found uncovered they covered with garments, and so placed our Lord thereon. When holy preachers find any persons at all without the clothing of holiness they imbue them with examples of their own virtues so that they gain faith in and love for their Maker.[35] For our Lord did not wish to get on an uncovered donkey, nor did he wish to get on an uncovered foal, because whether Jew or gentile, unless one be adorned with the sayings and deeds of the saints, he cannot have our Lord as his guide, but instead sin reigns in his mortal body to make him obey its concupiscences.[36]

A large part of the crowd spread their garments on the road. This large crowd designates the innumerable host of martyrs who have given their bodies (which are the covering

---

30. Mt 11:29   31. Ps 37:11 (36:11)   32. var.: 'that is, Christ'
33. Is 66:2   34. Ps 132:9 (131:9)
35. Ambr., *Expos. evang. sec Luc.* 9, 8-11 (CC 14: 334, 57 - 336, 99)
36. Rm 6:12

of their souls) for our Lord, in order to make a smoother path of right living for the elect who follow, lest any of them should hesitate to place the foot of his good actions there [during a time of] peace, where he saw that many martyrs had preceded him [during a time of] war.

Others cut branches from the trees and spread them on the road. The branches of the trees are the sayings of their ancestors who went before [them]. Everyone who makes known what the prophets and the apostles and the rest of the saints said or did, as an example of right belief and works, cuts branches from the trees with which to make smooth the way for the donkey carrying our Lord. He gathers statements from the books of the saints with which he builds up the hearts of Christ's simple ones lest they stray from the path of the truth.[37]

The crowd which went ahead and which followed kept crying out, saying, 'Hosanna to the son of David'. Those who went ahead and those who followed exalted our Lord with one and the same voice of praise, for undoubtedly the faith of those who were approved before our Lord's incarnation and of those after it is one [faith], although they had sacraments that differed according to the customs of the times. Peter bears witness [to this] when he says, *But we believe that we are being saved in the same way as they also were, through the grace of the Lord Jesus.*[38] As for their saying, '*Hosanna,'* that is, 'salvation' *to the son of David,* this is the same thing we read in the psalm, *The Lord is* [our] *salvation,* [let] *your blessing* [be] *upon your people.*[39] It is the same as the chorus which the saints re-echo with a chant of great praise in the Apocalypse, *Salvation to our God who sits upon the throne, and to the Lamb.*[40]

'*Blessed is he who comes in the name of the Lord'.* 'In the name of the Lord' signifies 'In the name of God the Father,' just as [our Lord] himself said elsewhere to the unbelieving Jews, '*I have come in the name of my Father, and you do not receive me; another will come in his own name, him you will receive'.*[41] Christ came in the name of God the Father, because in

37. Greg., *Hom. in Ezech.* 2, 5, 2 (CC 142: 276, 40/44)
38. Ac 15:11   39. Ps 3:8 (3:9)   40. Rv 7:10   41. Jn 5:43

everything that he did and said he was concerned with glorifying his Father, and with proclaiming to human beings that he is to be glorified. The antichrist will come in his own name, and although he may be the most wicked person of all and a boon companion of the devil, he will see fit to call[42] himself the Son of God, while *being opposed to and raised above everything which is said to be God and is worshipped.*[43] The crowd took this verse of praise from the one hundredth and seventeenth psalm,[44] and there is no one who doubts that it is sung about the Lord. Hence it is appropriate that there is previously sung of him in the same psalm, *The stone which the builders rejected has become the corner stone,*[45] for Christ, whom the Jews rejected as they were building the decrees of their own traditions, became a memorial[46] for believers from among both peoples, namely the Jews and the gentiles. For as to the fact that Christ is called the cornerstone in this psalm, this is what was being chanted in high praise in the gospel by the voice of those who followed and those who went ahead.

What was added in continuing this praise, 'Hosanna' (that is, 'salvation,' or 'save [us]') *'in the highest,'* obviously teaches us that our Lord's coming in the flesh was the salvation not only of the human race upon earth, but also of the angels in heaven.[47] When we the redeemed were led back to the heavenly regions, their number was being filled, since it had been made less by the fall of Satan. So indeed Paul said that *All things were restored in Christ, both what was in heaven and what was on earth—everything was restored in him.*[48] Rightly, then, was 'Hosanna in the highest' being chanted in praise of him, for the entire dispensation of his incarnation was for the sake of fulfilling the glory of his heavenly Father.

Accordingly, my brothers, we must direct our course with all the devotion of our minds toward the homeland that has

---

42. 'see fit to call' = *dignatur...cognominare*; var.: 'scorn to be called' = *dedignatur...cognominari*
43. 2 Th 2:4   44. Ps 118:26 (117:26)   45. Ps 118:22 (117:22)
46. 'memorial' = *monimentum*; var.: 'fortification' = *munimentum.*
47. Jer., *In Matth.* 21, 9 (CC 77: 185, 1252/72)
48. Eph 1:10

been promised us, recollecting always that, although the road is narrow[49] along which we make our way, happy is the dwelling place to which we are hastening. It is more blissful to be led over a hard route to the kingdom than by an agreeable and easy one to chastisement. It is more blissful to win everlasting joy by temporary self-restraint of the flesh than to undergo eternal punishment for the sake of wanton pleasure that lasts but for a brief time.

Behold, with the Lord's help, we have now for the most part finished our fast of forty days. The conscience of each one of us is witness that the more strictly each has remembered to devote himself to the Lord during these holy days, the more joyfully he awaits the holy time of our Lord's resurrection. But even if anyone's conscience still accuses him of being imperfectly purified, let no one hesitate to wait in expectation, with fear and trembling, for the arrival of this important solemnity. And yet if there be such a one, let him not be fearful concerning his salvation; and, if he is disturbed by the large number or the enormity of his evil deeds, let him not fall into the pit of despair, in accordance with that [saying] of Solomon, *When a wicked person comes to the depth of his reprehensible actions, he despises* [himself].[50] Let him rather solicitously deliberate upon this: that if the time of this yearly festival, during which we are filled with gladness because of the resurrection of our Maker, brings so much joy to the chaste and fills the impure with apprehension and confusion, so much the more at the time of that strict examination when the general resurrection of all will be carried out—even before the Judge's sentence is heard—will a clean conscience, excusing the former, gladden them, while a guilty conscience, accusing the latter, will condemn them forever.

Therefore, dearly beloved brothers, let all those who, girded with the armor of continence, began contending with the proud tempter right from the beginning of Lent, carefully see to it that they do not discontinue what they have begun before they have been given into the care of angels,[51]

---

49. Mt 7:14   50. Pr 18:3   51. Mt 4:11

when the enemy has been overthrown. But let one who up to this time has not clothed himself with the armor[52] of the virtues at least start today; today let him take on the works of faith, together with the multitude of those who believe. Let him, by crying out *'Hosanna in the highest,'* implore the benevolence of him who, coming in his Father's name, brought blessing to the world, and let him beg to be saved in the heavenly fatherland. Let him spread his garments on the road, that is, let him humble the members of his body for the present [time], so that God may exalt them in the future,[53] mindful of David's [saying], *The bones which have been humbled will exult.*[54] Let him cut branches from the trees and spread them for himself on the road, that is, let him painstakingly recall to his memory the writings of the saints with which they strengthen those who are standing lest they fall,[55] encourage those who have slipped lest they lie there for a longer time, instruct those who are rising up so that they may be trained in the virtues, and rouse those so trained so that they may hope for their reward in heaven. And let him fortify for them the course of their actions, lest they offend [by becoming] a stone of offence and a rock of stumbling.[56] Thus he, together with the rest of the believers, may follow in the footsteps of his Redeemer, and venerate with fitting purity of mind the mysteries of the passion and resurrection of the one who deigned to give to all the elect, his members, the remedy for their wounds, together with a pledge of heavenly joys, Jesus Christ our Lord, who lives and reigns with the Father in the unity of the Holy Spirit, God throughout all ages of ages. Amen.

---

52. Cf. Eph 6:13　　53. 1 P 5:6　　54. Ps 51:8 (50:10)
55. 1 Co 10:12　　56. 1 P 2:8

NOTE

1. 'Float on top of' = *excellere.* Bede here utilizes untranslatable word-play, since the verb has both a physical sense which applies in the present context, and a metaphorical sense, 'to excel,' which directs our attention back to the derivative *celsitudinem* earlier in the sentence (translated 'the *eminence* of our Lord's love'). Cf. *Hom.* I.25 (*CC* 122: 178, 19/20).

homily̆ II.4

The usual way for prudent persons to learn the virtue of prudence is not only from things that they recognize have been done or said properly and prudently, but also from things that have been done or said otherwise. They may imitate the former by following them, and escape the latter by avoiding them. Reason compels us, dearly beloved brothers, [after hearing] the reading from today's holy gospel, to act in this way—namely, not only to learn devotion to virtue from the example of those who loved Christ, but [also] to consider the lack of faith of those who persecuted [him], and, having considered it, to turn quickly away from it. We must follow the prudence of those women whom we recognize had clung [to him] with such great faith and love, and we must flee the ignorance of the high priests and Pharisees who sought to surround the Wisdom of God with snares and to kill [him]. Let us beware of the insanity of those who had come up to Jerusalem to be sanctified on the feast of the Jewish Passover, but, forgetful of sanctification, plotted the murder of our Savior in the very house of prayer. The Passover was drawing near, during which everyone, after being sanctified and cleansed, had to come to eat of the [paschal] lamb. Those very ones who had come

up to the temple to be sanctified now departed from it more
unclean than ever, as a result of their conspiracy to shed
blood.

Since the time of our own celebration of the Passover is
drawing near [that is, Easter], let us solicitously take care
that as it comes close we may approach the Lord's altar sanctified, not so as to eat the flesh of the [paschal] lamb, but
so as to partake of the holy mysteries of our Redeemer. *Let
us cleanse ourselves of all contamination of body and spirit, working
out our sanctification in the fear of God.*[1] Let no one turn the
house of prayer into a den of thieves;[2] let no one who is
preparing death traps for the members of Christ, no one
still abiding in death, presume to approach to receive the
holy mysteries of life. *The person who does not love remains
in death.*[3] Let us love Christ for himself, let us love him in
his members; let us seek the Lord, and our [souls] will live;[4]
let us seek him not as the wicked do, in order to kill him,
but as believers, in order to enjoy him forever.

[John] said, *They were seeking Jesus, and, standing in the temple they conversed with one another,* [saying] *'Why do you suppose that he is not coming for the festival day'?* The Jews were
seeking Christ, but seeking him with evil intent, that they
might put him to death when he came for the festival day.[5]
Let us seek him standing in the temple and *persevering with
one mind in prayer,*[6] and let us converse with one another
in psalms, hymns, [and] spiritual canticles,[7] imploring him,
with [the help of his] grace, that he may deign to come to
our festival day and illumine us with his presence by sanc-
tifying his gifts for us.

*For the high priests and Pharisees had given a command that
if anyone knew where he was, he should point him out, so that
they might apprehend him.* Let us also give a command to one
another, my brothers, that if anyone recognizes in the heart
of some brother the more fruitful feelings of mercy, greater
humility, generosity, forbearance, patience,[8] and a more
abundant supply of the rest of the virtues (which are indi-

1. 2 Co 7:1   2. Mt 21:13   3. 1 Jn 3:14   4. Ps 69:32 (68:33)
5. Aug., *Tract. in Ioh.* 50, 3 (CC 36: 434, 10/12)
6. Ac 1:14   7. Eph 5:19   8. Col 3:12

cations of Christ's presence), he should immediately indicate where such a one is, so that by faithfully imitating him
we may hold to the footsteps of Christ, once we have discovered them. But our Lord, though he was aware that the
Jews had conspired to kill him, did not flee the hands of
those who were plotting [against him]. Being sure of the
glory of his resurrection, he first came to Bethany, a town
near Jerusalem, where Lazarus was, whom he had raised
from the dead. Then [he came] on to Jerusalem, where he
himself was to suffer and rise from the dead. [He came] to
Jerusalem so that he might die there, but to Bethany so that
the raising up of Lazarus might be imprinted more deeply
on the memory of all. Then the wicked leaders might be
more and more confounded and shown to be inexcusable,
since they did not fear to kill him who was able to raise
[another] from the dead, nor were they either affected by
his graciousness in raising [another], or much frightened
by the power of the one who performed this raising up,
so as to withdraw from their intention of shedding his blood
unjustly. And lest these planners of false accusation might
say that Lazarus had only as an apparition been raised, a
dinner was prepared there for our Lord, and [Lazarus] himself was one of those reclining with him.[9] When they either saw or heard of [Lazarus's] being alive, speaking,
having a meal and talking intimately with his friends, they
might then acknowledge the power of the one who had
raised him up, and receive grace.[10]

Mystically, however, this dinner of our Lord, at which
Martha served and Lazarus reclined with the others, designates the faith of the Church which works through love.[11]
Hence our Lord says elsewhere to his disciples of the people who were to believe in him, *'I have food to eat of which
you do not know';* and explaining this he continued, *'My food
is to do the will of him who sent me, in order that I may carry
out his work'.*[12] Martha serves at this dinner when every

9. Aug., *Tract. in Ioh.* 50, 5 (*CC* 36: 435, 5/7)
10. Some MSS add: 'or, being unwilling because of the hardness of their
    hearts, to acquiesce to the truth, they might incur a penalty'.
11. Ga 5:6   12. Jn 4:32

faithful soul commits itself [to doing] the work of its devotion to the Lord. Lazarus becomes one of those who are
reclining [at table] with our Lord when those too who, after the death of sin have been restored to righteousness,
are one with those who have remained in their righteousness. Being repentant they exult in the presence of the truth,
and along with the innocent they are nourished with the
favors of heavenly grace.

It was appropriate that this dinner was held at Bethany.
This is a town on the slope of the Mount of Olives,[13] and
is interpreted 'house of obedience'.[14] The Church is the
house of obedience that complies faithfully with the Lord's
ordinances. She is the town that is established upon the
mount of mercy,[1*] and that can never be hidden.[15] She has
been produced from the side of her Redeemer, that is, imbued with the water of cleansing and the blood of sanctification which came forth from his side[16] when he was dying
for her sake.

Here also Mary, Lazarus's other sister, as an indication
of her great love (as the following section of this gospel reading demonstrates), took a pound weight of precious pure
ointment made from spikenard, and anointed Jesus' feet,
and wiped his feet with her hair. By this she not only gave
an indication of her devotion, but she also expressed the
holy service of other souls faithful to God.

But first we should note that, as Matthew and Mark tell
it,[17] Mary poured the ointment made from spikenard not
only over the Lord's feet, but also upon his head. We should
not doubt that this was that same woman, once a sinner,
who, as the evangelist Luke reports, came to our Lord[18] with
an alabaster vase of ointment *and, standing behind him at his
feet, began to bathe his feet with her tears, and she wiped them
with the hair of her head, and kissed his feet and anointed them
with ointment.*[19] This is the same woman, but there [in Luke's

13. Jer., *Sit.* (PL 23: 884)
14. Jer., *In Matth.* 26, 6 (CC 77: 246, 997/98), *Nom.* (CC 72: 135, 26/27)
15. Mt 5:14   16. Jn 19:34   17. Mt 26:7, Mk 14:3
18. Ambr., *Expos. evang. sec. Luc.* 6, 14 (CC 14: 179, 142/53)
19. Lk 7:37-38

gospel], she bent over and anointed only our Lord's feet,
and she did this amidst her tears of repentance; here [in
John's gospel], amidst the joy of her righteous action, she
did not hesitate both to anoint his feet and to stand up to
anoint his head also. There indeed she signified the initial
stages of repentance; here the righteousness of perfect souls.
Hence, rightly, the amount of the ointment was not mentioned there, but now mention is made that it was a pound
weight. What is represented by the pound weight of ointment but the perfection of righteousness? Then the type of
ointment was not mentioned; now indication is given that
it was compounded from spikenard which was pure (that
is, untainted and unadulterated with other different kinds),
and which was precious, to imply the chastity of perfect
faith and action.

By our Lord's head, which Mary anointed, is represented
the sublimity of his divinity, and by his feet the humility
of his incarnation. We anoint his feet when we proclaim
with due praise the mystery of the incarnation which he
took upon himself;[20] we anoint his head when we venerate the loftiness of his divinity with an assent that is worthy of what is being spoken of. For what is suggested by
the ointment but the good odor of assent? Paul bears witness to this when he says, *But thanks be to God who always
achieves his victory in us through Christ Jesus and through us
spreads the fragrance of the awareness of him in every place.*[21]
By the Lord's head can also properly be signified the very
Mediator between God and human beings,[22] who is the head
of the Church.[23] By his feet can appropriately be understood
his lowliest members, of whom he will say at the end [of
time], '*As often as you did this for one of the least of my brothers,
you did it for me*'.[24] We anoint our Lord's head when we cher-
ish the glory of his divinity, along with that of his humanity, with the worthy sweetness of faith, hope and charity,
[and] when we spread the praise of his name by living uprightly. We anoint our Lord's feet when we revivify his poor
by a word of consolation, so that they may not lose hope

20. Greg., *Hom. in evang.* 2, 33, 6 (*PL* 76: 1242/43)
21. 2 Co 2:14   22. 1 Tm 2:5   23. Col 1:18   24. Mt 25:40

when they are under duress; we wipe [the feet of] these same ones with our hair when we share some of what is superfluous to us [to alleviate] the wants of the needy.[25]

And there comes about in our case too what follows: *And the house was filled with the fragrance of the ointment.* In accord with our capacity will the world be filled with the renown of our devotion, by which we prove that we venerate and love God and our neighbors with a simple and pure heart. There is accomplished what the bride glories of in the canticle of love, *While the king was resting* [on his couch], *my spikenard gave forth its fragrance.*[26] Here it is clearly shown that what Mary once did as a type, the entire Church and every perfect soul should do always.

Then one of his disciples, Judas Iscariot, the one who was going to betray him, said, 'Why was this ointment not sold for three hundred denarii and [the money] *given to the needy'*? Woe to the wicked betrayer, woe to his accomplices in evil! Even now they persecute the members of Christ, they do not stop envying their neighbors' reputation for virtue, which they themselves do not deserve. We might be able to suppose that Judas spoke this out of concern for the poor, but for the truthful witness, [John], who divulged his [true state of] mind when he said, *But* [Judas] *said this, not because he had any interest in the needy, but because he was a thief, and, having the moneybox, he carried what was put* [in it]. Judas did not perish at the time when, corrupted by money, he handed over our Lord;[27] he was already morally lost when he was a follower of our Lord, and, having the Lord's moneybox, customarily carried[2*] what was put into it for their ministry and took it out by theft.[28] Our Lord saw that Judas's heart was already polluted by the stain of avarice, and foresaw that it would be [still more] polluted by the worse stain of betrayal, [yet] he entrusted to his keeping whatever he had in his moneybag and allowed him to do as he wished with it, to restrain [Judas's] mind from selling him, either by the memory of the honor he had bestowed [upon him],

25. Aug., *Tract. in Ioh.* 50, 6-7 (CC 36: 435, 10/19)
26. Sg 1:12 (1:11)   27. Mt 26:14-15
28. Aug., *Tract. in Ioh.* 50, 9 (CC 36: 437, 13/14)

or by his memory of having been the moneykeeper. But because *a greedy person always is in need,*[29] [Judas], being faithless and wicked, never remembered the trust [placed in him], but went on from the theft of the money which he was wont to carry to betraying our Lord, who showed confidence [in him].[30]

Jesus said, 'Let her alone, that she may keep it for the day of my burial'. As though Judas were asking an innocent question, our Lord simply and gently explained the mystery of what Mary's action meant,[31] namely that he himself was about to die, and that he was to be anointed for his burial with the spices. It was being granted to Mary (to whom it would not be permitted to anoint his dead body, although she greatly desired this) to render a service [to him while he was] still alive, since she would be unable [to perform it] after his death, for she would be prevented by his swift resurrection. Hence Mark appropriately bore witness that our Lord said of her, *'She has done what she could; she has anticipated the anointing of my body for burial'.*[32] This is to say clearly, 'She will not be able to touch my body once I am dead; she has done what she was able to do; she has anticipated, while I am still alive, the performance of the duty of burying me'.

'You shall always have the poor with you, but you shall not always have me'. Here also our Lord, with the restraint of great patience, did not accuse Judas of greed. He reasonably demonstrated that he was not speaking [merely] of money [offered] for the poor, but that no fault should be found with those who provided from their resources for him while he was still living among human beings. He was going to remain bodily with the Church for but a brief while, whereas the poor, for whom alms could be provided, were always to be found in it.

Therefore a large crowd of Jews learned that he was there, and came, not for Jesus's sake alone, but that they might see Lazarus,

29. Horace, *Epistle* I, 2, 56
30. var: 'who entrusted money to his keeping'
31. *'quo mysterium Mariae pertineret'*: var: 'what ministry pertained to Mary' (*quo ministerium Mariae pertineret*)
32. Mk 14:8

whom he had raised from the dead. It was curiosity and not
charity that brought them to Jesus.[33] Let us do the opposite, dearly beloved brothers. If we recognize where Jesus
is, where he is making his abode, where he has found
Bethany (that is, 'the home of the obedient soul'[34] in which
he dwells), let us go thither by contemplation, not merely
for the sake of [seeing] a man whose soul he allowed to live
spiritually after he raised him from the dead, but so that
by imitating the good life of [that] man, we may in this way
deserve to reach the sight of Jesus, because we have recognized for certain where Jesus is. He has risen from the dead,
and ascended after his death into heaven; there he has his
perpetual abode. This is the true Bethany, the heavenly city
which none but the obedient can enter. Let us strive with
all our strength of soul to arrive there. Let us make our way
thither by the inward affection of our heart. Let us long [to
arrive] there. Let us beg all together, and let us beg individually, of the Maker of that house, that we may dwell in his
house all the days of our life[35]—not that we may see Lazarus there, whom he raised from the dead, but that we ourselves, together with Lazarus and the rest of the saints who
have been revived from the dead, may see the delight of
the Lord and be shielded by his holy temple.[36]

*The chief priests took counsel how they might put Lazarus to
death, because on his account many were leaving the Jews and
believing in Jesus.* Blind cunning of the blind, to wish to kill
one who had been restored to life! As if [Jesus] could not
restore to life one who had been killed, when he had been
able to restore to life one who had died! And, indeed, he
taught that he was able to do both, since he restored to life
both Lazarus, who had died, and himself, who had been
killed. Let us, dearly beloved brothers, leaving behind the
malice of the faithless, follow the devotion of the faithful.
Let us leave the company of the wicked, let us not sit down
in the gathering of those who are vain, and not go along
with those who commit iniquity.[37] Let us believe in him who

33. Aug., *Tract. in Ioh.* 50, 14 (CC 36: 439, 4/5)
34. Jer., *Nom.* (CC 72: 135, 26/27)   35. Ps 27:4 (26:4)
36. ibid.   37. Ps 26:4 (25:4)

saves not only the body, but also the soul from death, and let us observe in our works what we believe, so that by believing we may have eternal life in his name,[38] for he lives and reigns with the Father and the Holy Spirit throughout all ages of ages. Amen.

38. Jn 20:31

NOTES

1. Elsewhere in his writings Bede sees a connection between the root of the Greek word for olive-tree, *elaía*, and that for the word for mercy, *éleos* (*Hom.* I.25 (*CC* 122: 178,16).
2. Faithfully following his reading of Saint Augustine's *Tractates on John's Gospel* at this point, Bede makes use of the play on words there, namely *porto,* 'carry,' and *exporto,* 'take out'.

homily II.5

When John the evangelist was going to write about that memorable service[1] of our Lord, in which he deigned to wash the feet of his disciples at the Passover [meal] before he went forth to his passion, he first took care to make clear what the name 'Passover' mystically expressed. He started thus: *Before the festival day of the Passover, Jesus, knowing that the hour had come for him to pass from this world to his Father, since he had loved his own who were in the world, loved them to the end.* 'Passover' means passing over.[2] It derives its ancient name from the Lord's passing over on this [day] through Egypt, striking the first-born of the Egyptians[3] and freeing the children of Israel, and from the children of Israel's passing over on that night from their slavery in Egypt,[4] in order that they might come to the land which had once been promised to their heirs as one of peace. Mystically it signifies that on this [day] our Lord would pass over from this world to his Father; and that, following his example, the faithful, having cast off temporal desires, and having cast off their slavery to vices by their continual

---

1. 'service' = *ministerium*; var.: 'mystery' = *mysterium*
2. Aug., *Tract. in Ioh.* 55, 1 (CC 36: 463, 11 - 464, 21)
3. Ex 12:11-12, 23-27   4. Ex 14:21-29

practice of the virtues, should pass over to their promised heavenly fatherland.

How Jesus passed over from this world to his Father, the evangelist designates in fine and appropriate language when he says, *Since he had loved his own who were in the world, he loved them to the end,* that is, he loved them so much that by that very love he would end his bodily life for a time, and he would soon pass from death to life, from this world to his Father. *No one has greater love than this, that he should lay down his life for his friends.*[5] Hence each passing over (namely, that under the law, and that under the gospel) was consecrated with blood—the former with that of a paschal lamb, the latter with that of the one about whom the Apostle says, *For Christ, our paschal* [lamb], *has been immolated;*[6] the latter with his blood poured out on the cross, the former with its blood sprinkled in the manner of a cross in the middle of the lintel and the middle of the door posts.

[John] says: *And when the meal was finished (the devil having now put into the heart of Judas Iscariot, the son of Simon, that he should hand him over), [Jesus], knowing that the Father had given all things into his hands, and that he had come forth from God and was going back to God, rose from the table and put aside his* [outer] *garments.* When [John] was about to speak of the greatest act of humility of the humanity that [Christ] had taken upon himself, he first recalled the eternity of his divine power. This was to demonstrate that he is both true God and true man, and to admonish us by [Christ's] commands that the greater we are, the more we should humble ourselves in everything.[7] He was truly human since he could touch and wash the feet of [other] human beings, be handed over by [another] human being, and be crucified by human beings; he was truly God since into his hands the Father had given everything, he had come forth from God, and he was returning to God.

Our Lord knew that the devil had now put it into the heart of Judas to hand him over. He knew that his Father had given all things into his hands—among these being the

5. Jn 15:13   6. 1 Co 5:7   7. Si 3:18 (3:20)

betrayer himself and those to whom he would be handed over, and the death which he was about to suffer after he had been handed over—so that he could do as he willed concerning them all, and by his power turn their wickedness into good. He knew that through the humility of his incarnation he had come forth from God, and that through the victory of his resurrection he was going to return to God, neither abandoning God when he came forth from him, nor abandoning us when he returned [to him]. He knew all these things. Yet as an indication of his great benevolence [toward us], and as an example of his great humility for us [to follow], he rose from the table, put aside his [outer] garments, and washed his disciples' feet, fulfilling the office not of the Lord God but that of a human being, a servant. He even humbly washed the feet of the one whose hands he knew were to be shamefully polluted by his betrayal.[8]

If anyone should take delight in investigating this most humble service[9] of our Savior at a more profound level, the sacred meal at which our Lord reclined with his disciples represents the entire time in which he remained bodily in the Church. He himself fed everyone far and wide with the banquet of his saving words and the sweetness of his miracles, and was himself fed by the faith and love of those who heard him. By converting to the grace of the truth all those who make up his body, which is the Church,[10] he caused an increase [in it], as if in the manner of those who partake of food. He rose from the table and put aside his [outer] garments when, ceasing the fuller sharing of his life in time with human beings, he put aside on the cross the bodily members which he had assumed. He took up a linen towel, with which he girded himself, when, after having taken up for us the mandate of suffering which he had received from his Father, he covered his body with the torment of his passion. A linen towel, which is woven by the endless labor of twisting [flax], is usually taken to signify the pain of suffering. When our Lord had laid aside his [outer] gar-

8. Aug., *Tract in Ioh.* 55, 5-6 (CC 36: 465, 2 - 466, 17)
9. 'service' = *ministerium;* var: 'mystery' = *mysterium*
10. Col 1:24

ments, he girded himself with a linen towel to signify that
he was putting aside the clothing of the body which he had
put on, [and that he was doing this] not without the distress of sorrow, but with the prolonged anguish of the cross.
He poured water into a basin, and began to wash his disciples' feet and to dry them with the linen cloth with which
he was girded, when, after he was dead on the cross, he
poured forth onto the ground water along with blood from
his side.[11] With these he would cleanse the works of believers, and he deigned not only to sanctify these works by
the sacramental [mystery] of his passion, but also to
strengthen them by the example of his own passion.

But as for the fact that after he had commenced the washing of the feet, it is said, *He came therefore to Simon Peter,*
this is not to be understood as meaning that he came to him
after some of the rest, but rather that [Jesus] began with
him who was the first among the apostles, and that [Peter],
with good reason, shrank from such an act of service because he did not grasp [the meaning of] the mystery. We
should not doubt that others of them would have reacted
in the same way if they were not deterred by the statement
that was spoken to Peter, *'If I do not wash you, you will have
no part with me'.* Here it is clearly being pointed out that
this washing of the feet implies the spiritual purification of
body and soul without which we cannot arrive at fellowship with Christ.

Hence, on hearing this, Peter, having been reproved, answered immediately with his usual warmth of divine love:
'Lord, not only my feet, by my hands too and my head,' as if
he were clearly saying, 'Since I now understand through
your pointing it out to me, that by washing my feet you
affirm that you are cleansing my misdeeds, I offer you not
only my feet, but also my hands and my head, to be washed.
I do not deny that, not only by walking, but also by my
actions, my vision, my hearing, tasting, smelling and touching, I commit many deeds which must be forgiven by you'.

But let us hear the answer our Lord made to this ardent
love, [and] how he gradually stirred him up to a mystical

11. Jn 19:34

understanding of the washing. [Jesus] said, *'The person who has bathed needs only to wash his feet, and he is completely clean'.* [Jesus] is giving clear notice that this washing of the feet indicates pardoning of sins, and not only that which is given once in baptism, but in addition that by which the daily guilty actions of the faithful, without which no one lives in this life, are cleansed by his daily grace. Our feet, by which we move about [and] touch the ground (and for this reason we cannot keep them free from contact with dirt, as [we can] the rest of our bodies) signify the necessity of our living upon earth, by which we who are idle and negligent are daily affected to a great extent. Even outstanding men who live the highest kind of life are distracted from the heavenly contemplation which they love so much, so that *if we say that we have no sin, we deceive ourselves, and the truth is not in us.*[12]

'The person who has bathed needs only to wash his feet, and he is completely clean'—the person who has been cleansed in the baptismal font and [has received] pardon for all his sins has no need to be cleansed again; moreover he cannot be cleansed again in the same way. He finds it necessary only to have the daily defilements of his worldly life wiped away by the daily forgiveness of his Redeemer. His whole body, together with its actions, is clean, with the exception merely of those things which cling to the mind because of the necessities of temporal cares. For their daily polluting and cleansing we say daily in prayer, *And forgive us our debts as we also forgive our debtors.*[13]

But these things are said of the apostles and those like them, those namely who are blessed and unspotted, who fear the Lord and walk in his ways.[14] Since we are often forgetful of divine fear, and we go in the wrong direction, we cannot be freed by this easy daily rite of prayers from the baseness [that results from] our wrong turns. Our greater impurity needs to be purified by a greater practice of prayers, vigils and fasting, of tears and almsgiving. He

12. 1 Jn 1:8
13. Mt 6:12, Aug., *Tract. in Ioh.* 56, 4 (CC 36:468, 4/19)
14. Ps 119:1 (118:1)

undoubtedly cleanses inwardly the traces [of sin] in our
hearts who, sitting at God's right hand, daily makes intercession for us[15] through the nature of the humanity which
he assumed.

After our Lord had washed his disciples' feet he put his
[outer] garments back on. When he had reclined again he
made clear in words [the meaning of] the service[16] of washing [their feet], which they had not understood a little earlier
when he had done it. After he had consecrated for us the
washing of pardon by his suffering on the cross, he put back
on the members, now immortal, which he had laid aside
when they were mortal. When he appeared to his disciples
after his resurrection, and kept company familiarly with
them, even eating [with them], during a period of forty
days, he explained to them[17] the benefit of his passion. They
still feared its outcome up to that time, because they did
not understand its mystical power.

He said, *'If I, your Lord and master, have washed your feet,
you also ought to wash one another's feet'.* We should take this
statement in both its literal sense and its mystical sense, and
we ought to devoutly carry it out. Its literal sense is that
we should serve each other in charity, not only by washing our brothers' feet, but also by aiding them in any of their
needs. The mystical sense is that, just as our Lord is wont
to forgive the sins of those who repent, so also should we
hasten to forgive our brothers when they sin against us.
Just as he washes us from our sins[18] by interceding with
the Father on our behalf,[19] so also should we, if we know
that our brother is committing *a sin* [which is] *not to death*,
ask that *life* be *given to him who is sinning not to death.*[20] And
as the apostle James advises, we should confess our sins
to one another, and pray for each other, that we may be
saved.[21] Just as he laid down his life for us, so we also, if
the occasion arises, should lay down our life for our
brothers.[22]

---

15. Rm 8:34
16. 'service' = *ministerium;* var.: 'mystery' = *mysterium*
17. Ac 1:3-4   18. Rv 1:5   19. Rm 8:34
20. 1 Jn 5:16   21. Jm 5:16   22. 1 Jn 3:16

There follows: *'Truly, truly I say to you, a servant is not greater than his Lord, nor an apostle greater than the one who sent him'*. He said this because he, the Lord, had washed the feet of his servants, and he who sent [them washed the feet] of those he sent. [The word] 'apostle' in Greek means in Latin 'one who is sent'. [He said this] to show that what he, the Most High, humbly did was much more to be humbly carried out by those who were humble and weak. In a spiritual sense too, he would advise [us] that if he *who committed no sin nor was there found any deceit in his mouth*[23] makes intercession for our aberrations, all the more ought we to pray for each other; if he, to whom we have nothing to forgive, forgives us, all the more should we forgive one another our debts. The Apostle also commands this very thing, saying, *Be generous and merciful toward each other, requiting each other just as God also in Christ has requited you.*[24]

Jesus said, *'If you know these things, blessed will you be if you do them'*. This statement of our Saviour is very helpful for salvation, and we must ponder it attentively. We will be blessed if we know the heavenly commands, yet still more so if we eagerly pursue in our works the things that we know. One who neglects to keep his known commandments is not capable of being happy; one who scorns finding out about these [commandments] is separated much further away from the heritage of the blessed. The psalmist agrees with this. Weighing the hearts of mortals, and in like manner perceiving that everyone loves happiness but few ask where it is, he clearly testified as to what is the greatest happiness of human beings in this life, saying, *'Blessed are those who are undefiled in the way, who walk in the Lord's law'*.[25] And lest it be supposed that this way of the undefiled and blessed can be laid hold of indiscriminately by the ignorant and the untaught, he subsequently continued and said, *'Blessed are they who search his testimonies and seek him with their whole heart'*.[26]

Wherefore, dearly beloved, let us ask him for his clemency, who commanded that his commandments be kept

23. 1 P 2:22   24. Eph 4:32   25. Ps 119:1 (118:1)
26. Ps 119:2 (118:2)

strictly,[27] that he may direct our ways toward keeping his righteousness.[28] After we have kept his commandments, may he bring us to the blessedness of the everlasting sight of him, Jesus Christ, our Lord and God, who lives and reigns with the Father in the unity of the Holy Spirit throughout all ages of ages. Amen.

27. Ps 119:4 (118:4)   28. Ps 119:5 (118:5)

homily II.6

The deaf-mute, of whose marvelous cure by our Lord we have just now heard when the gospel was read, represents those members of the human race who merit being freed by divine grace from the error brought on by the devil's deceit. Man became deaf, unable to hear the word of life after, puffed up [as he was] against God, he listened to the serpent's deadly words; he was made mute [and unable to declare] the praises of his Maker from the time when he presumed to have a conversation with his seducer.[1] Rightly did [God] close [man's] ears from hearing the praises of his Creator along with the angels—those ears which the unsuspected enemy by his speech had opened to hearing denunciation of this same Creator; rightly did [God] close [man's] mouth from proclaiming the praises of his Creator along with the angels—that mouth which the proud [deceiver] had filled with his lies about the forbidden food, in order, [as the devil said], to improve upon the work of this same Creator. And alas, the unfortunate rebellion of the human race, which sprouted in a corrupt manner at the root, began to spread in a much more corrupt

---

1. Gn 3:1-7

way in shoots from the branches, so that when our Lord
came in the flesh, with the exception of a few of the faithful from among the Jews, almost the entire world, now deaf
and mute, was wandering away from recognition and confession of the truth.

But *where sin abounded, grace abounded all the more.*[2] Our
Lord came to the Sea of Galilee, where he knew that there
was a disabled person whom he would heal. He came by
his benevolent grace to the proud, disordered and incon-
stant hearts of the nations, since he knew that among them
were some who would be receptive to his grace. And it is
well said that he came through the district of the Ten Cit-
ies to the Sea of Galilee, where he would heal the disabled
man: because of their lack of faith he left the people who
had received the ten commandments and came to the gentiles, so that, as John says, *He might gather together the children of God who had been scattered.*[3]

*And they brought to him a deaf-mute, and entreated him to lay
his hands upon him.* Because that man, being deaf, was unable to know about our Savior, and being mute, was unable to ask [anything of him], his friends led him [to our
Lord] and made supplication to the Lord for his restoration
to health. Thus in the case of a spiritual cure, we must see
that if someone cannot be converted to hearing and confessing the truth by human efforts, he should be brought
to the attention of divine benevolence, and we should beg
for the help of the hands of the Most High to heal him. The
mercy of the heavenly physician is not slow, if the insis-
tent prayers of the petitioners do not hesitate or fail.

Hence it is at once added that Jesus *took* the disabled man
*aside from the crowd, put his fingers into his ears, and spitting,
touched his tongue.* He puts his fingers into the ears of a deaf
person to make him hear when, through the gifts of spiritual
grace, he converts to the hearing of his word those who
for a long while have not believed. Spitting he touches the
tongue of a person who is mute to enable him to speak
when, through the ministry of preaching, he endows [some-

2. Rm 5:20   3. Jn 11:52

one] with the grasp of the faith he must confess. That by the fingers of the Lord the gifts of the Holy Spirit are signified he himself teaches, saying, *'If I by the finger of God cast out demons,'*[4] which another evangelist puts more clearly, *'If I by the Spirit of God cast out demons'.*[5] And [there is] the psalmist when he says, *'Since I shall see the heavens, the works of your fingers,'*[6] that is, 'I shall see the saints lifted up from earthly things, not by the merit of their own virtue, but by the gift of your Spirit, and elevated by their [participation in] the heavenly way of life'. The spittle from our Lord's head and mouth is the word of his gospel, which he deigned to take from the hidden mystery of his divinity and administer visibly to the world, so that it could be healed.[7]

We should note that before our Lord touched the ears and tongue of the disabled man who was to be healed, he took him and led him aside from the crowd. The first hope of salvation for anyone is to desert those with vicious habits, and the commotion of the crowds, and so humbly bow his head to receive the gift of healing. We must not in any way suppose that salvation is possible[8] as long as one is not afraid to cling to his disordered habits, to be delighted by pointless words, [or] to be impaired by disturbing thoughts. But there lies in store for a person who, with God's mercy and aid, has changed the disturbed ways of his former life, who has conceived in his heart the inspiration of divine grace, who has learned from the word of heavenly teaching to confess the true faith, to secure immediately the longed-for joys of good health.

Hence it is appropriate that, after our Lord separates the disabled man from the crowd, after he puts his fingers into his ears, after he touches his tongue with his spittle, there is added: *And looking up toward heaven he groaned and said, 'Effeta,' which means 'be opened'. And at once his ears were opened and the ligament of his tongue was loosened.* It was proper that, as he was about to heal the disabled man, our Lord looked up toward heaven and groaned. This was to indicate from

4. Lk 11:20   5. Mt 12:28   6. Ps 8:3 (8:4)
7. Greg., *Hom. in Ezech.* 1, 10, 20 (CC 142: 153, 335 - 154, 347)
8. var.: 'that one can please our Savior'

where healing was to be hoped for, and with what zeal for
compunction and tears it was to be sought after and reached
out for. He looked up toward heaven and groaned because
he grieved that we, whom he had created to possess heavenly things, were cast far away, [entangled] in earthly matters. He looked up toward heaven and groaned to suggest
to us, who had withdrawn from the joys of heaven through
being gratified by earthly things, that our return to these
joys must be accomplished by groaning and sighing.

As to his saying 'Effeta' (that is, 'be opened'), he did this
in order to heal the ears which a longstanding deafness had
closed up, but which his touch now opened that they might
hear. Hence I believe a custom has prevailed in the Church
that his priests, first among all the elementary stages of con-
secration [that they perform] for those whom they are
preparing to receive the sacrament of baptism, touch their
nostrils and ears with saliva from their mouth, while they
say, 'Effeta'. By the saliva from their mouth they symbolize the taste of heavenly wisdom to which they are being
introduced. By touching the nostrils [they indicate] that,
once they have cast aside all harmful delights, they should
always embrace only the odor of Christ, about which the
Apostle says, *We are the good odor of Christ to God in every
place*,[9] and they should remember that, following the example of blessed Job, they are not to speak falsehood with
their lips, nor with their tongue meditate on lying, as long
as breath is in them and the Spirit of God is in their nostrils.[10] Moreover, by the touching of the ears [they indicate]
that, once they have left off listening to wicked tongues,
they are to listen to the words of Christ and do them, like
the prudent man who built his house upon a rock.[11]

Each one of us, dearly beloved brothers, who has received
the baptism of Christ according to the sacred rites, has been
consecrated in this way. All who are going to receive this
healing and saving[12] bath according to the sacred rites, either
at the approaching time of Easter, or at some other time,
will be consecrated in this way. Hence it is most necessary

9. 2 Co 2:15   10. Jb 27:3-4   11. Mt 7:24
12. 'healing and saving' = double meaning of *salutare*

that we should fear to defile thoughtlessly what the Lord has propitiously deigned to cleanse and sanctify in us, and to profane it as though it were of little account; but if any of us has partaken of a meal of disgraceful wickedness, let us hurry to cleanse ourselves once more at the font of tears and repentance. Let us renew the purity which has been divinely bestowed upon us *through faith in what we have heard,*[13] avoiding that [sentence] of the Apostle which he said in reproach of some individuals, *And they will turn away their ears from the truth, and will be turned toward false tales.*[14] Let us restrain our tongues from evil, since they have been sanctified by our confession of faith.[15] Let us fear to use that [tongue] with which we bless our God and Father to curse human beings, who have been made according to God's likeness. *For if anyone supposes that he is religious and does not bridle his tongue, his religion is worthless.*[16]

Behold, it is said that his ears were opened and the ligament of his tongue was loosed, and that he spoke rightly. Since we learned to speak rightly at the time of our baptism by believing in our heart, we must take the utmost care to [arrive at the state of] righteousness, and by making a confession with our mouth to [achieve] salvation,[17] lest after our baptism we turn aside to unrighteousness and offensive words. If, according to the testimony of our Judge himself, *'Every person who speaks an idle word will give an account of it on the day of judgment,'*[18] what do you suppose will happen to those who speak not only idle words, but also those that are blameworthy? Or to those who do not fear to indulge in utterances of an unchaste, boastful, or blasphemous sort, or (what is especially and exceedingly pleasing to them) slanderous utterances? Or to those who, like false witnesses, speak lies? Or to those who sow discord among brothers? It is not sufficient to keep our ears and our tongues only from what is evil if we do not also (as the psalmist says) incline our ears to the words [that come] from the mouth of God,[19] if our mouths do not ex-

---

13. Ga 3:2   14. 2 Tm 4:4   15. Ps 34:13 (33:14)
16. Jm 1:26   17. Rm 10:10   18. Mt 12:36
19. Ps 78:1 (77:1)

press wisdom, and the meditation of our hearts prudence.[20] But we should also keep all our senses, of our inner as well as our outer selves, pure, and adorned always with good works, since all of us have been washed [in the waters of] baptism.

Let us see what follows when the deaf-mute has been cured: *And [Jesus] charged them not to tell anyone. But the more he charged them, the more did they proclaim it. They wondered greatly, saying, 'He has done all things well; he has even caused the deaf to hear and the dumb to speak'.* What should we believe was the reason, dearly beloved brothers, that these things were done? Should we judge that God's only-begotten Son wrought this sign and wanted it to remain hidden, that it was disclosed to the crowds against his will, and that he could not have cloaked this sign in silence if he so chose, since he could do what he chose when he chose [to do it]? Is it not possible that he wanted to give us an example, so that, when we perform acts of virtue, we would avoid the vice of boasting and, most of all, we would avoid human praise, lest our good deed be deprived of the gift of heavenly reward as a result of the empty favor of the general public?

Yet we should be aware that if our good deeds are worthy of imitation they cannot be hidden, but will be revealed for the purpose of fraternal correction, by the divinely-arranged plan of the one who said, *'A city situated on a mountain top cannot be kept from sight';*[21] and elsewhere, *'Wherefore what you have said in the darkness will be spoken of in the light'.*[22] And in truth our Lord's divinely-arranged charge is to be so understood in every detail. For no one should judge that what was said [means that] when we perform good deeds we ought to avoid the sight of our brothers, since our Lord said, *'Let your light shine before men, that they may see your good deeds.'*[23] What follows, *'And that they may give glory to your Father who is in heaven,'*[24] indicates that we should seek from the works which we show to our brothers not their praise, but advance [in virtue]. Those who show

20. Ps 49:3 (48:4)   21. Mt 5:14   22. Lk 12:3
23. Mt 5:16   24. ibid.

their good works with the intention that they alone be praised, not that those who praise them may advance in good [habits], or that their Father who is in heaven may be glorified, are the sort who are to be punished with that terrible rebuke in which it is said, *'Truly I say to you, they have received their reward'.*[25]

This too must be said, that if those who received the charge to be silent were unable to keep silent about our Lord's virtues, much more should we, who are charged to refresh each other with the daily food, the heavenly word, always devote ourselves to proclaiming [the workings] of divine grace, since the apostle John says, *Let the one who hears say, 'Come'.*[26] He means, let the one who conceives the grace of heavenly inspiration in his mind, the one who has learned words of encouragement with which he may be capable of comforting his neighbor, by no means hide the good that he knows under silence, but he should share [this] by opening himself up straightaway to his brothers. If we do not neglect to speak generously to our neighbors about the good things we know of, he *in whom all the treasures of wisdom and knowledge are hidden*[27] will deign to make known to us the perfect light of truth which we now know only in part,[28] Jesus Christ our Lord, the only-begotten Son of the Father, who lives and reigns with [him] in the unity of the Holy Spirit, God throughout all ages of ages. Amen.

25. Mt 6:5   26. Rv 22:17   27. Col 2:3
28. 1 Co 13:9

homily II.7

Matthew 28:1-10   *The Easter Vigil*

The resurrection of our Lord and Savior has consecrated the vigil of this most sacred night[1] for us, dearly beloved brothers, as we have heard from the gospel reading. Rightly do we celebrate[2] this [night] with watching and hymns, out of love for him who, out of love for us, willed to spend it in the sleep of death and to be raised from the dead. As the Apostle says, *He died for our transgressions and rose to make us righteous.*[3]

He revealed this by the times at which he died on the cross and rose from the dead. He brought the mystery of his victorious passion to fulfillment about three o'clock in the afternoon,[4] when day was already declining toward evening and the rays of the sun were becoming cooler after the midday heat. This is a clear suggestion that he had submitted to the gibbet of the cross in order to take away the wicked

---

1. *Gregorian Sacramentary*, ed. H.A. Wilson, *HBS* 59 (London, 1915), p. 58; *Bobbio Missal*, ed. E.A. Lowe, *HBS* 58 (London, 1920), no. 258, p. 77; *Missale Gallicanum Vetus*, ed. L.C. Mohlberg, *RED*, ser. maior, Fontes, 3 (Rome, 1958), no. 179, p. 42; *Sacramentum Gelesianum*, ed. L.C. Mohlberg, *RED*, ser. maior, Fontes, 4 (Rome 1960), nos. 453-54, p. 75. See also Bede, Homily II. 7, p. 226, line 48, page 230, line 181.
2. Aug., *Serm.* 1-4, ed. Morin, 457-60   3. Rm 4:25, 1 Co 15:3
4. literally 'about the ninth hour'

deeds by which we fell away from divine light and love into the night of this estrangement [from him]. He rose on the morning of Sunday,[5] which is now called the Lord's day, clearly teaching that he would bring us, once we had been raised up again from the death of our souls, into the light of everlasting bliss.

But he took care to suggest to us another remarkable mystery by the times of his passion, burial and resurrection. He was crucified on Friday, rested in the sepulcher on Saturday, and rose from the dead on Sunday, indicating to his elect that they must toil by good works throughout the six ages of this world amid the dangers of persecutions, and that they should hope for a [period of] rest for their souls in the next life, [enjoying] a kind of perpetual sabbath. Besides this, on judgment day, the Lord's day as it were, they are to celebrate the recovery of their immortal bodies, in which their souls may thenceforth enjoy heavenly happiness without end.

As to its being said in the gospel reading that holy women came to see the sepulcher 'on the evening which was growing on toward the dawn of Sunday,' we should understand this thus: they started to come during the evening, but reached the sepulcher as the morning of Sunday was dawning; that is, they prepared the spices with which they desired to anoint our Lord's body on [Saturday] evening, but brought the spices which they had prepared in the evening to the sepulcher in the morning. Matthew, for the sake of brevity, wrote this more obscurely; but the other evangelists[6] show more distinctly the order in which it was done. After our Lord had been buried on Friday, the women went away from the tomb and prepared spices and ointments for as long as it was permitted them to work; and they refrained from activity on the sabbath, in accord with the commandment,[7] as Luke clearly reports.[8] When the sabbath was over, as evening was coming on, the time for working had returned. Being resolute in their devotion, they bought the spices which they had not prepared [earlier] (as

5. *prima sabbati*   6. Mk 16:1-2, Lk 24:1   7. Ex 12:16, 20:8-10
8. Lk 23:56

Mark records it[9]) so that they might come and anoint him. *And very early on the first day of the week they came to the tomb.*[10]

But we must inquire why, when he is describing the night of our Lord's resurrection, the evangelist says, *On the sabbath evening which was growing on toward the dawn of Sunday,* when the customary order of time would have the evening darkening into night, rather than growing on toward dawn. Speaking mystically, the evangelist was striving to suggest the great dignity this most sacred night acquired from the glory [of our Lord's] victory over death, when he mentioned that its inception, when the women devoted to Christ began to be watchful about performing their service for him, had already begun to grow on toward the following dawn. Our Lord, the author and controller of time, he who rose [from the dead] during the final part of the night, surely caused the whole of it to be festal and bright by the light of his resurrection.

From the beginning of the world's creation until this time, the course of time was so divided that day preceded night, according to the order of its primeval making.[11] On this night, because of the mystery of our Lord's resurrection, the order of time was changed.[12] He rose from the dead during the night, and on the following day he showed the effect of his resurrection to his disciples. Having shared a feast with them, he proved the truth of his power as they wondered[13] and rejoiced.[14] Most properly was night joined to the light of the following day, and the order of time so settled that day would follow night. It was once appropriate that night follow day, for by sinning the human race fell away from the light of paradise into the darkness and hardships of this age. It is appropriate that day follow night now, when through faith in the resurrection we are led back from the darkness of sin and the shadow of death[15] to the light of life by Christ's gift. Wherefore, dearly beloved brothers, we who have come to know that this special night has been illumined by the grace of our Lord's resurrection

9. Mk 16:1-2   10. Mk 16:2   11. Gn 1:3-5
12. Aug., *Serm.* 221 (*PL* 38: 1089-90)
13. Lk 24:41-43   14. Jn 20:20   15. Lk 1:79

must also take particular care lest any least part of it become dark in our hearts. All of it should become light as day for us, especially now when we are keeping vigil with the devotion of worthy praise, and are awaiting with a pure and sober conscience the feast of Easter Sunday when we have completed this vigil.

Mary Magdalene and the other Mary came to see the sepulchre. Two women with the same name, and with the same love and devotion, who came to have a look at our Lord's sepulcher, represent two faithful peoples (Jews and gentiles), who with one and the same zeal desire to celebrate their Redeemer's passion and resurrection wherever his Church has spread throughout the globe. That there was a great earthquake when our Lord rose from the sepulchre, just as when he was dying on the cross,[16] signifies that formerly earthly hearts, and those deprived of heavenly hope, were to be violently agitated by belief in his passion and resurrection and [moved] to repentance. When thoroughly stirred by a most salutary trepidation, they would be lifted up to perpetual life.

As for the angel's coming, [this indicates that] he was performing an act of service that he owed to our Lord. Because Christ is both God and man, along with the activities of his humanity there is never a lack of angelic ministries due to God,[17] as an examination of the history of the holy gospels proves most abundantly.[18] [The angel] rolled back the stone not to throw open a way for our Lord to come forth, but to provide evidence to people that he had already come forth. If as a mortal human being he could at his birth enter the world although the Virgin's womb was closed, without any doubt, now that he had become immortal, he could at his rising leave the world although the sepulcher was closed.[19]

---

16. Mt 27:51
17. *semper angelorum ministeria Deo debita non desunt,* the reading of several manuscripts
18. Mt. 4:11, Lk 2:13-14, 22:43, Jer., *In Matth.* 28, 3 (*CC* 77: 279, 1919 - 280, 1935).
19. Aug. *Serm.* 191, 2 (*PL* 38:1010), 247 (*PL* 38:1157)

Nor must we pass over the reason the angel, as a witness to our Lord's resurrection, appeared [to the women]
sitting, when we read that the one who brought the joyful
news of his nativity to the world stood before the
shepherds.[20] Standing is appropriate to one fighting, sitting to one ruling.[21] It was fitting that the angel who
proclaimed the coming of our Lord into the world appeared
standing, that by his standing [position] he might express
the fact that the one he was proclaiming was coming to do
battle with the prince of this world. It was fitting that the
herald of his resurrection is reported to have been sitting,
so that by sitting he might prefigure him who, having triumphed over the author of death, would ascend to his seat
in his everlasting kingdom. Concerning this he said a little
later, as he appeared to his disciples, *'All power in heaven
and on earth has been given to me';*[22] and the evangelist Mark
says, *The Lord, after he had spoken to them, was taken up into
heaven and sat down at God's right hand.*[23] [The angel] was
sitting upon the stone with which the tomb was closed, but
which had been rolled away, to teach that [Christ] had cast
down and triumphed over the closed places of the lower
world by his power, so that he might lift up to the light and
the rest of paradise all of his own whom he found there,
according to the prophet's [statement], *You also because of
the blood of your covenant, have led your prisoners back from the
pit, in which there is no water.*[24]

His appearance was like lightning and his clothing like snow.
This was to signify by his clothing and countenance that
he, the glory of whose resurrection he was announcing, is
both dreadful in condemning the reprobate, and generous
and kind in consoling the elect.[25] The terror brought on by
fear is expressed by lightning, kindness by the shining
brightness of snow. As an indication of the divine ability
to discriminate, the angel who appeared thoroughly terrified the wicked guards at the sepulcher, and cast them pros-

20. Lk 2:9
21. Greg., *Hom. in evang.* 2, 29, 7 (*PL* 76:1217)
22. Mt 28:18   23. Mk 16:19   24. Zc 9:11
25. Greg., *Hom. in evang.* 2, 22, 3 (*PL* 76:1171)

trate on the ground like dead men; whereas, by his generous consolation, he cheered the holy women who were visiting the sepulcher, and comforted them, so that they would
not be in a state of trepidation. In addition, he first said,
addressing them in a friendly way, that he knew they were
seeking Jesus, and added that he had already risen; next,
he also laid upon them the most honorable and glad mis-
sion of announcing the joyful news of his resurrection. How
filled with bliss were these women who, taught by the angel's account, were found worthy to announce the triumph
of the resurrection to the world and to proclaim that the
sovereignty of death, to which Eve became subject when
she was seduced by the serpent's speech, had been utterly
destroyed! How much more blissful will be the souls of men
and women equally, when, aided by heavenly grace, they
have merited to triumph over death and enter into the joy
of a blessed resurrection, while the condemned have been
struck with trepidation and well-deserved punishment on
the day of judgment!

As the women were running to take the good news to
the disciples, Jesus greeted them. He was revealing that he
comes with his assistance to meet all who are undertaking
the way of virtue, so that they may be able to reach salvation.[26]

They approached and took hold of his feet. Let us see in our
Lord's resurrection from the dead, brothers, the reality of
our own [human] flesh, let us see the glory [of his] new
[state] of incorruptibility. Earlier we read about his rising,
with the tomb still closed; now we read of the women taking hold of his feet and adoring him. He rose and came out
while the opening of the tomb remained closed in order to
teach that his body, which had been shut up in the tomb,
had now become immortal; he offered the women his feet
to take hold of, in order to make known that he was showing them a true body which mortals could touch.

---

26. some MSS: 'perpetual salvation'

'Go,' he said, '*Tell my brothers to go to Galilee; they will see me there*'. O wonderful benevolence[27] of our Savior! O his admirable generosity! Those whom before his passion he had been accustomed to call his disciples, and occasionally even his servants, after his resurrection he names his brothers! He did this to point out that in his rising he had resumed the condition of human being which he had had before, and to elevate them to meriting and hoping for the crown of immortality, with which he himself was preeminent, for their own bodies.

As to his predicting that he would be seen in Galilee (and as the following part of this holy gospel declares,[28] he did appear to them there), in this too he mystically suggested both the power of his resurrection and our own advance in the spiritual life. Galilee means 'a crossing over accomplished'.[29] It was good that he who had now crossed over from death to life, from corruptibility to incorruptibility, from punishment to glory,[30] was seen in Galilee by his disciples to set forth the victory of his resurrection, not only by his showing of his body and the encouragement of his discourse, but also by the name of the place in which he appeared and spoke [to them]. But we ourselves will then be capable of taking delight in the joy of his resurrection only if we now attempt to cross over from the corrupting influence of vices to works of virtue. Hence we must take the utmost care, my brothers, that, as we have come to know the time of the resurrection of our Lord and Savior, [and] as we celebrate his solemnity by constantly advancing in good works, we cross over to the contemplation of his preeminence. We do not know the time of our own resurrection, although we are in no way uncertain that it will come to pass; and so at all times let us keep careful watch while we wait for it, and particularly on this special night. Let us entreat the mercy of him who quickly triumphed resplen-

---

27. *Missale Gothicum Vetus*, ed. L.C. Mohlberg, *RED*, ser. maior, Fontes, 3 (Rome, 1958), no. 134, p. 35, lines 29/30; *Missale Gothicum*, ed. L.C. Mohlberg, *RED*, ser. maior, Fontes, 5 (Rome, 1961), no. 225, p. 60, line 19
28. Mt 28:16   29. Jer., *Nom.* (CC 72: 131, 2)
30. Greg., *Hom. in evang.* 2, 22, 5 (*PL* 76: 1172)

dently over death, which he humbly underwent for our sakes, that he may grant us to cross over from death to life at the time of our own resurrection. Let us ask him who is the Christ, who was immolated for us as our paschal [lamb],[31] to grant us to bring to worthy completion the solemnity of Easter joy which we have entered upon, and through this to attain eternal joys.[32]

In truth, as we are engaged upon these matters we should note that the solemnity of this most sacred night and of our redemption, which we are observing, was already once mystically represented among the ancient people of God. When this people had been long weighed down by their slavery in Egypt, and the Egyptians did not want to permit them to go forth to freely serve their Maker, at length the Lord commanded [his people], in celebration of the Passover, to immolate a lamb and to roast and eat its flesh during this night; to smear both doorposts of their houses, the lintel and the threshold, with the blood [of the lamb] which had been poured out; and to wait within, being watchful for the hour of their redemption. While they were doing this, behold, the Lord came in the middle of this night, and struck the firstborn of the Egyptians. He freed his people from the burden of their long slavery, and brought them to the fatherland which had formerly been promised, ordering them to observe this night every year by the immolation of the paschal lamb as a solemnity in memory of their salvation.[33]

The redemption of that people unquestionably bore within it a type of our spiritual redemption, which was brought to completion on this night by our Lord's rising from the dead.[34] So too that people's carnal oppressors, the Egyptians, represent the cruel arms of the spirit of wickedness,[35] with which it oppressed the human race that had become subject to it by virtue of its wicked domination.[36] But the

---

31. 1 Co 5:7
32. *Gregorian Sacramentary*, ed. H.A. Wilson, *HBS* 49 (London, 1915), p. 65
33. Ex 12:3-50
34. Greg., *Hom. in evang.* 2, 22, 7 (*PL* 76:1178)
35. *nequitiae spiritalis*, cf. Eph 6:12
36. 'by virtue of its wicked domination' (*impia dominatione*); var. *impius dominator* = 'with which the wicked dominator oppressed the human race that had become subject to him'

unspotted Lamb came and deigned to be immolated for us; he gave his blood as the price of our salvation, and by undergoing death for a time he condemned the sovereignty of death forever. The Lamb that was innocent was killed, but by a wonderful and longed-for display [of his power] he efficaciously weakened the strength of the lion that had killed him. The Lamb that took away the sins of the world[37] brought to naught the lion that had brought sins into the world. It was the Lamb that restored us by the offering of his flesh and blood, so that we would not perish, [that brought to naught] the lion which, roaring, surrounded us and sought out from among us someone it might cause to perish.[38] It was the Lamb that put the sign of his death on our foreheads, in order to ward off the weapons of the death-bearing enemy.

It was for this reason that the blood of the lamb [enjoined by] the law was ordered to be placed upon the lintel and both doorposts and on the threshold of the houses in which it was being eaten. This fourfold division of the blood was to represent the four-pronged standard of our Lord's passion by which we who have been signed are set free. It cast down the opponent of our freedom and peace, who was lying in wait for us in secret, like a lion in its den. Just as after the lamb had been immolated on this night in Egypt, the homes of the believers had been marked with its blood, and its flesh had been consumed, the Lord came suddenly and punished those who had no share in this mystery, while at the same time[39] redeeming the people he saw to be imbued with the salvation-bearing sign:[40] just so did our Lord and Redeemer, when he had offered his body and blood as a sacrificial victim to his Father for us, overthrow the might of the devil and his minions by crushing the effrontery of the unclean spirits. He broke open the bulwarks of the lower world, rescued those of his elect who were held there (albeit in a state of repose), and, by rising from the dead on this very night, brought them to the joys of the heavenly kingdom.[41] [Thus] was the prophecy fulfilled

37. Jn 1:29   38. 1 P 5:8
39. 'at the same time' = *e contra*   40. *sacramentis*
41. Greg., *Hom. in evang.* 2, 22, 6 (*PL* 76:1177)

which said, *Ascending on high, he led captivity captive.*[42] He
not only brought away the righteous whom he found in the
lower world, but also those whom, though still alive in the
flesh, he recognized as belonging to him; and by his death
and resurrection he procured the means of salvation for us
whom he foresaw were going to believe in him at the end
of time. He consecrated for us, even before we were created,
the spiritual food of life by which we are to be refreshed;
he prepared for us the sign of victory by which we were
to be protected from the snares of our enemies; and he
opened up for us the way by which we were to follow him
to everlasting life.

Hence, let us, as is right, mindful of our redemption, devote ourselves during this night to a worthy vigil to God,
and give our attention as we listen to the prayers and divine readings that tell of the favors of the grace given to
us. Let us celebrate the new people of a spiritual adoption,[43]
taken away from Egyptian domination,[44] to the one true
Lord at the font of regeneration. Let us immolate anew to
God, as a means of advancement toward our salvation, the
most holy body and precious blood of our Lamb, by which
we have been redeemed from our sins. And since we are
made glad by this annual solemnity [that commemorates]
the mysteries of our Lord's resurrection along with our own
redemption,[45] let us strive, dearly beloved, to lay hold of
these mysteries by the interior love of our minds, and always to keep a grasp on them by living them. Let us preserve them like clean animals,[46] at one time ruminating by
murmuring them with our mouths, at another recollecting
them in the inner recesses of our hearts. And above all, let
us take care to conduct our lives, with actions by which we
may merit to behold joyfully the outcome of our own resurrection too. Thus when the last trumpet arouses the entire
human race, and summons it before the tribunal of the just

---

42. Ps 68:18 (67:19)   43. Rm 8:15
44. 'domination' (*dominio*), a well-attested ms. variant for *domino*, 'by
    the Lord'
45. *redemtionis*; var.: 'rescue' (*ereptionis*)
46. Gn 7:2, Lv 11:2-3, Dt 14:6

Judge, the sign of our Judge with which we were made holy
may separate us from the lot of the condemned, and the
vigil in which we have awaited his coming may separate
us from the punishment due to those who are negligent.
When the latter have received fitting chastisement, he himself will lead us into the dwelling place of heavenly peace
which he promised us from of old, he who lives and reigns
with the Father in the unity of the Holy Spirit, God throughout all ages of ages. Amen.

homily II.8

Matthew 28:16-20   *Easter*

he gospel reading which we have just now heard, dearly beloved brothers, shines out full of joy even in its literal sense, because it describes in precise words the triumph of our Redeemer, and at the same time the gifts of our redemption. And if we choose to treat of it by going more to the heart of the matter, we will learn the more pleasing fruit of the spiritual meaning contained in its literal sense. God's word [is] indeed like spices—the more finely it is crushed by handling and sifting, the greater is the fragrance of its inner power that it gives forth.

Now it is clear and delightful for the holy to hear that *the disciples went into Galilee, to the mountain where Jesus had directed them, and upon seeing him, they adored* [him]. It is not lacking in mystery that after his resurrection our Lord appeared to his disciples on a mountain, and that it was in Galilee. This was to make known that the body which at his birth he had assumed from the earth common to the rest of the human race he had now, at his resurrection, clothed with heavenly power after it had been raised above everything earthly. He appeared on a mountain to advise[1] his faithful

---

1. var.: 'remind'

ones that if they wished to see the loftiness of his resurrection there [in heaven], they should pass over [below] from their lowly cravings to heavenly desires. What the name 'Galilee' connotes in relation to the salvation-bearing mystery is well known from the frequent explanations of the fathers, but it is not irrelevant to repeat quite often what we must keep in our minds. Galilee means 'a crossing over accomplished' or 'revelation'.[2]

Each interpretation of the name leads to a single conclusion. We read above that the angel said to the women, *'Go, tell his disciples that he has risen, and behold, he will go before you into Galilee; you will see him there'*.[3] And now, as the evangelist tells, we know that *the disciples went into Galilee, and upon seeing him, they adored* [him]. What does it mean that the Lord Jesus goes ahead of his disciples into Galilee in order to be seen by them, that they follow, and upon seeing him they adore [him], except that *Christ rose from the dead, the first-fruits of those who have fallen asleep?*[4] Those who are Christ's follow [him], and they themselves in their turn pass over into life; and, seeing him there, they adore him whom they contemplate in his divine form, and praise him for ever. The fact that Galilee also means 'revelation' accords with this vision. Then indeed, *we, with unveiled face,* as the Apostle bears witness, *beholding the glory of the Lord, are changed into the same likeness,*[5] all of us who now commit our way to him[6] and follow his footsteps with sincere faith.[7]

And upon seeing him, they adored [him]; *but some of them remained doubtful.* If we seek the source of the doubt of those who were doubtful upon seeing our Lord, no other reason comes to mind than that of which Luke makes mention when he tells that on the very day of his resurrection when he appeared to his disciples, *They were extremely disturbed and thoroughly frightened, thinking that they were seeing a spirit.*[8] Therefore, *upon seeing him,* they recognized the Lord; and because they had learned that he is God, they lowered their

---

2. Greg., *Hom. in evang.* 2, 22, 5 (*PL* 76:1172); Jer., *Nom.* (*CC* 72:94, 26; 131, 2)
3. Mt 28:7　　　　　　　4. 1 Co 15:20　　　　　5. 2 Co 3:18
6. Ps 37:5 (36:5)　　　　7. 1 Tm 1:5　　　　　　8. Lk 24:37

faces to the ground and adored. But there was still present in their minds a doubt that was not to be disregarded, for they supposed that they were seeing, not the revived body in which he suffered, but the spirit he gave up when his passion was over. Hence the benevolent master immediately confirmed the faith of those who already believed, and summoned those who were still doubtful to the grace of faith. He made known to all of them the height of glory that the humanity he had taken on for the sake of human beings and given over to death had reached. *'All power in heaven and on earth'*, he said, *'has been given to me'*. He was not speaking here about the divinity coeternal with the Father but about the humanity he had assumed. By putting it on he was made a little lower than the angels; by rising in it from the dead he was crowned with glory and honor, and set over the works of his Father's hands, with all things brought into subjection under his feet.[9] Among all the things [brought into subjection under his feet] was death itself, which seemed to prevail in him for a time, but which was made subservient beneath his feet.

What the psalmist said to the Father concerning our Lord as he rose from the dead, *You have put all things under his feet*,[10] is surely the same as what our Lord himself said to his disciples as he rose, *'All power in heaven and on earth has been given to me'*. Indeed even before he rose from the dead the angelic virtues in heaven knew that they were rightfully subject to the human nature they saw had been specifically assumed by their Maker. Blind human beings on earth, however, disdained to be brought into subjection to one they knew had put on mortality in common with themselves; they declined to understand the divine power in his miracles, since they discerned that there was human weakness present in his sufferings.

On this account, *the Mediator between God and men*[11] himself, generously wishing that it become known also to human beings on earth that all power in heaven and on earth had been given to him, so that they might have everlasting

---

9. Ps 8:5-6 (8:6-7)   10. Ps 8:6 (8:7)   11. 1 Tm 2:5

life with the angels in heaven, sent teachers to proclaim the word of life to all countries throughout the earth. *'Go,'* he said, *'teach all nations, baptizing them in the name of the Father and of the Son and of the Holy Spirit, teaching them to observe everything that I have commanded you'*. This is the most correct order of preaching, the one that is to be followed most diligently even by present-day preachers in the Church: first the listener is to be taught; next he should be imbued with the sacraments of the faith; then according to circumstances he should be more fully instructed in observing our Lord's commandments.[12] It is not possible that anyone uninstructed and ignorant about the Christian faith can be purified by the sacraments of this faith, nor is it sufficient that one be cleansed from his sins in the bath of baptism if he does not strive to devote himself to good works after his baptism. Therefore, he commanded them first to teach the nations, that is, to educate them in knowledge of the truth, and so to baptize them, because *without faith it is impossible to please God*,[13] and *unless one is born again of water and the Holy Spirit, one cannot enter the kingdom of God*.[14]

'Teaching them,' [Jesus said], *'to observe everything that I have commanded you,'* for, *as the body apart from the spirit is dead, so too faith apart from works is dead*.[15] He subsequently suggests the greatness of the reward for a holy way of life and the kind of pledge of future blessedness that await the faithful even in the present, saying, *'Behold, I am with you all days, even to the consummation of the world'*.

I would like, however, to compare with this testimony what Mark says, *And the Lord, after he had spoken, was taken up into heaven, and sat down at the right hand of God*.[16] Because he who was taken up into heaven is both God and a human being, he remains on earth with the saints in the humanity which he took from the earth, but in the divinity with which he fills earth and heaven equally he remains *all days, even to the consummation of the world*. From this it is understood that even up to the end of the world, the world will not lack those worthy of the divine abiding and

12. Jer., *In Matth.* 28, 19-20 (*CC* 77: 282, 2001/10)
13. Heb 11:6   14. Jn 3:5   15. Jm 2:26   16. Mk 16:19

indwelling. Nor should we doubt that those struggling in this world will deserve to have Christ abiding in their hearts as a guest, and will abide with Christ in his kingdom after the contests of this world.

Nevertheless we should note that the divine majesty, while existing everywhere, is present in one way to the elect, in another to the condemned.[17] It is present for the condemned in the power of [God's] incomprehensible nature, by which he knows everything, the most recent happenings and the former ones, understands [human] thoughts from afar, and foresees all the ways of each one.[18] It is present for the elect in the grace of his benevolent protection, by which he draws them, guiding each one individually by his present gifts and chastisements to the possession of their future inheritance as a father guides his children. It is present for the elect, as it is written, *The Lord is near to those with a troubled heart, and he will save the humble in spirit.*[19] It is present for the condemned, as is set down before that [line], *The countenance of the Lord is upon those who do evil, that he may destroy their memory from the face of the earth.*[20] Hence the evil should always be anxious as regards their wretched works, since even each of their thoughts lies open to the view of the strict Judge. The good should always rejoice in their performance of works of righteousness, and in what they suffer for righteousness' sake, since for those *who love God, all things work together for good.*[21] When they suffer any tribulation, there is never lacking the benevolence of him to whom it is chanted in the psalm, *The poor person commits himself to you; you will be the helper of the orphan. Shatter the arm of the sinner and the wicked.*[22]

It was not by his words alone that he promised us the presence of his benevolence, but he also made it evident by obvious indications when he appeared frequently to his disciples after his resurrection, right up to the day on which he betook himself to heaven. He strengthened their minds

17. Aug., *Serm. Dom. in Monte* 2, 5, 18 (CC 35: 108, 383/405)
18. Ps 139:2-4 (138:3-5)   19. Ps 34:18 (33:19)
20. Ps 34:16 (33:17)   21. Rm 8:28
22. Ps 10:14-15 (9:35-36)

by admonishing them, rebuking them, and bestowing upon them the gift of the Holy Spirit. We find only ten of these apparitions in the writings of the evangelists, but the Apostle teaches that there were more when he says, *And he rose on the third day, according to the scriptures, and was seen by Cephas, and after this by the eleven; then he was seen by more than five hundred brothers at the same time; next he was seen by James, and then by all the apostles; last of all, he was seen also by me, as by one who was prematurely born.*[23] But we do not know the places or times of these appearances that [Paul] records. We know only that, as regards his affirmation that he was the last one to see our Lord after his ascension, this occurred either when, addressing him from heaven, [the Lord] made him a teacher in the Church from being a persecutor of the Church,[24] or when he was caught up into paradise and the third heaven and heard hidden mysterious words which it is not permitted for human beings to speak.[25] As he says elsewhere, [there is] a mystery of the good news which he did not receive from human beings but learned through the revelation of Jesus Christ.[26] The history [recorded in] the gospels and in the Acts of the Apostles relates that after his resurrection our Lord was seen ten times, as I have said. There we read that he appeared five times on the very day of his resurrection: first, to Mary Magdalene as she was weeping at the tomb;[27] next, he appeared to the same Mary and to another woman of the same name, when he came to meet them as they were returning from the tomb to announce to his disciples what they had discovered there;[28] third, to Simon Peter;[29] fourth, to Cleopas and his companion, with whom he was proceeding on foot toward Emmaus—there he was recognized [by them] in the breaking of bread, and they soon went back to Jerusalem and found the disciples saying, '*the Lord has truly risen and has appeared to Simon*'[30] (although we do not read more fully elsewhere when he had appeared to Simon); fifth, he

23. 1 Co 15:4-8
24. Ac 9:4-6; Aug., *Serm.* 278, 1, 1 (*PL* 38: 1269)
25. 2 Co 12:2-4   26. Ga 1:11-12   27. Jn 20:11-17
28. Mt 28:9-10   29. Lk 24:34; 1 Co 15:5   30. Lk 24:13-35

appeared to them in this same place, when the doors were closed and Thomas was not there.[31] Sixth, [he appeared] after eight days, when Thomas was also with them;[32] seventh, when they were fishing at the sea of Tiberias;[33] eighth, on the mountain in Galilee, which we heard about in today's reading;[34] ninth, he appeared to the eleven as they were reclining [at table] on the day on which he ascended into heaven;[35] tenth, they saw him on that same day no longer remaining on earth but raised up into the air and betaking himself to heaven, as the angels said to them, *'He will come in the same way as you have seen him going into heaven'.*[36]

By the frequent occurrence of his bodily manifestations our Lord wished to show, as I have said, that he is present by his divinity in every place to the desires of those who are good. He appeared at the tomb to those who were grieving; he will also be present to us when we are salutarily saddened at recalling his absence. He came to meet those who were returning from the tomb so that, having learned of the joy of his resurrection, they might proclaim it; he will also be present to us when we rejoice in faithfully announcing the good things that we know to our neighbors. He appeared in the breaking of bread to those who, supposing that he was a stranger, invited him to share their table; he will also be present to us when we willingly bestow whatever goods we can on strangers and poor people; and he will be present to us in the breaking of bread, when we partake with a chaste and simple conscience of the sacrament of his body, namely, the living bread.[37] He appeared in secret to those who were speaking of his resurrection; he is also present to us now, whenever we do this same thing by his gift; he will always be present to us when, free for a time from outside works, we come together in order to speak of his grace. He appeared when they were staying inside, with the doors closed out of fear of the Jews; he appeared when this same fear abated and they sought him

31. Jn 20:19-25   32. Jn 20:26-29   33. Jn 21:1-13
34. Mt 28:16-17   35. Mk 16:14-19   36. Ac 1:11
37. Jn 6:51

with steps unconcealed on the top of the mountain. Formerly he was present in order to comfort his Church with his Spirit when it was oppressed by unbelievers, and was being prevented from coming out in public and being spread abroad; he is present to this same [Church] even now when royal personages in political power are well-disposed toward the faith, the terror of persecution has died away, and the whole superior portion of the world is predisposed to following in the apostles' footsteps. He appeared to those who were fishing, and, by appearing to them aided them by his divine goodness; he will also be present to us when we are taking care of the necessities of our lives here on earth with an upright intention, and he adds his benevolent help to our righteous labors. He appeared to those who were reclining [at table]; he will also be present to us when, in accordance with the Apostle's suggestions, whether we eat or drink, or whatever else we do, we do all for the glory of God.[38]

He appeared first in Judaea, then in Galilee, and after this in Judaea again on the day on which he ascended into heaven. He was present to the Church when it was first enclosed within the limits of Judaea alone; he is present now when, after abandoning the Jews on account of the fault of unbelief, he has crossed over to the gentiles; he will be present in the future, when he will return to Judaea before the end of the world, and (as the Apostle says), when the multitude of the nations has come in, thus will all Israel be saved.[39] Lastly, he appeared to them as he was ascending into heaven; he will also be present to us so that after death we may deserve to follow him to heaven, if before death we take care to follow him to Bethany, from where he ascended (that is, to the 'house of obedience').[40] Indeed, when he was about to ascend into heaven, he came to Bethany, because, as the Apostle says, *He became obedient even to death, death on a cross; wherefore has God also exalted him.*[41] We too come to the same place if we do what he has advised us, if we direct ourselves toward what he promised—

38. 1 Co 10:31
40. Jer., *Nom.* (CC 72: 135, 26/27)

39. Rm 11:25-26
41. Ph 2:8-9

'Be faithful even to death, and I will give you the crown of life'.[42]
And so it comes about, by the bestowal of his grace, that
the one who remains with us until the conclusion of this
life[43] will raise us up after this life to see with him the rewards of the heavenly life, in which he lives and reigns with
the Father in the unity of the Holy Spirit, God throughout
all ages of ages. Amen.

42. Rv 2:10
43. var: 'to death, the conclusion of this life'

homily̆ ɪɪ.9

Our Lord and Redeemer revealed the glory of his resurrection to his disciples gradually and over a period of time, undoubtedly because so great was the virtue of the miracle that the weak hearts of mortals could not grasp [the significance of] this all at once. Thus he had regard for the frailty of those seeking him. To those who came first to the tomb, both the women who were aflame with love for him and the men, he showed the stone rolled back.[1] And since his body had been carried away, he showed them the linen cloths[2] in which it had been wrapped lying there alone. Then, to the women who were searching eagerly, and who were confused in their minds as to what they had found out about him, he showed a vision of angels[3] who were to disclose by certain evidence the fact that he had risen again. Thus, with the report of his resurrection, already accomplished, going ahead of him, the Lord of hosts and the King of glory[4] himself at length appeared and made clear with what great might he had overcome the death he had temporarily tasted.

1. Mk 16:4
3. Mt 28:1-5; Mk 16:1-6; Lk 24:1-10

2. Lk 24:12; Jn 20:5-7
4. Ps 24:10 (23:10)

We find out too, in the course of the gospel reading, how often he was seen by human beings on the very first day of his resurrection—five times. The first was when it was said to Mary Magdalene at the tomb, as she was desirous of embracing his feet, *'Do not touch me, for I have not yet ascended to my Father'.*[5] Then [he appeared] to two women as they were running from the tomb to announce to his disciples what they had learned from the angels about his resurrection which had been accomplished. Of them it is written that *they approached and took hold of his feet and adored.*[6] He appeared on that day, as it was drawing toward evening, to the two who were going to the town of Emmaus.[7] On calling him to [partake of their] hospitality, they recognized him in the breaking of bread.[8] He appeared also to Peter, and although the evangelist did not describe when and where this occurred, nevertheless he was not silent about its occurrence. He wrote that when the two forementioned disciples returned at once to Jerusalem after recognizing the Lord at Emmaus, *they found the eleven gathered together, and those that were with them, who said, 'The Lord has truly risen, and has appeared to Simon'.*[9] And then he added, *And they told what had taken place on the way, and how they recognized him in the breaking of bread.*[10] And then he immediately attached [the account of] his fifth appearance, about which we have just now heard when the gospel was being read, starting thus: *While they were speaking about these things, Jesus stood in their midst and said to them, 'Peace to you. It is I. Do not fear'.*

Here first we must note and diligently commit to memory, that the Lord deigned to stand in their midst as his disciples were speaking about him, and to reveal his presence in a vision of himself. This is what he promised elsewhere to all the faithful, saying, *'Where there are two or three gathered together in my name, there am I in their midst'.*[11] In order to strengthen the constancy of our faith, which the presence of the divine benevolence always brings about, he wished

5. Jn 20:17   6. Mt 28:9   7. Lk 24:13
8. Lk 24:29-31   9. Lk 24:33-34   10. Lk 24:35
11. Mt 18:20

sometimes to show this by the presence of a physical vision of himself. In our case too, although we are lying far below the apostles' feet, we must trust that this very thing happens to us by his mercy, namely that he is in our midst as often as we come together and are gathered in his name. His name indeed is Jesus, that is, 'savior'.[12] When we come together to speak about acquiring our eternal salvation, it is undoubtedly true that we are gathered in the name of Jesus. Nor is it permissible to doubt that he is present among us as we are conferring about the things which he himself loves. And doubtless the more truly [he is present], the better we retain in a more perfect heart[13] what we profess with our mouth.

Then too we must see that when the Savior appeared to his disciples he immediately ordained for them the joys of peace, reiterating that selfsame thing [which is a part of] the celebrated glory of immortality, and which he had set forth as a special pledge of salvation and life when he was about to go to his passion and death, saying, *'Peace I leave to you, my peace I give you'*.[14] The angels who were seen soon after he was born also proclaimed the grace of this favor to the shepherds, praising God and saying, *'Glory to God in the highest, and on earth peace to men of good will'*.[15] Surely the entire divinely-arranged plan of our Redeemer's [coming] in the flesh is the reconciliation of the world—it was for this purpose that he became incarnate, for this he suffered, for this he was raised from the dead—that he might lead us, who had incurred God's anger by sinning, back to God's peace by his act of reconciliation. Hence he was rightly given the name 'Father of the world to come' and 'Prince of peace' by the prophet;[16] and the Apostle, writing about him to those from among the nations who had believed, said, *And coming, he brought the good news of peace to you who were from far off and peace to those who were near, since through him we both have access in one Spirit to the Father.*[17]

---

12. Jer., *Nom.* (CC 72: 6, 28)
13. vars: a) 'in a more developed heart,' b) 'the profession of the heart'
14. Jn 14:27   15. Lk 2:14   16. Is 9:6
17. Eph 2:17-18

But, when the Lord appeared to them the disciples were agitated and exceedingly frightened, and they supposed that they were seeing a spirit. They acknowledged, indeed, that it was the Lord who appeared, but they supposed that they were seeing him not in the substance of his body but in that of his spirit. That is, since they knew that his body was lifeless and buried, they did not suppose that they were looking at his body now raised up from death, but that they had before their eyes instead his spirit, which he had committed into the hands of his Father[18] when he left his body behind. But the most benevolent Master, by his generous gift of consolation and advice, took care to wipe away this mistake of theirs, together with the trepidation with which they had been struck at the new and unknown vision. *'Why are you upset,'* he asked, *'and why do thoughts arise in your hearts? See my hands and feet, that it is I myself'.*

It was not without cause that he ordered them to see and recognize his hands and feet instead of his countenance, which they knew equally well. [He ordered it] so that, when they saw the signs of the nails with which he had been fastened to the cross, they would be able to understand that it was not only a body which they saw, but the very body of their Lord, which they knew had been crucified. Hence John, when he mentions this appearance of the Lord, does well to testify that he also showed his disciples his side,[19] which had been wounded by the soldier, so that as they recognized many indications of the passion they knew so well and the death he had undergone, they might rejoice with more certain faith in the resurrection and destruction of death he had accomplished.

In order that he might render them more certain concerning their faith in his resurrection in all its details, he displayed his body, which he showed them was immortal, not only for them to look at with their eyes, but also to probe with their hands, saying, *'Touch* [me] *and see that a spirit does not have flesh and bones as you see that I have'.* [This was] so that those who were going to proclaim the glory of his

18. Lk 23:46   19. Jn 20:20

resurrection might be able to show to us without any ambiguity what kind of risen body we too are to hope for.
Hence the blessed apostle John, with great assurance, summons his hearers to follow the obscure matters of faith and
the truth which he learned, saying, *What was from the start,
what we have heard, what we have viewed with our eyes*[20] *and
what our hands have handled, concerning the word of life.*[21]

But the gentiles are accustomed at this point to lay traps
of deceit in front of the simplicity of our faith by saying,
'With what rashness do you trust that the Christ whom you
worship can bring back your incorrupt bodies from the dust,
when he could not cover the scars of the wounds which
he received on the cross and, as you say, he did not hide
the signs of his death, which were still on his body when
it was raised from the dead'? We answer them that since
Christ is almighty God, he will restore[22] our bodies, as he
promised, from corruption to incorruption, from death to
life, from the dust of the earth to heavenly glory, and he
called back to life his own body, which he had put off by
dying, as he wished it to be.

Although he could have shown his body to his disciples
with all indications of his passion abolished, he certainly
preferred to keep the indications of his passion on it, by
the grace of the divinely-arranged plan.[23] First of all [this
was] so that the disciples who saw these things could clearly
discern that what they saw was not a spirit without a body,
but a spiritual body, and that they might preach to the world
certain faith in his complete resurrection,[24] and certain hope
in the future resurrection of all human beings.[25]

Secondly, [it was] so that our very Lord and God, Jesus
Christ, who intercedes for us with the Father[26] in his [risen]

---

20. var.: 'and seen with our eyes, what we have viewed' = Vulg. rdg.
21. 1 Jn 1:1
22. 'he will restore' = *suscitabit,* a well-attested var. for *suscitauit,* 'he
    restored'
23. var: 'he preferred... by the certain grace,' or 'by the grace of the
    certain divinely-arranged plan'
24. var. 'in the glory of his resurrection'
25. Aug., *Serm.* 88 (*PL* 38: 539/40); 116 (658); *Serm.* ed. Morin (341, 21 ff.)
26. Rm 8:34

humanity, might demonstrate to him forever, by showing the scars of his wounds, how much he had labored for human salvation;[27] and so that he might, in a wonderful, and what to us is an indescribable, manner, ceaselessly counsel him, who can never forget, and who is always prepared to show mercy, how just it would be for him to show mercy toward human beings, of whose nature of sorrow and suffering the Son of God himself became a sharer, on whose behalf he struggled and by dying overthrew the sovereignty of death.

Thirdly, [it was] so that all the elect who have been received into everlasting happiness, when they see in their God and Lord the signs of his passion, may never stop thanking him, recognizing that it is by his death that they live; and so there can occur what the prophet sings of in the psalms, in the voice of the whole Church, *I shall sing for ever of your mercies, O Lord!*[28]

Lastly, [it was] so that even the damned may behold the signs of the passion in the [final] judgment, as it is written, *They will see him whom they have pierced,*[29] and may understand that they have been most justly condemned[30]—not only those who laid their wicked hands upon him, but also those who either received his mysteries and despised them as being worth nothing; or those who, when they were offered them, never took care to receive them; or those who, with even greater wickedness, labored by means of hatred and persecution to extinguish or spoil them in those who had received them.

Faith in the resurrection of Christ never misleads us, and hope in our own resurrection never deceives us, because God the Father both restored our Lord to life and will restore us to life[31] too by virtue of his power.[32] And as the Apostle says elsewhere, *If the Spirit of him who restored Jesus to life from the dead dwells in you, he who restored Jesus to life*

---

27. Ambr., *Expos. euan. sec. Luc.* 10, 170 (*CC* 14: 394, 1605/1609)
28. Ps 89:1 (88:2)   29. Jn 19:37
30. Quoduultdeus, *Sermo* 1, *De symbolo* (*CC* 60: 325, 5/19)
31. 'will restore' = *suscitabit*, a well-attested var. for *suscitauit*, 'restored'
32. 2 Co 4:14

from the dead will give life to your mortal bodies also through his Spirit which dwells in you.[33] This is surely said specially of the elect, for *we all indeed* will *rise,* and *not all will be changed.*[34] Only those who are now governed by the indwelling of the Holy Spirit are then raised up to the happiness of eternal life by this great gift of the Spirit. Thus the Lord, in order to confirm their faith in the resurrection, presented himself alive to his disciples, provided words of encouragement, and offered the traces of his passion not only for them to look at but also to touch. But their inmost hearts were still weak and unable to accept the newness of such great power, and so they began rather to marvel out of joy at what they saw than to believe what they were being taught.

Lest any uncertainty be left in their minds, the Lord also took food and consumed it in their presence. If they would not believe what they saw with their eyes or handled with their fingers, at least in his partaking of fleshly nourishment they would acknowledge that it was flesh which appeared to them. In this matter, dearly beloved brothers, we must beware of the stupid heresy of the followers of Cerinthus, lest anyone should judge in a childish and absurd way either that the body of God's Mediator and our Lord[35] stood in need of the support of food after it was raised from the dead, or that our own bodies will have to be restored with fleshly food in their life and spiritual mode of existence after their resurrection.[36] There the contemplation of the divine brightness[37] will not allow them to hunger or thirst, just as it will not allow them to suffer a lack of other good things. Hence that life's most ardent lover, certain in his devotion, joyfully speaks to God in hope: *I shall appear in your sight with justice; I shall be satisfied when your glory is made manifest.*[38] And Philip, aflame with the same love, said, 'Lord, show us the Father, and it will be enough for us'.[39]

Accordingly, we should simply and devoutly understand that the Lord's body, which was raised from death and had

33. Rm 8:11   34. 1 Co 15:51 (Vulg.)   35. 1 Tm 2:5
36. Aug., *Serm.* 242 (*PL* 38:1139)
37. var.: 'the brightness of divine contemplation'
38. Ps 17:15 (16:15)   39. Jn 14:8

now become immortal, had no necessity of taking food, yet did have that capability. So, when the occasion of proving his natural substance so required,[40] he was restored with food. Surely this food provided him with no physical sustenance, as it ordinarily does for the bodies of mortals; but, like water when it is cast into the fire, as soon as [the food] was consumed it was absorbed by his spiritual power. We must believe that our bodies too, after their resurrection, will be endowed with heavenly glory, and will have the greatest facility to do whatever they wish, and to go wherever they please. But because we will then have no necessity of or benefit from taking food, we can conclude that an immortal generation will enjoy no mortal food. There will be no other food and drink, life and health, joy, peace and all good things there for the children of the resurrection, than that which is chanted in the psalm, *Blessed are they who dwell in your house, O Lord, they will praise you for ever.*[41] And again, *The God of gods will be seen in Zion.*[42] Hence the Apostle too, describing the hidden mysteries of that age, says, *When God will be all in all.*[43]

However, when his [bodily] refreshment was ended, the Lord still added suggestions of encouragement, saying, *'These are the words which I spoke to you when I was still with you'* (that is, when I was similar to you, with a flesh that was still mortal and capable of suffering), *'that everything written in the law of Moses and in the prophets and in the psalms concerning me must be fulfilled'*. The Master of truth took away every slightest degree of dissimulation, and confirmed the duties of the truth in all respects. He was seen, touched, refreshed; a discourse of encouragement was presented in detail; and, lest it be supposed that his testimony alone might be insufficient, there was brought forth in their midst also the authority of Moses and the prophets, who had in their writings foreshadowed his incarnation, passion, and resurrection. In truth, lest perhaps they remain slow to understand their mystical sayings, he also clarified for them the sense in which they could understand these things.

40. var.: arose (*exiebat* for *exigebat*)
41. Ps 84:4 (83:5)   42. Ps 84:7 (83:8)   43. 1 Co 15:28

After this was done, he permitted nothing further of their former doubt to be left in their minds, nor did he then stop explaining to them the reason for his passion and resurrection. *And he said to them: 'For thus it was written, and thus was it necessary for the Christ to suffer and rise from the dead on the third day, and* [for you] *to preach repentance and forgiveness of sins in his name among all nations'*. It was necessary for the Christ to suffer and rise from the dead for this reason, that it was impossible for the world to be saved unless God came as a human being, appearing in the form of a human being; and unless he instructed human beings in divine things; and by undergoing death as a human being, he vanquished death by his divine power, and thus enkindled in those who believed in him a contempt of the death they had to undergo, and enlivened them by the certainty of the resurrection and eternal life they were to hope for.

By what other example could human beings more fittingly be aroused to faith in the glory in which they were to share, and in the immortal life which they were to merit, than by their acknowledging that God himself had been made a sharer in their humanity and mortality? By what means might they be more effectively stirred up to tolerate adversities of every kind for their salvation, than by their learning that their Maker had been subject to countless kinds of abuses at the hands of the wicked, and even to the sentence of death, for their salvation? For what other reason might they more fittingly receive the hope of their own resurrection, than by their remembering that through his sacraments they had been cleansed and sanctified, [and] united to the body of him who, when he had tasted death for them, presented an example of a speedy rising from death?

Accordingly, *'It was necessary for the Christ to suffer and rise from the dead on the third day,'* he said, *'and* [for you] *to preach repentance and forgiveness of sins in his name among all nations'*. Surely there was a necessary sequence, that first the blood of the Christ had to be shed for the redemption of the world; and through his resurrection and ascension there might be opened up to human beings the gate of the heavenly kingdom; and thus at last there might be sent those who would preach to all nations throughout the world the word of life and administer the sacraments of faith, by which they could be saved, and arrive at the joys of the heavenly fatherland, with the human being Jesus Christ, the very Mediator between God and human beings[44] working with them, he who lives and reigns for ever and ever. Amen.

44. 1 Tm 2:5

homily II.10

Luke 24: 1-9   *After Easter*

The reading concerning the resurrection of our Lord and Redeemer which has been narrated to us, brothers, is clear. There is no need to labor to explain here the well-known mysteries of our faith which are related in the gospel account, but rather to tell briefly what we should be doing in imitation of this reading.

On the first day of the week, very early in the morning, they came to the tomb. The first day of the week[1]* is the first day after the sabbath day, which now out of reverence we are accustomed to call the Sunday of the Lord's resurrection,[1] just as in sacred scripture the second day of the sabbath, the third day of the sabbath, and the rest of the days in their order are allotted a name according to their number. However, where day one of the sabbaths or the first day of the sabbaths is read, it signifies the same thing, showing us day one, or the first day after the sabbaths, that is the day of rest.

The fact that the women came to the tomb very early in the morning in order to seek the Lord proves the great devotedness of their love for him. In order to pay him service, as soon as the shadows of night had withdrawn and

---

1. *dominicae resurrectionis dominicam*

the ability to go [to the tomb] was given them with the appearance of the light, they strove to hurry [thither]. But they also present us with a typological example: if we desire to find the Lord, and to be strengthened by the presence of angels, *we should cast off the works of darkness and put on the armor of light, and we should walk honorably as in the day.*[2]

Just as it is proper for us to seek the Lord shining with the light of good works, so also is it proper for us to seek him abundantly provided with the gift of spiritual prayers. Hence it is good that the women who came to the tomb early in the morning are reported to have been carrying with them the spices which they had prepared. Our spices are our voices in prayer, in which we set forth before the Lord the desires of our hearts, as the apostle John attested in describing mystically the purest inmost longings of the saints, saying, *They had golden bowls full of incense, which are the prayers of the saints.*[3] What in Greek is called 'spice'[4] in Latin is called 'incense'.[5] We bear spices to the tomb of the Lord early in the morning when, mindful of the passion and death which he underwent for us, we show to our neighbor outwardly the light of our good actions, and are inwardly aflame in our heart with the delight of simple compunction. We must do this at all times, but especially when we go into church in order to pray, and when we draw near to the altar in order to partake of the mysteries of the body and blood of the Lord. If the women sought the Lord's dead body with such great care, how much more appropriate is it for us to stand with all due reverence before his sight as we celebrate his mysteries, since we recognize that he has risen from death, that he has ascended into heaven, and that the power of his divine majesty is present everywhere.

Carrying spices which they had prepared is well said. In our case the earlier preparation of the spices we carry to [perform] our service to the Lord is the purging of our hearts from pointless thoughts before the time of prayer, so that at the time of prayer we are able to admit nothing unclean into our minds, and to think of nothing that concerns transi-

2. Rm 13:12-13   3. Rv 5:8   4. spice: *aromata*
5. incense: *odoramenta*

tory matters beyond what we are making our entreaty for,
and to remember who it is whom we are supplicating, according to the example of him who said, *My heart is pre-*
pared, O God, my heart is prepared; I will sing and say my psalm
to the Lord.[6] One who enters a church to pray, and neglects
to drive away from his mind its usual superfluous thoughts
while he [pours forth] his words of entreaty, is like a person seeking the Lord without bringing with him the spices
he has prepared.

The women found the stone rolled away from the tomb, and on
entering they did not find the body of the Lord Jesus. According
to the historical sense, we know from what the evangelist
Matthew[7] tells us that an angel came down from heaven
and rolled the stone away from the mouth of the tomb. This
was not done so that he might make a way for the Lord
to go out, but so that the open and empty space of the tomb
might divulge to human beings that he had risen again.

Mystically, the rolling away of the stone implies the
disclosure[8] of the divine sacraments, which were formerly
hidden and closed up by the letter of the law. The law was
written on stone.[9] Indeed in the case of each of us, when
we acknowledge our faith in the Lord's passion and resurrection, his tomb, which had been closed, is opened up.
We enter the tomb, but do not find the body of the Lord,
when in our hearts we carefully think back over the order
[of events] of his incarnation and his passion, and recall that
he has risen from the dead and is no longer to be seen in
his mortal flesh. But the Jew and the pagan, who ridicule
the death of our Redeemer which they believe in, but refuse to believe further in the triumph of his resurrection,
continue to be like a tomb still closed by a stone. They are
not capable of entering to see that the body of the Lord has
disappeared by his rising, because by the hardness of their
infidelity they are prevented from becoming aware that a
dead person, who has destroyed death's right of entry and

6. Ps 57:7 (56:8)   7. Mt 28:2
8. disclosure: *reuolutio,* a metaphorical meaning of the word translated
   'rolling away' earlier in the sentence
9. Ex 24:12; 32:15; 34:1

has already passed into the heights of the heavens, cannot be found on earth.

It is also fitting that we imitate what happened when the women, on not finding the body of the Lord, were confused in their minds. Indeed we ought constantly to remember that we cannot find our Lord's body on earth. We are more humble as from the depths we cry to him[10] who dwells in the heavens. We are more confused in our minds as we see that we are still wandering far from him, in whose presence alone we are capable of living happily. May we be worthy to act with all the strength at our command,[11] and to be present before him.

Angels appeared to the women, saddened at the disappearance of Jesus's body, in order to bring them the remedy of consolation by disclosing the fact of his resurrection. We must have not the slightest doubt that this is now done, invisibly, in our case when we are afflicted for our own good concerning the length of our present tarrying [here on earth] and [our sadness at the lack of] the presence of our Maker. All at once we recall the eternal joys of the citizens on high, and at the recollection of their happiness (in which we hope also to share), we begin to bear more easily the hardship of the exile which we suffer; and we trust that we too, whom he deigned to redeem, can follow where our Redeemer, rising from death, ascended.

It is no secret that angels are frequently present, invisibly, at the side of the elect, in order to defend them from the snares of the cunning enemy, and uphold them by the great gift of heavenly desire. The Apostle attests to this when he says, *Are they not all ministering spirits sent to serve on account of those who receive an inheritance of salvation?*[12] Nevertheless, we should believe that the angelic spirits are especially present to us when we give ourselves in a special way to divine services, that is, when we enter a church and open our ears to sacred reading, or give our attention

---

10. Ps 130:1 (129:1)
11. *nisu uirtuis agere;* some MSS add: 'in order that we may better journey from the world'
12. Heb 1:14

to psalm-singing, or apply ourselves to prayer, or celebrate
the solemnity of the mass. Hence the Apostle advises
women to have a veil over their heads in church on account
of the angels.[13] And a prophet says, *I will sing psalms to you
in the sight of the angels.*[14] We are not permitted to doubt
that where the mysteries of the Lord's body and blood are
being enacted, a gathering of the citizens from on high is
present—those who were keeping such careful watch at the
tomb where [Christ's] venerable body had been placed, and
from which he had departed by rising. Hence we must strive
meticulously my brothers, when we come into the church
to pay the due service of divine praise or to perform the
solemnity of the mass, to be always mindful of the angelic
presence, and to fulfill our heavenly duty with fear and fitting veneration, following the example of the women devoted to God who were afraid when the angels appeared
to them at the tomb, and who, we are told, bowed their
faces to the earth.

In truth, we must note what it means that in this reading
it is testified that the angels stood beside the women, while
in the other evangelists it is recounted that they spoke to
them sitting.[15] Sitting on a throne is the act of a king, and
standing at a place of sacrifice is that of a high priest. Because our Redeemer deigned to become for us at the same
time both a king and a priest—a priest to cleanse us
thoroughly from our sins by being a sacrificial offering in
his passion, a king to bestow on us an everlasting
kingdom—the angels who proclaim his resurrection appeared while sitting to signify that he had gone to seek his
seat in the heavenly kingdom after having overcome death;
they appeared also standing to show that he also intercedes
for us in the mysteries of his Father as a high priest, according to what the Apostle says of him, stating, *He who
is at the right hand of God, who also intercedes for us.*[16]

The angels *said* to the women, *'Why do you seek the living
here among the dead? He is not here but has risen'.* To say this
clearly, 'Why do you seek in a grave, which is exclusively

13. 1 Co 11:10   14. Ps 138:1 (137:1)   15. Mt 28:3; Mk 16:5
16. Rm 8:34

a place for the dead, the one who is already risen from the dead to life'?

'Recollect how he spoke to you when he was still in Galilee, saying, ''The Son of man must be handed over into the hands of wicked human beings, and be crucified and rise on the third day.'' ' These words of the angels are plain and known to all faithful people, seeing that without knowledge of them they cannot be faithful. But there is something in [these words] about which we must counsel this brotherhood along with ourselves, so that we may recollect them very often, as the angels command, and turn them over solicitously in our mind: God's Son saw fit to become Son of man to make those of us who believe in him sons of God. He was delivered into the hands of sinful human beings to separate us from the company of sinful human beings, and at the same time to free us from the power of malignant spirits. He was crucified and rose on the third day, so that he might grant us the virtue of suffering for him, and the hope of rising and living with him. It is fitting that we retain these hidden mysteries of the Lord's divinely-arranged plan in our minds always, and more attentively than is usual when the sacraments of his most blessed passion are being commemorated, when the death of our Savior, which he obliterated forever by the very swift power of his resurrection, is renewed by its mystical reenactment[17] on the altar.

And we should not pass over without discussion why our Lord and Redeemer chose to rise on the third day; that is, why he chose to remain at rest for two nights and one day in the sepulcher. He suffered on Friday,[18] and was laid in the tomb late [on that same day] and rose in the morning on Sunday.[19] Human nature was held subject to two deaths, namely, of the soul and of the flesh. The death of the soul was on account of sin; the death of the flesh was on account of the penalty for sin. It is the death of the soul when, on account of its sin, [a soul] is deserted by God, who is its life; it is the death of the body when by divine judgment

---

17. *mysticis officiis*　　18. Friday: *sexta sabbati*
19. Sunday: *prima sabbati*

[a body] is deserted by the soul, which is its life.[20] Just as
the resurrection of the soul is to receive God back into itself after the blemish of sin has been removed, so the resurrection of the flesh is to receive the soul back into itself after
it has paid the penalty of corruption.

We were held subject to these two deaths [as a result of
the sin of] the first parent of our race. But *the Mediator between God and human beings, the human being Christ Jesus,*[21]
came and mercifully underwent one [death], and justly condemned both [kinds of death]. Having died in his flesh
alone, he rose in his flesh alone, because he never lost
through sinning the life of his soul, which he would have
recovered by repenting. This was to show, by the example
of his own resurrection, that the entire human race would
rise from the death of the flesh at the judgment, and to tell
us that all the elect are to be restored to life from the death
of the soul before the judgment by the sacrament of his
resurrection. He who destroyed our twofold death by his
single death rightly lay in the tomb for two nights and the
one day in between, to symbolize by the very time of his
burial that he was shattering the darkness of our twofold
death by his own single death.

*But the women, coming back from the tomb, told the apostles
what they had seen and heard there from the angels.* This act
of divine benevolence we recognize [is part of] the divinely-
arranged plan whereby the opprobrium of the transgres-
sion of our first [parents] might be removed from the fe-
male sex. You see that several [women], instructed by
angels, proclaim that the death which one woman, seduced
by the devil, had brought upon the world was now destroyed.[2*] One woman, coming out [of the garden] opened
a path away from heavenly joys; many, coming back from
their present exile, gave the information that the gate had
now been unbarred for regaining the heavenly fatherland.
But since it not unreasonably disturbs those who know only
simple tombs that it happened that the Lord's tomb had

20. Aug., *De trin.* 4, 2, 4 - 4, 3, 6 (CC 50: 164, 16 - 167, 52); Gregory the
    Great, *Moral.* 4, 16, 31 (CC 143: 183, 45 - 184, 53).
21. 1 Tm 2:5

room for so many human beings together with the angels, we think it appropriate to explain simply to you, dear ones, what we have ascertained about this, according to a description related by those of our contemporaries who have been in Jerusalem and who, upon their return, left a written record for us of what they saw there. Thus it was a vaulted chamber,[22] hollowed out of rock; its height was such that a person standing in the middle could touch the summit with his hand. Its entrance faced east, and the great stone about which the gospel tells us was placed over it. To the right as one enters was the place that was specially prepared as a resting place for the Lord's body, seven feet in length, about two feet[23] above the rest of the floor. The opening was not made like that of ordinary sepulchers, from above, but entirely from the south side, from which the body could be placed inside.[24] And this is what the evangelist Mark says, that the women, *as they went inside the tomb, saw a youth sitting on the right side.*[25] Uundoubtedly the angel who was sitting at the place where the Lord's body lay was at the right side of anyone coming into [the tomb], and he was seated at the right side of the sepulcher in the same place. However, all this is contiguous and not separated from any of the rest, seeing that is is hollowed out of one and the same rock.

We understand that such was the situation of the Lord's tomb at first. But they tell us that now there is a vaulted church there, of extraordinary workmanship, divided by a triple wall, with the tomb in the middle. This is sheathed on the outside with marble up to the very summit; the summit itself is covered with gold and is surmounted by a golden cross of no small size. To the east of this church is the church [erected over the place called] Golgotha. Among other ornaments that befit such a place it has a very large silver cross in the place where the Lord deigned to be crucified for our

22. *domus rotunda*
23. *septem quidem pedes longus trium uero mensura palmorum*
24. Adamn., *De locis sanc.* 1, 2, 3 - 1, 2, 10 (CC 175: 187, 15 - 188, 52);
    Bede, *De locis sanc.* 2, 1 - 2, 2 (CC 175: 254, 13 - 255, 31)
25. Mk 16:5

salvation, with a great chandelier hanging from above; a bronze circle, that is, with lamps on it, which surround the cross with the requistite homage of light.[26] In the area to the east of this is the church of Constantine, which is called by another name, the *martyrium,* where the Lord's cross was discovered by Helena, Constantine's mother. For this reason he built a church in the place with magnificent and royal ornamentation.[27]

Having explained these details about the site of the holy places to the extent that I was able to learn about them, I find it pleasing to consider the fact that the prophecy of Isaiah has been fulfilled, in which he predicted the burial and resurrection of the Lord, and at the same time our faith and salvation. *In that day the nations will entreat the root of Jesse, which stands as a sign for the peoples, and his sepulcher will be glorious.*[28] The Lord is indeed the root of Jesse, born of the stock of Jesse according to the flesh.[29] He *stands as a sign for the peoples,* because the sign of salvation, by which the people who believe are protected from the malice of the cunning enemy, was made holy by his passion. The *nations will entreat* him, because by the grace of his visitation he has not summoned the Jews alone, but us too, who are able to cry out to him from the ends of the earth. And *his sepulcher* is *glorious,* because he has kept the place in which he demolished the kingdom of death memorable by the signs of everlasting glory.[30]

Wherefore, dearest ones, having turned to him with our whole minds, let us entreat him to free us from the snares of the enemy by the sign of his protection, and to bestow upon us [the ability] to celebrate the sacraments of our redemption worthily and to come to the joys of a blessed resurrection, Jesus Christ our Lord, who lives and reigns

26. Adamn., *De locis sanc.* 1, 5, 1 (CC 175: 190, 3/8); Bede, *De locis sanc.* 2, 1 (CC 175: 254, 7/10)
27. 'ornamentation' = *cultu;* Adamn., *De locis sanc.* 1, 6, 1 (CC 175: 190, 5 - 191, 11); Bede, *De locis sanc.* 2, 1 (CC 175: 254, 2/6)
28. Is 11:10
29. var: 'according to his humanity, but Jesse's own Maker according to his divinity'
30. 'signs' = *indiciis,* a var. for *iudicii,* 'judgment'

with the Father in the unity of the Holy Spirit, God for all
ages and ages. Amen.

NOTES

1. 'First day of the week' = *Vna sabbati.* Bede is here concerned with
   the fact that the Latin *sabbatum* was sometimes used in the singular
   and sometimes in the plural, hence *una sabbati* in Luke 24:1 is equivalent to *una sabbatorum,* and in either case *una* is interchangeable with
   prima. All of these possibilities mean the day after the Sabbath, that
   is, Sunday. For another case where *sabbatum* itself means 'week,' see
   Lk 18:12.
2. See note 1 to Homily I.3.

homily II.11

John 16: 5-15   *After Easter*

s we have heard from the gospel reading, dearly beloved brothers, our Lord and Redeemer disclosed to
his disciples, when the moment of his passion was
near, both the glory of the ascension by which he was to
be honored after his death and resurrection, and the coming of the Holy Spirit, by which they were to be enlightened.
This was so that, as the hour of his passion was drawing
near, they might grieve less over his death. They would
have no doubt that he would be taken up to heaven after
his death; they would be less agitated over being forsaken,
since they would hope that, although the Lord was going
away, they were to be consoled by the gift of the Holy Spirit.

He said, '*I am going to him who sent me, and none of you
asks me, "Where are you going?"* ' It is as if he were clearly
saying, 'By my ascension I shall return to him who determined that I was to become incarnate; and so great and so
evident will be the honor of this ascension, that there will
be no need for any of you to ask where I am going, since
all of you will see that I am on my way to heaven'. But it
is good that when he had said regarding his ascension, '*I
am going to him who sent me,*' he added, '*And none of you asks*

me, *"Where are you going?"* ' Earlier on, when he was tes-
tifying publicly about his passion and saying, *'You are not
able to come where I am going,'*[1] Peter questioned him saying, *'Lord, where are you going'*?[2] He received the answer,
'Where I am going you cannot follow me now, but [you will follow me] *later on'*. This was undoubtedly because they were
not yet able to understand, not yet able to imitate the mystery of his passion and death; yet they truly recognized the
majesty of his ascension as soon as they saw it, and they
wished with the entire capacity of their minds[3] that they
might deserve to follow [him].

*'But because I have spoken these things to you, sadness has filled
your hearts'*. The Lord himself knew what these words of
his would bring about in the hearts of his disciples—that
they would produce more sadness over his departure, by
which he was forsaking them, than delight over his ascension, by which he was returning to the Father. Hence he
added kindly, by way of consoling them: *'But I tell you the
truth, it is expedient for you that I go'*. [That is,] 'It is expedient that my appearance as a servant be withdrawn from
your sight, so that your love of my divinity be fixed more
solidly in your minds. It is expedient that I take my appearance, which is well-known to you, to heaven, that through
this you may long with greater desire [to be] there. Thus,
with your hearts raised up to things on high, you may then
become capable of receiving the gifts of the Holy Spirit'.

*'For if I do not go away, the Paraclete will not come to you;
but if I go away, I shall send him to you'*. It was not because
he was unable to give the Spirit to his disciples while he
was still residing on earth that he spoke these things, since
we clearly read that when he appeared after his resurrection, *he breathed on them and said, 'Receive the Holy Spirit'.*[4]
It was because while he was still residing on earth and keeping company physically with them, they were unable to lift
up their minds to thirst after the favors of heavenly grace.[5]
But when he was ascending to heaven, they, in like manner,

1. Jn 13:33   2. Jn 13:36   3. *totis animi uotis*
4. Jn 20:22
5. Aug., *Tract. in Ioh.* 94, 4 (CC 36: 563, 2/33)

transferred all their desire there, according to what they had heard elsewhere, *'For where your treasure is, there will your heart be also'*.[6] They had then become capable [of receiving] the Spirit when they were no longer saddened at his death, but delighted at the favor he had promised, as Luke attests when he says, *And it came to pass, while he was blessing them, that he withdrew from them and was borne into heaven. And they, adoring [him], returned to Jerusalem with great joy, and were continually in the temple praising and blessing God.*[7]

It is evident, and there is no need of a lengthy explanation, why he calls this Spirit 'the Paraclete,' that is, 'the Consoler'. [The Spirit's] coming consoled and refreshed the hearts of the disciples, when [Christ's] departure had caused them to be sad. But also, when [the Spirit] inspires a hope of pardon and heavenly mercy in any individual believers who are saddened about the commission of sin, or are laboring under the ordinary afflictions of this life, he unquestionably relieves them of the anguish of their sorrow by enlightening their minds.

But since the Spirit not only [acts] internally, pouring the force of divine charity into the mind which it fills, but also [acts] externally, once bodily fear has been driven away, providing confidence for rejecting the depravity of evil deeds, [the reading] rightly goes on: *'And when he comes, he will convict the world of sin and of righteousness and of judgment'*. Now it is clear that the Son of God himself, our Lord Jesus Christ, convicted the world, that is, the adherents of the world, of the sin of its unbelief when he was in the world. He convicted it of righteousness because they were clearly unwilling to imitate the righteousness of the faithful. He convicted it of judgment because they were following the devil, who was already judged and condemned. But it was not without reason that he said that the Spirit would do this same thing when he came, for the minds of [Christ's] disciples were unquestionably going to be fortified by his inspiration, so that they should not fear to convict the world which was murmuring against them.

6. Lk 12:34   7. Lk 24:51-53

Therefore explaining his thought the Lord continued: *'Of sin because they do not believe in me'*. He considers the sin of unbelief something special. Just as faith is the origin of the virtues, so the basis of the vices is to persevere in unbelief,[8] as the Lord attests in a terrifying way when he says, *'But the one who does not believe is already judged, because he does not believe in the name of the only-begotten Son of God'*.[9] And on the other hand, *The righteous person lives from faith.*[10]

'Of righteousness because I am going to my Father, and you will no longer see me'. The righteousness of Christ's disciples consisted in this, that they believed that the Lord, whom they discerned was a true human being, was also the true Son of God, and that they worshipped always with a definite love the one whom they knew had been taken away bodily from them. The righteousness of other believers, that is, of those who have not seen the Lord in his human body, consists in this, that with their hearts they believe and love him whom they have never seen with their bodily vision as true God and man. Unbelievers are convicted of this righteousness, [which arises from] faith, for the reason that, when they hear the word of life in like manner [with believers], they are unwilling to believe [in a way which leads] to righteousness.

For that the wickedness of the evil is to be condemned is shown not only from their audacity, but also from a comparison of them with the upright. Thus it is written, *Virtue that has been tested reproves the unwise.*[11] The Holy Spirit convicts the world of its sin because it has not believed in Christ. He also convicts it of the righteousness of believers, because they have been unwilling to follow the example of those who knew that he had ascended to his Father and would no longer keep company [with them] bodily on earth; nevertheless they could not be separated from their love for him for any reason. For when he says, *'Because I am going to my Father, and you will no longer see me,'* this is what he means: 'After I have ascended, you will not see me in the manner in which you are now accustomed to see me,

8. Aug., *Tract. in Ioh.* 95, 3-4 (CC 36: 567, 30 - 568, 32)
9. Jn 3:18   10. Ga 3:11; Rm 1:17   11. Ws 1:3

enclosed in my mortal and corruptible body; [you will see me] coming to judgment in majesty, and once the judgment is finished, appearing to the saints in great glory'.

There follows: *'Of judgment because the ruler of this world is judged'*. He calls the devil 'the ruler of the world' because he rules over those who, in a perverse way, love the world rather than the world's Maker. He was judged by the Lord when he said, *'I saw Satan falling like lightning from heaven'*.[12] He was judged by [the Lord] when he was casting out demons, and when he gave his disciples the power of treading upon all the power of the enemy.[13] Accordingly, the world is convicted of the judgment by which the devil is judged when human beings are frightened by the example of the archangel, who was condemned on account of his pride, lest they presume to resist the will of God. The Holy Spirit convicts the world of the judgment by which the ruler of the world has been judged when the apostle Jude, speaking in the Holy Spirit, in order to correct the wickedness of evil human beings, records the punishment of the proud angels, saying, *'The angels who did not preserve their place of leadership, but left their dwelling place, he has kept in eternal chains in darkness for the judgment of the great day'*.[14]

There follows: *'I have still many things to say to you, but you are not able to bear them now. When the Spirit of truth comes, he will teach you all truth'*. It is certain that when the Spirit came from above, the apostles obtained a much more intimate knowledge of the truth than that which they had been able to obtain hitherto when they were fleshly-minded, and they were enkindled with a greater desire to strive for the truth. Nevertheless, we must not suppose that in this life anyone can comprehend all truth, since we were promised this reward for our faith in another life. Truth himself said, *'This is eternal life, that they may come to know you, the only true God, and Jesus Christ whom you have sent'*.[15] And elsewhere [he said] to the Jews, *'If you remain in my word, you will truly be my disciples and will come to know the truth'*.[16] Hence the Apostle also, who was caught up to the third

12. Lk 10:18　　　　　13. Lk 10:19　　　　　14. Jude 6
15. Jn 17:3　　　　　　16. Jn 8:31-32

heaven[17] and *heard secret words which it is not permitted for a person to speak,*[18] says, *We know* [the truth] *partially and we prophesy partially.*[19] We must understand, therefore, that when he says of the Spirit, *'he will teach you all truth,'* it is as if he were saying, 'He will pour forth charity in your hearts;[20] and after you have been taught inwardly by his instruction, you will advance from virtue to virtue, and become worthy to come to a life in which the eternal brightness of the highest truth and of true loftiness, that is, the contemplation of your Maker, may appear to you'.[21]

'For he does not speak on his own, but speaks whatever he hears'. The Spirit does not speak on his own, that is, without the participation of the Father and Son, for the Spirit is not divided or cut off [from them]; *he speaks whatever he hears.* Clearly he hears because of the unity of his substance [with them], and his sharing of their knowledge. He does not speak on his own, because he does not exist on his own. The Father is the only one who does not have existence from another, for the Son is born of the Father, and the Holy Spirit proceeds from the Father. The Spirit hears from the one from whom he proceeds, for he does not exist on his own but as [coming] from the one from whom he proceeds. From the one from whom he derives his essence he also derives his knowledge. From him, then, he derives his hearing, which is the same as his knowledge.[22]

As to what he adds, *'And he will make known to you the things which are to come,'* it is true that a countless number of the faithful have foreknown and proclaimed things which are to come as a result of the gift of the Spirit. There are some who, filled with the grace of the Spirit, cure the sick, raise the dead, command demons, and shine forth with many virtues; they lead an angelic life on earth; nevertheless they do not know by a revelation of the Spirit the things that are to come about there.[23] We can also take these words of the Lord to mean that when the Spirit comes, he may

---

17. 2 Co 12:2   18. 2 Co 12:4   19. 1 Co 13:9   20. Rm 5:5
21. Aug., *Tract. in Ioh.* 96, 4; 98, 8 (CC 36: 571, 1 - 572, 44; 581, 7/21)
22. Aug., *Tract. in Ioh.* 99, 7-8; 100, 4 (CC 36: 586, 1 - 587, 12; 590, 1/21)
23. var.: 'come about for them'

announce to us *the things which are to come* when he brings
back to our memory the joys of the heavenly fatherland,
when he makes known to us the feasts of the common-
wealth on high through the gift of his breathing upon [us].
He announces to us *the things which are to come* when he
draws us away from the delights of present things, and kin-
dles within us the desire for the kingdom which has been
promised us in heaven.

   *'He will honor me, because he will take from what is mine and
make it known to you'.* The Spirit honored Christ because
through him such great charity was enkindled in the hearts
of the disciples that they cast aside fleshly fear and reso-
lutely preached the effect of the resurrection of him from
whom they had fearfully fled at the time of his passion.[24]
Hence it is written, *And they were all filled with the Holy Spirit, and spoke the word of God with confidence.*[25] The Spirit honored Christ, when holy teachers, filled with spiritual grace,
worked so many and such great miracles in Christ's name,
in order that by them they might convert the entire world
to faith in Christ; when they bore so many and such great
contests of suffering for the name of Christ, until even the
necks of proud persecutors submitted to the most sweet
yoke of Christ. The Spirit honors Christ when by his inspiration he enkindles in us a love of the vision of him, and
when he impresses upon the hearts of the faithful that he
is to be believed equal to the Father in his divinity.

   'Because he will take from what is mine', he said, *'and declare
it to you'.* The Holy Spirit received what he has from the
same source as the Son, namely, the Father, because, in
this Trinity, the Son is born of the Father, and the Holy Spirit
proceeds from the Father. It is the Father alone, however,
who is born of no one and proceeds from no one.

   *'All things that the Father has are mine. Therefore I have said
that he will take from what is mine and declare it to you'.* He
spoke of those things which belong to the very divinity of
the Father, in which he is equal to him: 'All things that the
Father has are mine because I have them too'. It was not

---

24. Aug., *Tract in Ioh.* 100, 1 (CC 36: 588, 12/25)
25. Ac 4:31

that the Holy Spirit was going to receive [something] from a created being, subject to the Father and the Son, that caused him to say, '*He will take from what is mine,*' but doubt-lessly [because he was going to receive it] from the Father, from whom the Spirit proceeds and from whom the Son is born.

But because by the Lord's gift we have completed our ex-planation of the reading from the holy gospel, following in the footsteps of the fathers, there remains [the task] of ad-vising your fraternity, dearly beloved, along with myself, always to keep the remembrance of it [in our minds] with solicitous concentration, to explore its sweetness with faith-ful hearts, and to ruminate upon it frequently with a chaste mouth. Of what advantage is it [for us] to come together to hear God's word, and once it is over, to return right away to empty and wordly conversation and actions? Let us re-call, as this reading advises us, that as soon as his passion was completed our Lord returned to the Father from whom he was sent, that he neither deserted the Father when he came to us, nor deserted us when he returned [to his Father].[26]

Let us follow his footsteps thither with the entire effort of our minds. And so that we may deserve to come to the gate of his kingdom there, let us seriously consider enter-ing by that course of actions by which he proceeded when he was spending his life on earth. *For he who says that he abides in Christ ought himself also to walk as he walked.*[27] He himself came to his crown of glory by means of the strug-gles of his sufferings. Therefore it is rightly impressed upon us that in our case too *we must enter into the kingdom of God through many tribulations.*[28] Hence the apostle Peter too, when some of his brothers were beset by the heat of temp-tations, consoled them and said, '*Do not be afraid as if some-thing new were happening to you; rejoice as you share in the sufferings of Christ, that you may also rejoice and exult when his glory is revealed*'.[29]

---

26. Aug., *Tract. in Ioh.* 55, 5; 102, 6 (CC 36: 466, 9/10; 597, 4/6)
27. 1 Jn 2:6   28. Ac 14:22   29. 1 P 4:12-13

Let us call to mind that he promised that he would send the grace of the Spirit to his disciples, and he did send it. And let us take care with all watchfulness, lest by our seductive thoughts we grieve the Holy Spirit of God, in whom we have been sealed for the day of redemption.[30] For so it is written, *The Holy Spirit will flee the pretense of discipline, and will remove himself from thoughts which are without understanding.*[31] When the psalmist was burning with the desire to receive this Spirit, he providently sought first [to have] the guest-chamber of a clean heart in which he could receive him, and so at length sought the entry of so great a guest. *'Create a clean heart in me, O God,* he said; *renew an upright spirit in my inmost parts'.*[32] He entreated that first a clean heart be created in him, and then that an upright spirit be renewed in his inmost parts, because he knew that an upright spirit could have no place in a defiled heart.

Let us painstakingly retain in our hearts [the awareness] that the Spirit convicts the world of sin and of righteousness and of judgment. Let us beware lest by seeking what is below we belong to the world, because *the world will pass away with its concupiscence.*[33] Let us seek the things that are above, let us taste the things that are above, *where Christ is, seated at the right hand of God.*[34] Let us have our way of life in heaven with the Apostle,[35] and, lest we be convicted of the sin of unbelief, let us carry out what we believe in our works: *Faith without works is worthless.*[36] Lest we be judged more strictly in comparison with the righteous whom we have been unwilling to imitate, let us carefully retain in our minds[37] what the Lord said of those who reject this grace: *'The queen of the south will rise in judgment with this generation and condemn it, because she came from the ends of the earth to hear the wisdom of Solomon, and behold, there is one greater than Solomon here'.*[38] Lest we be condemned with the ruler of the world,[39] let us resist him bravely with our faith,[40]

---

30. Eph 4:30
31. Ws 1:5
32. Ps 51:10 (50:12)
33. 1 Jn 2:17
34. Col 3:1-2
35. Ph 3:20
36. Jm 2:20
37. following the well-attested var. *memoremus* for *meminimus*, 'we retain in our minds'
38. Lk 11:31
39. 1 Co 11:32
40. 1 P 5:9

and let him flee from us. Let us speak the truth in our hearts and not practise treachery with our tongues,[41] so that by pouring forth charity more and more in our hearts,[42] the Spirit of truth may teach us the recognition of all truth.

Let us entreat the help of the grace of this Spirit in all our actions, dearly beloved. Let us all, individually and collectively, say to the Lord, *'Let your good Spirit lead me in the right way'*.[43] And so it will come to pass that the one who came down upon the apostles, and declared to them the things that were to come, may disclose also to our minds the joys of the life to come. May he kindly set us on fire to seek these joys, with the cooperation of the one who is accustomed both to promise and to give him to his faithful, Jesus Christ our Lord, who lives and reigns with the Father in the unity of the Holy Spirit, God for ever and ever. Amen.

41. Ps 15:2-3 (14:3)   42. Rm 5:5   43. Ps 143:10 (142:10)

homily̅ II.12

John 16:23-30   *After Easter*

It can disturb hearers with weak [faith] that, at the beginning of this reading from the gospel, the Savior promises his disciples, *'If you ask anything of the Father in my name, he will give it to you'*. Not only do people like us not receive many things they seem to ask of the Father in Christ's name, but even the apostle Paul himself asked the Lord three times that the angel of Satan with which he was tormented might depart from him, and he was not able to obtain what he asked.[1] But the perplexity caused by this question has already been resolved by the old explanation of the fathers. They understood truthfully that those people alone ask in the name of the Savior who ask for those things which pertain to eternal salvation. They understood, therefore, that the Apostle did not ask in the Savior's name [when he asked] to be relieved of the temptation which he had received as a protection for his humility. If he had been relieved of it, he could not have been saved, as he affirmed when he said, *'And lest the greatness of the revelations should make me proud, there was given to me a goad of my flesh, an angel of Satan to buffet me'*.[2]

1. 2 Co 12:8   2. 2 Co 12:7

108

Whenever we are not listened to when we ask, it happens either because we are are asking [for something] contrary to what would aid our salvation, and for this reason the grace of his kindness is denied us by our merciful Father because we are unsuitably asking[3] (which is represented as happening to this Apostle, to whom the answer was given when he was asking for the third time: '*My grace is sufficient for you; for virtue is perfected in weakness*'[4]); or [it happens because] we are asking things that are indeed useful for and connected with true salvation, but we ourselves, by our evil lives, divert away from us the voice of the just Judge, falling into what was said by Solomon, *The person who turns away his ear from hearing the law, his prayer will be an abomination;*[5] or [it happens because] when we pray for certain sinners, that they may recover their senses and return to themselves, that although we are asking [for something] pertaining to salvation, and we deserve to be heard for our own merit, yet their obstinacy stands in the way of our obtaining what we ask.

It also sometimes happens that we seek things entirely related to salvation with our eager petitions and devoted actions, and yet we do not immediately obtain what we ask. The result of our petition is postponed to some future time, as when we daily ask the Father on bended knees, saying, *Your kingdom come,*[6] and nevertheless we are not going to receive the kingdom as soon as our prayer is finished, but at the proper time.[7] It is a fact that this is often done with benevolent foresight by our Maker, so that the desires [inspired by] our devotion may increase by deferment. When they have advanced more and more by daily growth, at length they embrace perfectly the joys they are seeking.

In this respect we should note that when we pray for those who sin, although we are unable to obtain our request for their salvation, still we are not in the least deprived of the fruit of our petition. Even though they do not deserve to be saved, we will nevertheless be rewarded for the love

---

3. Aug., *Tract. in Ioh.* 73, 2-4 (CC 36: 510, 14 - 511, 16)
4. 2 Co 12:9   5. Pr 28:9   6. Mt 6:10
7. Aug., *Tract. in Ioh.* 73, 4; 102, 1-2 (CC 36: 511, 3/6; 594, 15 - 595, 24)

which we expend on them. And so in such a petition there will be fulfilled for us the promise of the Lord who said, *'If you ask anything of the Father in my name, he will give* [it] *to you'*. We must see that he did not simply say, *'He will give* [it],' but *'He will give* [it],' he says, *'to you'*. Even if he will not give [what we ask for] to those on whose behalf we ask, nevertheless when we mercifully intercede for the lapses of others, he will grant us a reward for our generosity.

There follows: *'Up to now you have not asked anything in my name'*. They had not up to then asked in the name of the Savior, because, while they enjoyed the visible presence of the Savior himself, they had not lifted up the gaze of their minds to the invisible gifts of salvation. But our weakness, asking of the Father, does not ask in the name of Jesus, that is, the Savior, when it asks [for something] contrary to the object of its salvation—not held back from asking for eternal salvation by the bodily sight of their Savior, like the simplicity of the apostles, but hindered from gazing upon the will of God by the obstacle of its own longing.

The Lord makes evident what is chiefly to be asked for, and what is to be hoped for without any doubt, from the Father, by those who persevere faithfully in asking, by appending and saying: *'Ask, and you will receive, that your joy may be full'*. The sequence of his meaning is: 'Ask that your joy may be full, and you will receive it'. He calls the happiness of lasting peace 'full joy'.[8] Let us pass over the joy of the damned, by which they purchase for themselves eternal sorrow. Even in the present [life] the saints possess joy from their hope of heavenly goods when they are harassed by earthly adversities for the Lord's sake; they possess joy when, persuaded by love for their brothers, they learn *to rejoice with those who rejoice, to weep with those who weep*.[9]

But that is not full joy, because it is intermingled with alternating weeping. Full joy occurs when no one weeps, when it is given *to rejoice with those who* only *rejoice*. Accordingly he says, *'Ask, and you will receive, that your joy may be*

8. Aug., *Tract. in Ioh.* 102, 2 (CC 36: 595, 3/29)
9. Rm 12:15

full,' as if he were saying unmistakably: 'Ask of the Father
not the uncertain joys of [this] age, which are always mixed
with sorrow, and are held subject to a definite end; ask of
the Father that singular joy whose fullness is not lessened
by the touch of any sort of unrest, and whose eternity is
never destroyed by any termination'. For if you persevere
in asking, without doubt you will receive what you ask for.
Peter wrote concerning the fullness of this joy to those who
believed, saying, *Because you believe, you will exult with un-
speakable and exalted gladness, acquiring as the outcome of your
faith the salvation of your souls.*[10] To ask joy of this sort is not
to plead only with your words for entry into the heavenly
fatherland, but also to strive with labor to receive it. Praying well does not contribute anything at all useful in the
search for heavenly things, if one does not stop being involved, by living wickedly, in things that are below.

*'I have spoken these things to you in parables. The hour is com-
ing when I shall no longer speak to you in parables but tell you
plainly about the Father'.* He was undoubtedly pointing to
that hour when, after his passion and resurrection were
over, he would give them the gift of the Holy Spirit. Then,
spiritually taught within, and inflamed by spiritual love,
they took care to ask for and to desire more ardently those
things alone which would aid their attaining the sight of
him, so that they began [to comprehend] everything that
was to be comprehended by mortal human beings concerning the knowledge of his divinity.

This is what he added: *'On that day you will ask in my name'.*
We can understand the hour that he foretells [as that] in
the future life in which he plainly tells his elect about the
Father; that is, he plainly shows the Father to them when,
as the Apostle says, *We shall see* him *face to face.*[11] Concerning this telling John also speaks: *Dearly beloved, we are now
the children of God, and it has not yet appeared what we shall
be; we know that when he appears, we shall be like him, for we
shall see him as he is.*[12] The elect truly ask in the name of Jesus
when they make intercession on behalf of our weakness,

10. 1 P 1:8-9   11. 1 Co 13:12   12. 1 Jn 3:2

so that we may reach the lot of salvation [which they have obtained], from which we [are absent] being still on our journey on earth amidst the snares of the enemy. He promised that [the granting of] this petition of the saints would most fittingly come about on that future day, saying, *'On that day you will ask in my name'.* They ask in the day because their intercession on our behalf is poured forth, not amid the darkness of distress, as ours is, in the present [life], but in the light of everlasting peace and the glory of the blessed spirits.

The spirits of the elect who dwell in that heavenly city can be understood as asking in the name of the Savior on their own behalf too, since they clearly desire the coming of the period of universal judgment and the resurrection of their bodies, in which they have striven for the Lord's sake. Hence John says, *I saw under the altar the souls of those who had been slain for the word of God and for the testimony they had* [borne]. *And they cried out with a loud voice, saying, 'O Lord, holy and true, how long will you not judge and avenge our blood on those who live on earth'?*[13] And there is immediately added, *And they were each given a white robe and were told to rest yet a little longer, until the number of their fellow servants and of their brothers should be filled.*[14] Each soul now has a white robe, when each enjoys his bliss alone. They will then receive two, when the number of their brothers has been filled at the end, and they are gladdened by receiving their own immortal bodies.

'And I do not say to you that I shall pray to the Father for you'. Because our Lord Jesus Christ is both God and a human being, at one time he indicates the height of his divinity as he speaks, at another the humility of his humanity. When he says that he will not pray to the Father for his disciples, he is speaking of the power of his divinity because he is of the same substance as the Father; in this regard he was not wont to pray to the Father himself, but to grant, with the Father, what was prayed for. When he said to Peter, *'I have prayed for you, that your faith may not fail,'*[15] and when

13. Rv 6:9-10   14. Rv 6:11   15. Lk 22:32

John said of him, *We have an advocate with God the Father, Jesus Christ, the righteous,*[16] [these things] were said in view of the divinely-arranged plan of the humanity which he assumed. And when he reveals the triumph of [his humanity] to the eyes of his Father, he propitiously intervenes on our behalf. When he said, *'And I do not say to you that I shall pray to the Father for you,'* he did not use the present tense 'I pray,' but the future tense 'I shall pray'. [This saying] can be appropriately taken to mean that when the saints are received into internal peace, there will be no need for anything to be prayed for on their behalf, since they will have been endowed with such great happiness that it could not be greater.

'For the Father himself loves you, because you love me and believe that I have come forth from God'. This must not be understood in such a way that the love and belief of the disciples preceded the love with which the Father loved them, and that the merit of human beings may be prior to the favors of heavenly grace, since the Apostle says most clearly, *Or who has first given to him, and it shall be repaid him? For all things are from him and through him and in him.*[17] It must be understood instead thus, that the Father anticipated them with his gratuitous love, and by loving them he sustained their love and belief in the Son; and that they, once they acknowledged him, preserved their love for and faith in the Son with devout and eager hearts, and were rewarded with greater gifts of the Father's love.[18]

We must not, however, hold the opinion that the Father can love and give his gifts of love without the Son and the Holy Spirit. Nor again must we judge that the Son can be loved and believed in without the Father and the Holy Spirit. Therefore his saying, *'for the Father himself loves you,'* must be understood as meaning that it is with the Son and the Holy Spirit that he loves those whom he deems worthy of his love. And when he continues, *'Because you love me,'* this must be understood in the same way, that whoever loves the Son properly loves him together with the Father

16. 1 Jn 2:1   17. Rm 11:35-36
18. Aug., *Tract. in Ioh.* 102, 5 (CC 36: 597, 2/17)

and the Spirit of both [Father and Son], because the gifts
of virtue coming from those whose divine nature is indivisible are one and the same.

*'I have come forth from the Father and I have come into the
world. Again I leave the world and go to the Father'.* He came
forth from the Father and came into the world, because he
made himself visible to the world in his humanity, who in
his divinity was invisible along with the Father. He came
forth from the Father, because he appeared, not in that form
in which he is equal to the Father, but in the lesser one of
a created being, which he took on himself. And he came
into the world because, in the form of a servant which he
accepted, he offered himself to be seen even by those who
love this world. Again, he left the world behind and
returned to the Father because he removed from the sight
of those who love the world what they had seen, and he
taught to those who love him that he should be believed
to be equal to the Father. He left the world behind and
returned to the Father because by his ascension he brought
the humanity which he had put on to [the place of] invisible realities.[19]

These words of the Lord are mystical, and, as he himself
bore witness, spoken as parables. But the disciples to whom
they were spoken were still so fleshly-minded that they did
not grasp their deeper meaning. Not only did they not understand the hidden mysteries of his words, but they did
not even understand their own ignorance. They supposed
that what were parables for those who did not understand
them were delivered simply and lucidly. Hence they immediately answered, *'See, now you are speaking plainly and
you are not speaking a parable'.* They were affirming that he
spoke 'plainly'; they were not yet able to grasp the mysteries underlying his words.

When they added, *'Now we know that you know all things,
and there is no need for anyone to inquire of you; by this we believe that you have come forth from God,'* they clearly showed
that the Lord, in speaking to them, discussed those matters

19. Aug., *Tract. in Ioh.* 102, 6 (CC 36: 597, 3/10)

particularly which it delighted them to hear; by anticipating these matters he voluntarily delivered to them the answers to the questions which they wished to ask him. Hence they rightly believed and confessed that as God he knew all things, and that as the Son of God he had come from God. It is a clear indication of divinity to know the secret things of another's thoughts, as Solomon affirmed when he said in supplication to God, *For you alone know the hearts of all the children of human beings.*[20] Hence Jeremiah too said, *You, O Lord of Sabaoth, are the one who judges righteously and probes the loins and hearts* [of human beings].[21]

We must not recall these things cursorily or unconcernedly, but we ought to keep watch meticulously, my brothers, so that we may render not only our words and works, but also the very secrets of our hearts, worthy of divine inspection. Let not the blight of hatred or of envy remain in the temple of our breast; let not the beginning of any base or slanderous utterance arise from there; let not meditation upon any harmful deed be born there. Let us be mindful of the Lord's threat wherein he says, *'I am coming to gather their works and their thoughts'.*[22] When the traces of chaotic vices have been driven out of our heart, let us prepare a dwelling wherein he, who is its ineluctable examiner and judge, may deign to abide.

We should be aware that there are three degrees of evil thoughts: one, of those which contaminate the mind by the deliberate choice and purpose of sinning; another, of those which confuse the mind by the delight of sin, yet do not allure it to consent to sin; the third, of those which move across the mind in a natural way yet do not entice it to give in to vices, though they keep it from the good things it ought to reflect on.[23] This occurs, for example, when we bring back to mind the phantasms of things which we know were once idly done or spoken. A frequent recalling of these matters, like the troubling annoyance of flies, tends to swirl about the eyes of the heart; it does more to disturb its spiritual vision than to blind it.

20. 1 K 8:39   21. Jr 11:20   22. Is 66:18
23. Bede, *In epist. VII cath.*, Jm, 1, 15 (*CC* 121: 188, 192/200); Greg., *Hom. in evang.* (*PL* 76:1135 C)

Solomon convinces us to chastize all these kinds of evil thoughts when he says, *Guard your heart with all vigilance, for life comes forth from it.*[24] Following his suggestion, let us act quickly, that if we transgress in any way in our thoughts by consenting to carry out something wicked, we may swiftly wipe away this [transgression] by confession and fruits worthy of repentance.[25] If we perceive that we are being tempted by delight in committing sin, let us drive away this noxious delight by our frequent prayers and tears, and by our frequent recollection of everlasting bitterness; if we see that we are not capable of ridding ourselves of it on our own, let us seek the help of our brothers, that we may accomplish by their advice and intercession what we are unable to do by our own strength. *For the continuous expiation of a righteous person can accomplish much.*[26] And as the same [apostle, James] mentioned before, *The prayer of faith will save a sick person, and the Lord will comfort him; if he [has committed] sins, they will be forgiven him.*[27]

Because we cannot totally avoid idle thoughts, we should put them to flight, as far as we can, by stirring up good thoughts, and especially by frequent meditation on the scriptures, according to the example of the psalmist who said, *Oh, how I have loved your law, O Lord; it is my meditation all the day.*[28] Let us ask for heavenly clemency, which is truly to ask in the name of the Savior, that he may provide us with both purity of heart and the efficacy of good works. And above all, let us recall with an attentive mind that hour, and let us wish for it to come very quickly, wherein the Lord will no longer speak to us through the scriptures, but will plainly make known to us the Father, with whom he lives and reigns, God, in the unity of the Holy Spirit throughout all ages. Amen.

24. Pr 4:23
27. Jm 5:15
25. Mt 3:8; Lk 3:8
28. Ps 119:97 (118:97)
26. Jm 5:16

homily II.13

John 16:16-22   *After Easter*

We ought to receive these joyful promises of our Lord and Savior, dearly beloved brothers, with joyful ears of our heart, and we ought to persevere [in desiring them] with attentive intention, so that we may be worthy to experience them. For what is there that can be heard that is more rightly joyful than that we can come to a joy that can never be taken away? We must note, however, that the entire sequence of these gospel readings is appropriate to those who heard them from the Lord in person, whereas part of them is most suitably fitting also to us who have come to believe in the Lord after his passion and resurrection.

This that he said, *'A little while and you will no longer see me, and again a little while and you will see me, because I am going to the Father,'* was especially relevant to those who were worthy to stay close by him as his disciples when he was preaching in the flesh, and to be made joyful after the sorrow of his passion by seeing his resurrection and ascension.[1] For since he spoke these words on the night on which he was betrayed,[2] it was *a little while,* that is, the [remaining]

1. Aug., *Tract in Ioh.* 101, 2 (CC 36: 591, 8/9)
2. 1 Co 11:23

time of that same night and that of the following day, until
the hour [came] when they would begin not to see him.
For he was arrested on that night by the Jews, and crucified the next day when it was late; he was taken down from
the cross and shut off from human sight within the con-
fines of the sepulcher. *And again* it was *a little while* until
they saw him again, for he rose from the dead on the third
day and appeared to them with many proofs throughout
forty days.[3] As to why there had to be *a little while* when
they would not see him, *and again a little while* and they
would see him, he added the reason, saying, *'Because I am
going to the Father,'* as if he were saying unmistakably, 'After a little while I am going to be hidden from your sight
within the closed space of the grave, and again after a little
while I am going to appear for you to look at, after the sovereignty of death has been destroyed. This is so that I may
now return to the Father, since the divinely-arranged plan
of my taking mortality upon myself has been fulfilled, together with the triumph of my resurrection'.

[Christ's] saying, *'A little while and you will no longer see
me, and again a little while and you will see me,'* can also be
understood another way. There was going to be *a little while*
when they would not see him—that [time] when he was
going to be at rest in the grave—*and again* there was going
to be *a little while* when they would see him, namely those
forty days after his passion during which he appeared to
them frequently, up until the time of his ascension. But his
adding, *'Because I am going to the Father,'* according to this
way of understanding, refers back specifically to what he
had mentioned before, *'And again a little while and you will
see me'*. It is as if he were clearly saying: 'You will see me
revived from the dead for a short time on this account, that
I am not going to remain always bodily on earth, but in the
humanity which I have assumed I am soon going to ascend
to heaven'. These words of the Lord are appropriate, as I
have said, explicitly to those who were able to see his resurrection.

3. Ac 1:3

What he added by way of explanation to those inquiring of him, *'Truly, truly, I say to you that you will lament and weep but the world will rejoice; you will be sorrowful, but your sorrow will be changed to joy,'* is fitting both to their condition and to that of the entire Church. Those who loved Christ lamented and wept when they saw him apprehended by his enemies, bound, led before the Sanhedrin, condemned [to death], scourged, exposed as an object of derision and finally crucified, his side pierced with a lance, and buried. Those who loved the world—those whom, on account of their base thoughts, the Lord called 'the world'—rejoiced when they condemned him who was troubling for them even to look at[4] to a shameful death.[5] The disciples were sorrowful when their Lord was put to death, but when they acknowledged his resurrection, their sorrow was changed to joy. And when they saw the mighty power of his ascension, they were raised up to an even higher level of joy, praising and blessing God, as the evangelist Luke bears witness.[6]

But this discourse of the Lord is also appropriate to all believers who are striving to arrive at eternal joys through the tears and distress of the present [life]; who rightly lament and weep and are sorrowful during the present [time], since they are not yet capable of seeing him whom they love. As long as they are in their body they recognize that they are on a journey and [absent] from their fatherland and kingdom. They have no doubt that they must reach their crown by labors and contests.[7] Their sorrow will be changed to joy when, after the struggle of this present life is over, they receive the prize of everlasting life, about which it is said in the psalm, *Those who sow in tears will reap in joy.*[8]

But, while the faithful weep and are sorrowful, the world rejoices. Those who either have no hope of joy in another life, or despair of being able to attain it, justifiably have some sort of joy in the present [life]. This can especially be understood in relation to those who persecute the Christian

---

4. Ws 2:15   5. Ws 2:20   6. Lk 24:53
7. Aug., *Tract in Ioh.* 101, 5-6 (CC 36: 592, 1 - 594, 31)
8. Ps 126:5 (125:4)

faith, because after martyrs have been tortured and killed,
they rejoice that they have triumphed for a time. But it is
not long after this that the [martyrs] are crowned in secret,
and the [persecutors] undergo eternal punishment for their
lack of belief together with their act of committing murder.
It is properly said to them through the prophet, as a divine
rebuke, *Behold, my servants will be glad, but you will be put
to shame; behold, my servants will exult with gladness, but you
will cry out for sorrow of heart and wail for misery of spirit.*[9]

There follows: 'When a woman gives birth, she is sorrowful
because her hour has come'. He refers to holy Church as a
woman on account of her fruitfulness in good works, and
because she never ceases to beget spiritual children for God.
He says also in another place about this, *'The kingdom of
heaven is like yeast which a woman took and hid in three measures of flour until the whole [mass] was leavened'.*[10] A woman
took some yeast when the Church, by the Lord's generosity, secured the energy of love and faith from on high. She
hid this *in three measures of flour until the whole [mass] was
leavened* when she performed her ministry of imparting the
word of life to parts of Asia [Minor], Europe and Africa,
until all the bounds of the world were on fire with love for
the heavenly kingdom. The one who said sadly to those
who were departing from the purity of the faith, *'My little
children, for whom I am again in travail, until Christ be formed
in you,'*[11] was indicating that he was among this woman's
members. They testified that they were among her members who were enkindled with heavenly desires, who cried
out in praise of their Maker, 'It is out of fear of you, Lord,
that *we have conceived and been in travail, and given birth to
the Spirit'.*[12]

This *'woman is sorrowful when she gives birth because her hour
has come; but when she has given birth to a son, she no longer
remembers her distress for joy that a human being has been born
in the world'.* As long as holy Church devotes herself to the
progress of spiritual virtues in the world, she never ceases
being harassed by the world's temptations; but when she

9. Is 65:13-14   10. Lk 13:21   11. Ga 4:19
12. Is 26:18

arrives at her reward, after triumphing in the struggle of her labors, she no longer remembers the distress that preceded it on account of the joy [she derives] from the recompense that she has received. For *the sufferings of this* [present] *time are not worthy of being compared with the glory that is to come, which will be revealed in you*.[13]

'*She does not remember her distress,*' he says, '*for joy that a human being has been born into the world*'. Just as a woman is glad when a human being has been born into the world, so the Church is filled with fitting exultation when a multitude of the faithful are born into the life to come. She labors and groans greatly at the present [time] over their birth, and she sorrows like [a woman] in travail. It should not seem odd to anyone that a person's departure from this life is said to be his birth. Just as it is customary to say that a person 'is born' when he comes forth from his mother's womb and emerges into the light here [on earth], so also can someone be perfectly appropriately referred to as 'born' when he is released from the bonds of the flesh and raised up to eternal light. Hence church practice has been that the day on which blessed martyrs or confessors of Christ departed from the world we call their birthday, and their solemn festival is not spoken of as their 'funeral' but as their 'birthday'.

In what follows, our Lord himself explains the parable that he proposed about the woman: '*So you have sorrow now, but I will see you again and your hearts will rejoice, and no one will take your joy from you*'. This is easily understood of the disciples themselves, since they were sorrowful when their Lord suffered and was buried, but when the glory of his resurrection was accomplished they *rejoiced at seeing the Lord*.[14] No one will take their joy from them because, although they afterwards suffered persecution and torture on behalf of Christ's name, yet being enkindled with hope over his resurrection and their sight of him, they willingly bore all adversities; moreover they thought it perfect joy when they encountered different kinds of temptations.[15] Accordingly, after they had been beaten by the rulers [of the

---

13. Rm 8:18   14. Jn 20:20   15. Jm 1:2

synagogue], as is written, *'They went away from the presence of the Sanhedrin, rejoicing that they were considered worthy to suffer indignity for the name of Jesus'.*[16] No one takes their joy from those who, by suffering such things for Christ, have merited to reign with Christ without end.

But the entire Church goes forward toward the eternal reward of heavenly joys through the labors and trials of this life, as the Apostle attests [saying], *We must enter the kingdom of God through many tribulations.*[17] In saying, *'I will see you again and your hearts will rejoice,'* he meant, 'I will snatch you from your adversaries, I will crown you as victors, I will prove that I saw you always while you were struggling'. When does he not see those with whom he promised to remain all the days of the world,[18] especially when they are beset with distress? But their tormentors were of the opinion that the faithful were without divine protection, when they said to them as they were dying in the midst of their tortures, *'Where is their God'?*[19] Hence a certain one of them, when he was surrounded by hardships, said, *'O Lord, see my affliction, for my enemy is resolute'!*[20] This is clearly to say: 'Since the enemy pursues and lifts up his proud neck against your humble [followers], do you, O almighty Maker, relieve us by your help; and when the enemy has been overcome and driven away, confirm that you have always seen our struggles, and that they have been pleasing to you'. Accordingly, the Lord sees his chosen ones after their sorrow, when, their assailant having been condemned, he rewards their patience.

His saying, *'I will see you again,'* can also be understood as if he were saying, 'Again I appear to you to be seen'. In the same way he said to Abraham, *'Now I know that you fear God,'*[21] wherein he was saying, 'Now I have made people (who up to now did not know) recognize what I, in my own mind, always held to be certain, [namely] that you fear God'.

Therefore, dearly beloved, if we are now tried by sorrow for our own good; if, according to the urging of the Apostle,

16. Ac 5:41   17. Ac 14:22   18. Mt 28:20
19. Ps 79:10 (78:10)   20. Lm 1:9   21. Gn 22:12

we are *patient in the face of trials, rejoicing in hope;* [22] if we weep bitterly for our own mistakes, and the miseries of our neighbors, with due lamentation—the Lord will see us again; that is, he reveals himself to be seen by us in the future, he who once deigned to see us by bestowing on us recognition of himself through faith. He *will see you* in order to crown you, having once seen you in order to call you. He will see you *and your hearts will rejoice, and no one will take your joy from you,* because this is the true and unique prize for those who become sorrowful for God's sake, to rejoice in seeing him forever. He himself promised this sublime prize when he said, *'Blessed are the pure of heart, for they shall see God'.* [23] The prophet ardently desired this when he said, *'My soul has thirsted for the living God; when shall I come and appear before the face of God'?* [24] The Apostle, with those like him, gave thanks that he was to receive this when, being aware of his struggles, he declared with absolute trust, saying, *'We see now as in a mirror and obscurely, but then face to face'.* [25] May he himself, the helper of those who strive and the rewarder of those who conquer, grant us faithfully to seek and truly to acquire this, Jesus Christ our Lord, who lives and reigns with the Father in the unity of the Holy Spirit, God for ever and ever. Amen.

22. Rm 12:12   23. Mt 5:8
24. Ps 42:2 (41:3)—one MS has "psalmist" for "prophet"
25. 1 Co 13:12

homily‚ II.14

The Greater Litanies

Our Lord and Saviour, desiring that we arrive at the joys of the heavenly kingdom, taught us to ask these joys of him, and promised that he would give them to us if we asked for them. *'Ask,'* he said, *'and it will be given to you, seek and you will find, knock and it will be opened to you'*. We must ponder these words of our Lord, dearly beloved brothers, earnestly and with our whole heart, because he bears witness that the kingdom of heaven is not to be given to, found by, and opened to those who are idle and unoccupied, but to those who ask for it, seek after it and knock [at its gates]. The gate of the kingdom must be asked for by praying; it must be sought after by living properly; it must be knocked at by persevering. It is not sufficient to ask in words only if we do not also seek diligently how we ought to be living, so that we may be worthy to obtain that for which we plead, as he bears witness when he says: *'Not everyone who says to me, "Lord, Lord," will enter the kingdom of heaven; but he who does the will of my Father who is in heaven, he will enter the kingdom of heaven'.*[1] And it is of no avail to have begun good [deeds] if such a one does not strive to

1. Mt 7:21

124

bring the matters which one has begun well to a firm conclusion. Rather, *It were better not to recognize the way of righteousness, than after acknowledging it to turn back.*[2]

Hence, my brothers, we must ask painstakingly and pray
without respite.[3] *Let us fall down before God; let us weep before
the Lord who made us.*[4] And that we may become worthy to
be hearkened to, let us eagerly see how he wishes us to live,
and what he who made us has ordered us to do. Let us seek
the Lord and be strengthened; let us seek his face continually.[5] And that we may deserve to find him and see him,
let us cleanse ourselves of every defilement of flesh and spirit,[6]
for only those with a chaste body are capable of being raised
up to heaven on the day of the [final] resurrection, and only
those with a pure heart are capable of looking at the glory
of the divine Majesty.

Let us pierce the ears of our benevolent Maker with our
unwearying desire for eternal happiness, and let us not falter
in what we have begun before he opens [the gates], and
we become worthy to be snatched from the prison of this
death and to enter the gate of the heavenly fatherland. May
no one delude himself in regard to his innocence; and may
no one, trusting in his own actions, cease from his prayers
as if he has no need of the mercy of the righteous Judge.
Rather, even when someone recognizes that he has performed a good deed, since he does not know with what
severity this may be judged let him with trembling cry out
with the prophet, *'Do not enter into judgment with your servant, because no one living will be justified in your sight;'*[7] and
with blessed Job, *'If I wish to declare myself righteous, my own
mouth will condemn me; if I view myself as innocent, he will prove
that I am evil'.*[8] [Let him be] mindful always of the utterance of the apostle [John] that *If we confess our sins, he is faithful and just to forgive us our sins and to cleanse us thoroughly
from all iniquity; if we say that we have not sinned, we make him
a liar, and his word is not in us.*[9]

On the other hand, may no one in despair change his
mind, and decide not to ask for pardon after he has re-

2. 2 P 2:21   3. 1 Th 5:17   4. Ps 95:6 (94:6)
5. Ps 105:4 (104:4) 6. 2 Co. 7:1   7. Ps 143:2 (142:2)
8. Jb 9:20   9. 1 Jn 1:9-10

flected upon the nature and number of his sins. Let not the
odiousness of the sight of his wounds, or the seriousness
of his illness, prevent anyone from seeking salvation. Our
Maker deigned to become our physician, to come to us himself in the flesh, to take our infirmities upon himself in order to heal them, to carry our sorrows in order to take them
away: may these facts provide us with great confidence that
we can obtain healing! He poured forth his blood on our
behalf; he offered his death for our life. He showed [us]
that great remedy, repentance, for the great sins which have
been committed, saying through [the mouth of] his precursor, *'Offspring of serpents, who showed you how to flee from the
wrath to come? Bring forth fruits worthy of repentance;'*[10] and
a little further on, *'Let him who has two garments give* [one]
*to the person who has none, and let him who has food do like-
wise'.*[11] He put forward the daily medicine of confession and
mutual intercession for our lesser and daily faults, without
which we cannot pass through this life, as he said through
[the mouth of] the apostle James, *'Confess your sins to one
another and pray for each other, that you may be saved'.*[12] He
loves to be asked so that he can give—he who, as a generous donor, raises up the minds of the needy to ask of him,
saying, *'Everyone who asks receives, and the one who seeks finds,
and to him who knocks it will be opened'.* Because the truth who
made this promise cannot mislead [us], we must not doubt
that those of us who ask receive, those of us who seek find,
and to those of us who knock it will be opened.

But we must look attentively at this—that not everyone
who seems to pray before other people is proven to ask or
to seek or to knock at the entrance of the heavenly kingdom in the sight of the searcher of hearts.[13] The prophet
would not have said, *'The Lord is near to all who call upon
him in truth,'*[14] unless he recognized that there are some
who call upon the Lord, but not in truth. They do indeed
call upon the Lord in truth who do not contradict in their
lives what they say in their prayers. They call upon the Lord
in truth who, as they are about to offer their petitions, first

10. Lk 3:7-8   11. Lk 3:11   12. Jm 5:16
13. *interni arbitris*   14. Ps 145:18 (144:18)

busy themselves with carrying out his orders. Those who, as they are about to say to him in prayer, *'And forgive us our debts, as we also forgive our debtors,'*[15] have fulfilled that mandate of his which says, *And whenever you stand to pray, grant pardon*[*] *if you have anything against anyone, so that your Father too who is in heaven, may forgive you your sins.*[16] Hence about such persons the prophet appropriately adds, *He will fulfill the will of those who fear him, and will hearken to their prayers, and will save them.*[17] Accordingly, they call upon the Lord in truth who are acknowledged to fear him. He hearkens to their prayers when they cry out [to him]; he accomplishes their pious desires when they long for him; he raises them up to eternal salvation when they have passed from this life.

But there are, on the other hand, those who call upon the Lord but not in truth. James convicts these people when he says, *'You ask, and you will not receive, because you ask wrongly'.*[18] Now they ask wrongly who persevere in sins, and ill-advisedly entreat the Lord to forgive them the sins they do not at all forgive [others]. He condemns such as these through [the mouth of] Isaiah, saying, *'And when you reach out your hands, I will turn aside my eyes from you, and when you increase your prayers, I will not hearken to you; your hands are full of blood'.*[19] Still, having regard for such as these, he shows in what way they can obtain what they plead for when he goes on, *'Wash yourselves, be clean, take away the evil of your thoughts from* [before] *my eyes'.*[20] They ask wrongly who refuse to hear the voice of the Lord when he orders [something] by not obeying him; and nevertheless they earnestly ask their Lord to hearken to the voice of their supplication by having mercy [upon them]. He himself rejects them, saying in the gospel, *'But why do you call me, "Lord, Lord," and not do what I say'?*[21] Solomon also says of them in the book of Proverbs, *'The person who turns his ear lest he hear the law, his prayer will be abominable'.*[22] They ask wrongly

15. Mt 6:12
16. Mk 11:25; cf. Greg., *Hom in evang.* 2, 27, 28 (*PL* 76:1209)
17. Ps 145:19 (144:19)   18. Jm 4:3   19. Is 1:15
20. Is 1:16   21. Lk 6:46   22. Pr 28:9

who[23] apply themselves to long prayers, not with a reward
from on high in mind, but, after the example of the
Pharisees, for the sake of human praise. The Witness and
Judge himself bears fearful testimony about such as these,
[saying that] *'They have received their reward'.*[24]

They also ask wrongly who in their prayers demand
earthly rather than heavenly goods. The apostle [James] specially censures the prayers of these people in that expression of his of which I have [already] spoken. After he had
said, *'You ask, and you will not receive, because you ask wrongly,'*
he immediately continued, *'That you may indulge in your concupiscences'.*[25] The citizens of the heavenly fatherland, while
they are pilgrims on this earth, are not forbidden to ask the
Lord for peaceful times, bodily health, abundant crops, good
weather, and other necessities of this life, if these things
are not asked for inordinately, and if they are asked for only
for this reason, that with abundant food for the journey in
this present [life], they may more freely reach out toward
future gifts.[26] But because there are some who look for temporal rest and prosperity from their Creator, not that they
may obey their Creator with more devoted souls, but that
they may be free for more abundant eating and drinking,
that they may serve their concupiscences and the allurements of their flesh with less anxiety and restraint: such
people as these are rightly said to be asking wrongly.

But because all petitioners of this sort are not worthy to
receive what they ask in that they do so wrongly, let us
strive, dearly beloved, both to ask well and to be worthy
to obtain what we ask. This will come about if we seek in
our prayers what the Lord has ordered and proceed to our
prayers as the kind of persons he has taught us to be, and
if we devote ourselves attentively to our prayers until we
obtain what we ask. If we are eager to know what he wants
us to ask for, let us listen to what [is written] in the gospel:
*Seek first the kingdom of God and his justice, and all these things
shall be given you as well.*[27] To seek the kingdom of God and

23. 'who' = *qui*, an attested var. for *quia* ('because')
24. Mt 6:5   25. Jm 4:3
26. Greg., *Hom. in evang.* 2, 27, 7 (PL 76:1208)
27. Mt 6:33

his justice means desiring the gifts of the heavenly fatherland, and ceaselessly searching by what just merits one
should attain them, lest, if by chance we wander away from
the way that leads thither, we be unable to arrive at the des-
tination toward which we are struggling.

But if we diligently look into the words of our Lord and
Savior, in which he exhorts us to ask God our Father, after
the example of an earthly parent, we quickly recognize what
especially is the justice which can open for us the way to
the heavenly kingdom. *'Which one of you'*, he says, *'if* [his
son]*asks his father for bread, will give him a stone? Or if he asks
for a fish, will give him a serpent in place of the fish? Or if he
asks for an egg, will hand him a scorpion'*? This is indeed a clear
comparison, and one easy for all hearers to understand: if
any human being, mortal and weak and still burdened with
sinful flesh, does not refuse to give the good things which
he possesses, though they be earthly and weak, to the children whom he loves, much more does our heavenly Father
lavish the good things of heaven, which do not perish, upon
those who ask of him and are endowed with fear and love
[of him].

According to the typological understanding, bread signifies love. Just as the former is the chief kind of food, so
that a table seems to be empty without it, so the latter is
the chief of the virtues, so that the rest of the virtues are
unable to appear as spiritual virtues without it. Whatever
good thing is done is made perfect only by love. Hence the
Apostle says that if he were to speak with the tongues of
human beings and of angels, and if he were to have [the
gift of] prophecy and were to know all mysteries and all
knowledge, and if he were to have all faith so that he might
move mountains, and if he were to distribute all his possessions as food for the poor, and if he were to hand over
his body to be burnt, but if he had not charity, it would
profit him nothing.[28]

True charity is that by which we are commanded to love
God with our whole heart, our whole soul, our whole

---

28. 1 Co 13:1-3

strength, and our neighbor as ourself.²⁹ Any perfect person ought to impart the kindness of love not only to his
neighbors and friends, but also to his enemies, as the Lord
says: *'Love your enemies, do good to those who hate you, pray
for those who persecute and slander you, that you may be the children of your Father who is in heaven'.*³⁰

By the fish, faith that is *not insincere*³¹ is represented. Just
as a fish is born, lives, and is nourished beneath a covering
of water, so also faith which is in God, and which seeks
the joys of the other life through the weeping and tears of
the present one, is begotten invisibly in the heart, is consecrated by the invisible grace of the Spirit through the water
of baptism, [and] is nourished by the invisible help of divine protection so that it may not fail. It works all the good
things it is capable of for invisible rewards, mindful of that
[saying] of the Apostle that *the things which are seen are temporal, but the things which are not seen are eternal.*³² We can
also say that a fish is a type of faith, inasmuch as it is struck
repeatedly by the waves of the sea but is not destroyed,
so in the same way firm faith can be assailed by much distress from the world which opposes it yet remain unshaken;
moreover, it even emerges from the contest more glorious,
with the help of the one who told his disciples, when they
were being sent to preach about the gifts of faith, *'In the
world you will have distress; but be confident, I have overcome
the world'.*³³

The certainty of our hope is prefigured by the egg. No
offspring is yet discernible in the egg, but the birth of the
bird to come is hoped for. The faithful do not yet look upon
the glory of the fatherland on high, in which they believe
at the present [time], but they await its coming in hope.
Hence the Apostle says, *'But if we hope for what we do not
see, we await it through patience'.*³⁴

These, dearly beloved brothers, are the good things which
we ought particularly to ask for from God; this is the justice of the kingdom of God which we ought to seek above
all things: faith, hope and charity. So it is written: *The just*

29. Mk 12:30-31   30. Mt 5:44-45   31. 1 Tm 1:5
32. 2 Co 4:18   33. Jn 16:33   34. Rm 8:25

person lives by faith;[35] *but mercy will surround those who hope in the Lord;*[36] and *the fullness of the law is love;*[37] *for the entire law is fulfilled in one utterance: You shall love your neighbor as yourself;*[38] and again: *The love of one's neighbor works no evil.*[39] We must not be apprehensive that, if we seek the gift of love from the Lord with deep devotion, [and] if we say from the bottom of our hearts, *'Give us today our daily bread,'*[40] he will permit our hearts to be narrowed by the rigidity of hatred. Indeed he implies this rigidity through the hardness of the stone, when he says, *'Which one of you, if* [his son] *asks his father for bread, will give him a stone'?*

We must not be afraid that, if we entreat him for strength against the temptations of the ancient enemy, saying with our whole heart, *'Lord, increase our faith,'*[41] he will allow us to perish from the venom of unbelief. By the word 'serpent' the poison of unbelief with which he infected the human race is rightfully represented, when it is said, *'Or if he asks for a fish, will give him a serpent in place of the fish'?* If we implore the Lord for the hope of heavenly goods, through which we may be able to scorn both adversity and prosperity in the present, we must not fear that he will turn away his ears, and allow us, in our despair over what is to come, to look back, that is, to look for the poisonous advantages of the tottering world which we have left behind. The harmful change of a good intention, and the turning back to fleshly concupiscence, is rightly compared to the venom of a scorpion which it carries behind, that is, in its tail, when it is said, *'Or if he asks for an egg, will hand him a scorpion'?*

Accordingly, dearly beloved, let us ask these things of the Lord, that he may grant the fresh nourishment[42] of pure charity, sincere faith, and certain hope; and that he may take from us the hardness of hatred, the poison of faithlessness, the sting of despair which tends to drag us back to the things that pass. Without any doubt we will receive what we ask for. The apostle John says with unerring voice *that whatever we ask for according to his will, he hears us.*[43]

35. Ga 3:11; Rm 1:17   36. Ps 32:10 (31:10)   37. Rm 13:10
38. Ga 5:15   39. Rm 13:10   40. Lk 11:3
41. Lk 17:5   42. var.: 'grant us the nourishment'
43. 1 Jn 5:14

But the Lord himself gives us sure confidence of obtaining what we properly ask when he adds: *'Therefore if you, although you are evil, know how to give good gifts to your children, how much more will your Father from heaven give his good Spirit to those who ask him'*? His disciples were good, as far as human judgment can see; he calls them 'evil' because there is surely no one in this life who is capable of being free from moral faults, as Solomon states when he says, *'There is not a just person on earth, who does good and does not sin'.*[44] Hence the Lord, who providently points out the weightier medicine of repentance for the serious crimes of sinners, himself teaches that the daily faults of the elect, which occur especially in word or thought, must be taken care of by the daily practice of prayer.

He commanded them, among other things, to pray as follows: *'And forgive us our debts as we forgive our debtors'.*[45] Or [it may be that] he calls his disciples 'evil' because, in comparison with the divine goodness, every creature is judged to be evil,[46] as the Lord says, *'No one is good except God alone'.*[47] It is only by participation in the divine goodness that a rational creature is recognized as being capable of becoming good. Hence the Lord also bears witness by a benevolent promise that *your Father from heaven will give his good Spirit to those who ask him.* This is to point out that those who of themselves are evil can become good through receiving the gift of the Spirit. He pledged that his good Spirit would be given by the Father to those asking for him, because whether we desire to secure faith, hope and charity, or any other heavenly goods at all, they are not bestowed upon us otherwise than by the gift of the Holy Spirit. So it is that the same Spirit, in Isaiah, is named the Spirit of wisdom and understanding, the Spirit of counsel and fortitude, the Spirit of knowledge and piety, the Spirit of the fear of the Lord;[48] and in another place, the Spirit of love and peace,[49] [and] the Spirit of grace and prayers.[50] Un-

44. Qo 7:21   45. Mt 6:12
46. Jer., *In Matth.* 7, 11 (CC 77: 42, 924 - 43, 927)
47. Mk 10:18   48. Is 11:2-3   49. 2 Co 13:11
50. Zc 12:10

doubtedly whatever good we truly have, whatever we do well, this we receive from the lavishness of the same Spirit. When a prophet who understood this was seeking purity of heart, saying, *'Create a pure heart in me, O Lord,'* he immediately added, *'Renew an upright Spirit in my inmost parts'*.[51] If the upright Spirit of the Lord does not fill our innermost being, we have no pure heart where he may abide. When in his eager longing for an advance in good for his work he had said, *'Lord, I have had recourse to you, teach me to do your will,'*[52] he at once showed in what way he had to secure this when he went on, *'Let your good Spirit lead me into the right way'.*[53]

Following closely in his footsteps to the best of our abilities, dearly beloved brothers, let us ask God our Father that by the grace of his Spirit he may bring us to the way of upright faith which works through love.[54] And that we may be worthy to obtain what we long for, let us strive to live in such a way that we may not be unworthy of so great a Father. Instead, let us keep the mystery of regeneration, by which we were made children of God in baptism, always unimpaired in its effect on our body and equally on our mind. It is certain that if we continually follow the mandates of our Father on high, he will reward us with the inheritance of everlasting benediction which he prepared for us before all time, through Jesus Christ our Lord, who lives and reigns with him in the unity of the Holy Spirit, God forever and ever. Amen.

51. Ps 51:10 (50:12)   52. Ps 143:9-10 (142:9-10)
53. Ps 143:10 (142:10)   54. Ga 5:6

NOTE

1. In this particular instance Bede uses the Latin verb *remitto,* which he may have observed in Gregory the Great's *Hom. in evang.* 2, 27, 8 (*PL* 76:1209), in place of the word normally found in the Latin Vulgate, *dimitto,* 'forgive'.

homily II.15

Luke 24:44-53   *Ascension*

When he was about to ascend into heaven, our Lord first took care to instruct his disciples diligently concerning the mystery of faith in him. Thus they might preach it with greater certainty to the world, insofar as they had received it from the mouth of Truth himself, and recognized that it had long ago been foreshadowed by the words of the prophets. When he appeared to them after the triumph of his resurrection, according to what we have heard just now when the gospel was read, he said, *'These are the words which I spoke to you when I was still with you'* (that is, 'when I still had a corruptible and mortal body like yours'), *'since everything written about me in the law of Moses and the prophets and the psalms must be fulfilled'.* He said that the mysteries[1*] which Moses, the prophets and the psalms proclaimed had been fulfilled in him. Hence it is perfectly evident that the Church is one in all its saints, that the faith of all the elect is the same—[of all,] namely, who preceded and who followed his coming in the flesh. Just as we are saved through faith in his incarnation, passion and resurrection which have been accomplished, so they, by believing most certainly in his

135

incarnation, passion and resurrection to come, hoped that they would be saved through the same Author of life.[1]

The two men who carried the cluster of grapes on a pole from the promised land to the waiting people in the desert[2] accurately suggest this.[2*] The cluster of grapes on the pole is our Lord exalted on the cross, he who said, *'I am the true vine'*.[3] And elsewhere, as he was extending the cup of wine to his disciples, he said: *'This chalice is the New Covenant in my blood, which will be poured out for you'*.[4] The Church says of him: *'My beloved is a cluster of cypros[3*] to me.*[5] The two men carry a cluster of grapes on a pole: by it they are to give information to the people about the fertility of the promised land. Preachers belonging to each of the two covenants, who learned of the glory of the heavenly father-land from the Lord's revelation, do not cease telling the people about the hidden mystery of his passion, so that from it they can infer how great are the rewards he is going to give to his people in heaven, he who sent his only-begotten Son to earth to suffer for their salvation.

As to the fact that the two men carrying the cluster were capable of carrying it in like manner, but were not capable of looking at it in like manner, this signifies what the Savior himself said to those of his disciples who were glorified by the gift of seeing him, *'Blessed are the eyes which see what you see. For I say to you that many prophets and kings have wished to see what you see and have not seen it, and to hear what you hear and have not heard it'.*[6] Or [it signifies] that first the prophets and Moses knew and proclaimed one and the same triumph of the Lord's cross as the apostles did; but the prophets did it from time to time, in figurative and cryptic utterances, whereas the apostles and their successors, once the light of the gospel was disclosed, always proclaimed it clearly. Thus the entire Christian people now ought to know and confess the faith which up to that time only some, and those the more perfect, knew—although even then the en-tire people of God could convey the mysteries of the faith

1. Greg., *Hom. in Ezech.* 2, 5, 2 (CC 142: 276, 56/59)
2. Nb 13:23   3. Jn 15:1   4. Lk 22:20
5. Sg 1:14 (1:13)   6. Lk 10:23-24

typologically in the ceremonies of the law. Hence it is here said that the Lord, when the mysteries of his incarnation had been brought to perfection, opened the minds of his disciples[7] so that they could understand the scriptures. He opened their minds so that they could understand plainly what the prophets had said obscurely, and could hand on to believers what they needed to understand. He opened their minds so that they could understand that whatever he had done or taught when he was in the flesh, these same things the prophets had predicted that he would do and teach.

And he said to them, 'Thus was it written, and thus did Christ have to suffer and to rise from the dead on the third day, and repentance and forgiveness of sins were to be proclaimed in his name among all nations, beginning from Jerusalem'. As I have said, the faith of the prophets and fathers in times long past, even before his passion and resurrection, knew the name of Christ, as Peter attested when he said of them, *'But we believe that we are saved by the grace of the Lord Jesus, just as they also were'.*[8] But once his passion and resurrection, and also his ascension into heaven, were brought to completion, not only was faith in his name proclaimed more widely and clearly to their posterity, namely to the nation of the Jews, but it was revealed by the same compassion from on high to foreign countries too. And so it was necessary for the Christ to come in the flesh, to suffer and to rise, because the human race was not capable of being restored to life, redeemed from death, [and] directed to the hope of its own resurrection, except by his presence, passion and resurrection.

It was opportune that the preaching of repentance and the forgiveness of sins through confession of Christ's name should have started from Jerusalem. Where the splendor of his teaching and virtues, where the triumph of his passion, where the joy of his resurrection and ascension were accomplished, there the first root of faith in him would be brought forth; [there] the first shoot of the burgeoning

7. Cf. Lk 24:25   8. Ac 15:11

Church, like that of some kind of great vine, would be planted. Just so, by an increase in the spreading of the word, [the Church] would extend the branches of her teaching into the whole wide world. Thus would the oracle of Isaiah be brought to fulfillment in which he said that *the law will go forth from Zion and the word of the Lord from Jerusalem, and he will judge the nations and convict many peoples.*[9] It was opportune that the preaching of repentance and the forgiveness of sins, good news to be proclaimed to idolatrous nations and those defiled by various evil deeds, should take its start from Jerusalem, lest any of them, thoroughly terrified by the magnitude of its offenses, should doubt the possibility of obtaining pardon if it performed fruits worthy of repentance,[10] when it was a fact that pardon had been granted even to those at Jerusalem who had blasphemed and crucified the Son of God.

'But you', he said, *'are witnesses of these things. And I send upon you the promise of my Father'*. He calls the gift of the Holy Spirit 'the promise of his Father'. He told them many things about him before his passion, [as is recorded] in the Gospel of John, among which is the following: *'But when the Paraclete comes, whom I am sending you from the Father, the Spirit of truth who proceeds from the Father, he will bear witness concerning me, and you will bear witness'.*[11] And [as is recorded] in the Acts [of the Apostles], *He commanded them not to withdraw from Jerusalem but to await the promise of the Father, 'which you have heard,'* he said, *'from my mouth; for John baptized with water, but you will be baptized with the Holy Spirit'.*[12]

Here [something] is added concerning their promised waiting when it is said: *'But do you stay in the city, until you are clothed with power from on high'*. He pledged that power would come down upon them from on high, because although they possessed the Holy Spirit before, yet they received him more fully once he had ascended into heaven. Even before his passion, by the power of the Holy Spirit they were casting out many demons, healing many sick

9. Is 2:3-4   10. Mt 3:8; Lk 3:8   11. Jn 15:26-27
12. Ac 1:4-5

persons, preaching the word of life to whom they could;[13] and once he had risen from the dead, they were more specially refreshed by the grace of the same Spirit, when, as John writes, *He breathed* [on them] *and said to them 'Receive the Holy Spirit; whose sins you shall forgive, they are forgiven them'.*[14] But they were clothed with a greater virtue of his from on high, when ten days after the Lord's assumption, they received him in fiery tongues;[15] they were inflamed with such great assurance of strength that they could not be prevented from speaking to all in the name of Jesus by any threats on the part of the rulers.[16]

Then he led them out to Bethany, and lifting up his hands he blessed them. Because our Redeemer appeared in the flesh to take away sins, to remove what [humans] deserved as a result of the first curse, [and] to grant believers an inheritance of everlasting blessing, he rightly concluded all that he did in the world with words of blessing, showing that he was the very one of whom it was said, *For indeed he who gave the law will give a blessing.*[17] [4*] And it is appropriate that he led those whom he blessed out to Bethany, which is interpreted 'house of obedience,'[18] because contempt and pride deserved a curse, obedience a blessing. The Lord himself was made obedient to his Father even unto death,[19] so that he might restore the lost grace of blessing to the world; and the blessing of heavenly life is bestowed only on those who strive in holy Church to comply with the divine commands.

We must not pass over the fact we are told that Bethany is situated on the slope of the Mount of Olives.[20] Just as Bethany represents a Church obedient to the mandates of the Lord, so the Mount of Olives quite fittingly represents the very person of our Lord. Appearing in the flesh, he excels all the saints, who are simply human beings, both by the loftiness of his dignity and the grace of his spiritual power. Hence it is chanted to him in the psalms that *God,*

13. Mt 10:1; Mk 3:15; Lk 9:1-2, 6
14. Jn 20:22-23   15. Ac 2:2-3   16. Ac 4:18-21
17. Ps 84:7 (83:8)   18. Jer., *Nom.* (CC 72: 135, 26/27)
19. Ph 2:8   20. Jer., *Sit.* (PL 23:884)

your God, has anointed you with the oil of happiness above your companions.[21] And he himself promised the favor of the same holy anointing to his companions (as the present reading of the holy gospel bears witness), that is, to the faithful; and he sent what he had promised, as we know, not long after.[22]

If it is delightful to hear how the house of obedience, that is, holy Church, is built on the slope of the Mount of Olives, let us read the gospel of John, where it is said that when his suffering on the cross was brought to fulfillment, *One of the soldiers opened his side with a lance, and immediately there came forth blood and water.*[23] These are indeed the sacraments by which the Church is born and nourished in Christ, namely the water of baptism by which she is cleansed from sins, and the blood of the Lord's chalice by which she is confirmed in her gifts.[24] And because she is also signed with the chrism of the Holy Spirit, that she may be capable of being perfected on the day of redemption, the mount on whose slope the holy city is situated, on which the gift of blessing is given, is properly called the Mount of Olives.

And it came to pass that while he was blessing them he parted from them and was borne into heaven. We must note that the Savior ascended into heaven after he had given his blessing to his disciples; and at the same time we must commit to memory that, as we read in the Acts [of the Apostles], angels appeared to them as they were watching his ascension and said to them, *'He will come in the same way as you have seen him going into heaven'.*[25] And we must labor with all earnestness [to understand] that, just as the Lord will descend to judge [us] in the same form and substance of flesh with which he ascended, so also, since he departed blessing his apostles, he will make us worthy of his blessing when he returns, and will allot us the same status as those to whom he is going to say as they stand at his right hand, *'Come, you who are blessed by my Father, receive the kingdom'.*[26]

21. Ps 45:7 (44:8)   22. Ac 2:2-4   23. Jn 19:34
24. Aug., *Tract. in Ioh.* 9, 10; 120, 2 (CC 36: 96, 34/36; 661, 6/12)
25. Ac 1:11   26. Mt 25:34

And they, worshipping, returned to Jerusalem with great joy, and were continually in the temple, praising and blessing God. It is right that we remember, always, but especially in this place, dearly beloved brothers, our Lord's utterance in which he said, as he was glorifying his disciples (as I have reported just above), *'Blessed are the eyes which see what you see'.*[27] Who indeed is capable of describing, who is capable of worthily imagining, how with blessed compunction they lowered to the earth the eyes with which they had looked at him whom the heavens were worshipping as their king, now that, with the conquered mortal nature that he had assumed, he was returning to the throne of his Father's glory? [Or] how sweet were the tears which they poured forth when, aflame with lively hope and gladness over the prospect of their own entry into the heavenly fatherland, they discerned that their God and Lord was now bringing [thither] part of their own nature? Rightly then [were they] restored by such a sight! After they had worshipped in the place where his feet stood,[28] [and] after they had wet with copious tears the place where he had most recently planted his footsteps, they immediately returned to Jerusalem, where they had been ordered to await the coming of the Holy Spirit.

And so that they might be worthy of the heavenly promises, *they were continually in the temple, praising and blessing God,* being most certainly aware that the Holy Spirit deigns to visit and inhabit only those hearts which he sees are devoted to frequenting the place of prayer and to divine praise and blessing. Hence it is read in their Acts concerning them, *They were all persevering with one accord in prayer.*[29] This testimony to the apostolic work must be meticulously imitated by us: we who have the heavenly promises, [and] are commanded to painstakingly offer supplication to receive them should all come together to pray, and should persist in prayer, and should entreat the Lord with single-minded devotion. And we must not doubt that our benevolent Maker will deign to lend us a hearing if we

27. Lk 10:23   28. Ps 132:7 (131:7)   29. Ac 1:14

pray in this way, and to pour forth the grace of his Spirit into our hearts. [And we must not doubt] that he will cause our eyes also to be blessed, although not in the same way as those of the apostles who merited to see the Lord when he was sojourning in the world, when he was teaching and performing miracles, [and] when after his triumph over death he rose and returned to heaven, but certainly like theirs of whom he said to the apostle Thomas, *'You have believed because you have seen me; blessed are they who have not seen and have believed'*.[30] For indeed all those who believe, whether they be those who by the time of their birth preceded his incarnation, or those who saw him in the flesh, or those who believe after his ascension, share in that most benevolent promise of his, in which it is said, *'Blessed are the pure of heart, for they will see God'*.[31]

I have completed my explanation of the [details] of the gospel reading to the best of my ability. But because we have heard in this reading that the disciples' minds were opened that they might understand the scriptures, I am disposed to bring to mind some things from the writings of the prophets, and to enlarge upon and develop the joy of the evangelical solemnity by the predictions and assertions of the prophets.

The psalmist spoke of this solemnity [when he said], *God has ascended with a shout of jubilation, and the Lord with the sound of the trumpet.*[32] He ascended with a shout of jubilation, since he sought heaven as the disciples rejoiced in the glory of his being lifted up. He ascended with the sound of the trumpet, since he went up to the throne of his heavenly kingdom as the angels heralded his return to judge the living and the dead.

How God, who is present always and everywhere and does not change from place to place, ascended, the same [prophet] declares elsewhere, saying, *He who makes a cloud his stairway, and walks upon the wings of the winds.*[33] He calls the substance of human weakness with which *the sun of righteousness*[34] clothed himself, that [the sight of him] might

30. Jn 20:29   31. Mt 5:8   32. Ps 47:5 (46:6)
33. Ps 104:3 (103:3)   34. Ml 4:2

be borne by human beings, a cloud. Hence Isaiah says, *'Be-hold, the Lord will ascend upon a swift cloud and will enter Egypt, and the idols of Egypt will be shaken before his face'.*[35] The Lord ascended upon a swift cloud so that when he entered Egypt he might overturn its idols, when *the Word was made flesh and dwelt among us.*[36] He took upon himself a body immune from all stains of iniquity, and entered the world in it, so that he might destroy the cult of idolatry, and make clear the true light of divinity to the shadowy and dark hearts of the gentiles.[37] He who is not enclosed in a place willed to go from place to place by means of this cloud, his human nature; in it he who always remains invisible[38] in his divinity willed to suffer mockery, scourging and death; by means of it he who fills the heavens in the power of his divinity ascended into heaven, crowned with the power of his resurrection. He lifted up this earth upon the wings of the wind when he elevated what he had taken from the earth not only above all the whole bulk of the lower air, but even above the entire height of the upper air,[39] and stationed it at the right hand of the majesty of his Father.

Amos too speaks of the glory of the humanity he had assumed: *He who builds a means of ascent in heaven and founds his promise on earth.*[40] He built a means of ascent in heaven when he created for himself a human body and soul in which he would be able to mount up to heaven. He founded his promise on earth when by sending the Spirit from above he filled all the ends of the earth with the gift of his faith, as he had promised. The psalmist, foreseeing in his spirit that the gift of this promise would come, and desiring that it come quickly, said, *'Be exalted, O God, above the heavens, and let your glory be over all the earth'!*[41] Here he clearly means that before our Redeemer assumed a mortal body and demolished the kingdom of death, *God* was *known* only *in Judah,* and *in Israel* was *his name great.*[42] But when the

---

35. Is 19:1   36. Jn 1:14
37. See Jer., *Nom.* (CC 72: 143, 28/29), where he interprets the word Egypt as 'darkness'.
38. *inuisibilis;* var.: 'not subject to suffering' (*impassibilis*)
39. 'lower air' = *aeris;* 'upper air' = *aetheris*
40. Am 9:6   41. Ps 57:5 (56:6)   42. Ps 76:1 (75:2)

God-man rose from the dead and penetrated the heights of heaven, then the glory of his name was proclaimed and believed throughout the whole wide world.

The prophets proclaimed the mystery of the Lord's ascension not only by their words but also by their actions. Both Enoch, the seventh [in the line of descent] from Adam,[43] who was transported from the world,[44] and Elijah, who was taken up into heaven,[45] gave evidence that the Lord would ascend above all the heavens. Enoch, in that he was engendered seventh [in the line of descent] from Adam, prefigured that the Lord would be conceived and born not in the usual way of mortal nature, but by the power of the Holy Spirit; and that the full grace of the Holy Spirit, which is described by the prophet as sevenfold,[46] would come to rest upon [Christ] in a special way when he was about to be born; and that he would baptize in the Holy Spirit,[47] and give the gifts of the Spirit to those who believe in him. In that [Enoch] lived for three hundred and sixty-five years (which is the number of days in the solar year) among human beings before he was transported,[48] he symbolized [Christ's] future way of life in the flesh: he, when on the point of ascending into heaven, pointed out that he was the unique light of the world, saying, *'I am the light of the world; one who follows me does not walk in darkness but will have the light of life'.*[49] Hence he is called *the sun of righteousness* by the prophet,[50] since he deigned to enlighten all parts of the world, from the rising of the sun to its setting,[51] from the north even to the south, by the grace of his faith and truth. Moreover, Enoch, who was transported, means 'dedication,'[52] and this indicates that he who rises from the dead and ascends into heaven gives the pledge of his Spirit to consecrate the hearts of the faithful, and in the future [will] bring the Church fully from every part [of the world] to the joy of the resurrection and of an everlasting solemnity.

Elijah presented an image of this festivity of the Lord by a miracle with richer significance. When the time in which

---

43. Gn 5:6-18   44. Gn 5:24   45. 2 K 2:11
46. Is 11:2-3   47. Mt 3:11   48. Gn 5:23
49. Jn 8:12   50. Ml 4:2   51. Ps 50:1 (49:1)
52. Jer., *Nom.* (CC 72: 65, 17)

he was to be taken away from the world was near, he came to the river Jordan[53] with his disciple Elisha. With his rolled-up cloak he struck the waters, they were divided, and both of them crossed over on dry [land]. And he said to Elisha, *'Ask what you want me to do for you before I am taken away from you,'* and [Elisha] said, *'I entreat you that your spirit may become double in me'.* As they went on conversing together, behold Elijah was suddenly snatched away, and, as the scripture says, *he ascended as if into heaven.* By this action of his soaring aloft[54] it is meant that [Elijah] was not taken up into heaven itself, as was our Lord, but into the height of the air [above the earth], from where he was borne invisibly to the joys of paradise. Elisha took up the cloak of Elijah which had fallen from him; and, coming to the river Jordan, he struck the water with it, and after calling upon God he divided [the water] and crossed over.[55]

Let your love take note, my brothers, how the symbolic event agrees point by point with its fulfillment. Elijah came to the river Jordan, and having laid aside his cloak, he struck the waters and divided them. The Lord came to the stream of death, in which the human race ordinarily was immersed, and laying aside from himself for a time the clothing of flesh which he had assumed, struck down death by dying, and opened up for us the way to life by rising. The change and decline of our mortal life is properly represented by the river Jordan, since the meaning of 'Jordan' in Latin is 'their descent,'[56] and since as the river flows into the Dead Sea, it loses there its praiseworthy waters.[57] After [the water of the river] Jordan was divided, Elijah and Elisha crossed over on dry land: by his rising from the dead the Savior bestowed on his faithful ones the hope of rising too. After they had crossed over the river Jordan, Elijah gave Elisha the option of asking for what he wanted. The Lord too, after the glory of his resurrection had been fulfilled, implanted in his disciples a fuller comprehension of what he had promised

53. 2 K 2:6-11
54. *qua euectione*; var.: 'by this reading' (*qua lectione*)
55. 2 K 2:13-14 56. Jer., *Nom.* (CC 72: 67, 20)
57. Plin., *Nat. Hist.* 5, 15, 71

previously, that *whatever you ask in my name, I will do* [for you].[58] Elisha asked that the spirit of Elijah might become double in him. The disciples, thoroughly instructed by the Lord, desired to receive the promised gift of the Spirit, which would make them capable of preaching not only to the single nation of Judah, which he himself taught when he was present in the flesh, but to all countries throughout the globe as well. Did he not pledge the double grace of his Spirit when he said, *'A person who believes in me will himself also do the works which I do, and he will do even greater ones than these'?*[59] As Elijah and Elisha were conversing together, a chariot with fiery horses suddenly snatched Elijah as if into heaven. By the chariot and fiery horses we are to understand the angelic powers, of whom it is written, *He makes the angels his spirits, and his ministers a burning fire*[60] (Elijah, being an ordinary human being, had need of them in order to be raised up from the earth). The Lord too was suddenly taken up as he was speaking with his apostles, and as they were looking on; although he was not assisted by the help of angels, he was served by an angelic band of companions.[61] He was truly assumed into heaven with the angels also bearing witness to it, for they said [to the apostles], *'This Jesus who has been taken up from you into heaven'.*[62] When Elijah was raised up to the heavens, he let the cloak with which he had been clothed fall to Elisha. When our Lord ascended into heaven, he left the mysteries of the humanity he had assumed to his disciples, to the entire Church in fact, so that it could be sanctified by them, and warmed by the power of his love. Elisha took up Elijah's cloak and struck the waters of the river Jordan with it; and when he called upon the God of Elijah, [the waters] were divided and he crossed over. The apostles and the entire Church took up the sacraments of their Redeemer that had been instituted through [the apostles], so that, spiritually guided by them, and cleansed and consecrated by them, they too learned to overcome death's assault by calling upon the

---

58. Jn 14:13   59. Jn 14:12   60. Ps 104:4 (103:4)
61. Greg., *Hom. in evang.* 2, 29, 5 (*PL* 76: 1216)
62. Ac 1:11

name of God the Father, and to cross over to undying life, spurning the obstacle of death.

Let us then, with all devotion, dearly beloved brothers, venerate this glory of the Lord's ascension, which was first expressed by the words and deeds of the prophets, and was afterward brought to fulfillment in our Mediator himself.

And that we ourselves may become worthy of following in his footsteps and ascending to heaven, let us in the meantime become humble on earth for our own good, always mindful that, as Solomon says, *Humiliation follows the proud, and honor follows the humble in spirit.*[63] Behold, we have learned in our Redeemer's ascension whither all our effort should be directed; behold, we have recognized that the entrance to the heavenly fatherland has been opened up to human beings by the ascension into heaven of the Mediator between God and human beings.[64] Let us hurry, with all eagerness, to the perpetual bliss of this fatherland; since we are not yet able to be there in our bodies, let us at least always dwell there by the desire of our minds. In accord with the words of the great preacher, let us *seek the things that are above, where Christ is seated at the right hand of God; let us savor the things that are above and not those that are upon the earth.*[65] Let us *seek him and be strengthened;*[66] let us seek him by works of charity, and be strengthened by the hope of finding him. Let us *seek his face always,*[67] so that when he who ascended peacefully returns terrifying, he may find us prepared, and take us with him into the feasts of the city on high, Jesus Christ our Lord, who lives and reigns with the Father in the unity of the Holy Spirit throughout all ages. Amen.

63. Pr 29:23   64. 1 Tm 2:5   65. Col 3:1-2
66. Ps 105:4 (104:4)   67. *ibid.*

NOTES

1. The word *sacramentum* is used frequently by Latin writers to translate the Greek *mysterion* (e.g. Eph 1:9; Rv 1:20) to signify the hidden mystery, i.e., God's secret plan for the salvation of mankind.
2. The allegorical significance of this bunch of grapes goes back as far as Gregory of Nyssa. See Jean Danielou, *The Theology of Jewish Christianity* (London: Darton, Longman & Todd, 1964), p. 104. The pertinent passage from the writings of Gregory of Nyssa is to be found in *Gregorii Nysseni Opera* VII, 1, *De Vita Moysis*, Book II, 125, 16/21, ed. H. Musurillo (Leiden: E.J. Brill, 1964). No Latin translation of the *Life of Moses* by Gregory of Nyssa extant in the eighth century, to which Bede might have had access, is known.
3. *Cypros:* The usually unimpeachable *Thesaurus Linguae Latinae* lists this word at the end of Volume 4, containing after the ordinary words beginning with the letter C the proper words also starting with this letter, in column 798, line 41, with a reference to Sg 1:14, as meaning the name of a tree from which the island of Cyprus was thought to have derived its name. The *Oxford Latin Dictionary* (Oxford, 1982) has the Latin form *cyprus,* s. v., meaning 'the henna-tree or Egyptian privet, *Lawsonia inermis;* also its oil'. Henna oil, of course, is a reddish-brown dye used to tint or color hair. Pliny the Elder, in his *Natural History* 12, 51, 109, describes *cypros* as a tree found in Egypt as well as on the island of Cyprus akin to the thorny or privet-like shrub to be found in Italy—*Lawsonia alba*—and his translator into English in the Loeb Classical Library leaves the word in English, as I have done, 'cypros'. It is interesting, in connection with the passion motif of the juice of the grapes indicative of our Lord's blood, that the word 'Christ's thorn' is applied to small trees or shrubs of this sort with thorns because the legend about our Lord's crown of thorns has it that it was from one of these that it was woven.
4. This verse is found at the beginning of verse 8 of Psalm 83 (Hebrew Psalm 84) in the Old Latin or Roman psalter, but not in the Vulgate version of the psalms. Most of Bede's quotations from the psalms are taken from this older Latin (the so-called Roman translation) of the psalter, not from the Vulgate version (which is sometimes referred to as the Gallican psalter).

homily II.16

We find from many places in the holy gospel that before the coming of the Holy Spirit, the disciples were less capable of understanding the hidden mysteries of the divine sublimity, and were less brave in tolerating the adversities brought on by human depravity. When the Spirit came upon them with an increase of divine insight, there was given them the constancy [needed] to overcome human persecution as well. Hence it is said to them now, in the Lord's promise, *'When the Paraclete comes, whom I shall send you from the Father, the Spirit of truth who proceeds from the Father, he will bear witness about me; and you too will bear witness'.*

We must first note that the Lord testifies that the Spirit of truth is to be sent by him, and he then adds that the [Spirit] proceeds from the Father. This is not to say that the Spirit is sent by the Son in a different manner from that by which he proceeds from the Father, or that he proceeds from the Father at a different time from that in which he is sent by the Son; the Son says that [the Spirit] is *sent* by him, and *proceeds* from the Father, to indicate that his person is different from that of the Father; he also makes the point in this distinction of persons that his operation and

149

will is one with the operation and will of the Father. When
the grace of the Spirit is given to human beings, the Spirit
is unquestionably sent by the Father and sent by the Son,
and proceeds from the Father and proceeds from the Son,
since his sending is also the procession by which he proceeds from the Father and the Son. [The Spirit] also comes
of his own accord, because just as he is equal to the Father
and the Son, so he has the same will in common with the
Father and the Son. *The Spirit breathes where he wills;* [1] and,
as the Apostle says after listing the heavenly gifts, *One and
the same Spirit works all these things, distributing to each individual according as he wills.* [2]

The Spirit, upon his coming, bore witness concerning the
Lord. Breathing into the hearts of the disciples, he revealed
to them by his bright light everything about which mortals
were to have knowledge concerning [the Lord], namely, that
he was equal and of the same substance with the Father
before the ages; that he became of the same substance as
we at the end of the ages; that he was born of a virgin and
lived in the world without sin; that he went forth from the
world when he wished and by the kind of death that he
wished; that by rising from the dead he truly destroyed
death and raised up the true flesh in which he had suffered,
and at his ascension took it up into heaven, and established
it at the right hand of his Father's glory; that all the writings of the prophets bear witness to him; that the confession of his name was to be extended even to the ends of
the earth, and that the rest of the mysteries of his faith were
unlocked for his disciples by the testimony of the Holy
Spirit. Nor was whatever they correctly discerned conceded
to them alone by the gift of the Spirit, but also to all who
believe in the Lord through their word.

'He', Jesus says, *'will bear witness concerning me, and you
will bear witness'*. Once they had put aside their initial fear,
they ministered outwardly by telling others what they had
received inwardly by the Spirit's teaching. The Spirit himself both illumined their hearts by knowledge of the truth,

---

1. Jn 3:8   2. 1 Co 12:11

and by the preeminence of his power roused them to teach what they knew. Hence in Isaiah the Spirit is rightly called 'of strength and knowledge'.[3] He is indeed the Spirit of knowledge, since it is by his help that we rightly acknowledge what we must do and even think; he is also the Spirit of strength, since it is by his help that we receive [the strength] to carry out what we know well that we should do, lest we be driven away by some adversity from the good deeds we have begun.

'*And you*', he says, '*will bear witness, because you are with me from the beginning*'. When the grace of the Spirit was given, it helped the self-assurance of the disciples. They were with the Lord from the beginning, and so were capable of preaching without any ambiguity what they had seen and heard in his presence.[4] Hence Peter, when he wished to admit another apostle to the place of Judas, did well to choose for this position not a recent convert but someone proven by long experience, saying, '*And so one of the men who has been associated with us during all the time that the Lord Jesus went in and out among us must become with us a witness of his resurrection*'.[5] Thus it was that [Peter], bringing the good news of Christ to the nations, said with confidence, '*God restored him to life on the third day and made him manifest, not to all the people, but to witnesses who were preordained by God, to us who ate and drank with him after he rose from the dead*'.[6]

But with the increase in merit of the elect, the envy of the ancient enemy tends immediately to increase. Either imperceptibly by himself, or openly through human beings who have become subject to his malice, he tries to cut down the shoots of piety that have begun to spring up. The Lord, having promised confidence in their preaching, reveals to his disciples the persecution that will arise at the same time from those who would resist their preaching. He adds: '*I have spoken these things to you that you may not be scandalized. They will put you out of their synagogues*'. Their loving master took care to predict to his disciples their future battles with the wicked. They would be less inclined to stumble

3. Is 11:2   4. 1 Jn 1:1, 3   5. Ac 1:21-22
6. Ac 10:40-41

when they occurred, because adversities which can be known beforehand tend to be borne more calmly. Evils that afflict a mind that is unprepared and unforeseeing often cast it down more deeply from its state of integrity.[7] Hence Solomon does well to give this advice, saying, *Son, when you are approaching the service of God, stand firm in justice and fear, and prepare your soul for temptations.*[8]

The Savior warned his disciples ahead of time that they would not only be driven away from fellowship with their fellow- citizens, but that they would also suffer death at their hands, for there follows: *'The hour is coming when everyone who puts you to death will think that he is doing a service to God'.* The Jews thought that they were doing a service to God in pursuing the ministers of the New Covenant with hatred and death, because as the Apostle bears witness about them, *'They have zeal for God, but not according to knowledge;'*[9] and he says of himself, *'I myself was convinced that I ought to do many things in opposition to the name of Jesus of Nazareth, which I did at Jerusalem'.*[10]

Having foretold the distress brought on by their adversaries, as if consoling his disciples[11] he continued at once, *'The hour is coming when everyone who kills you will think that he is doing a service to God,'* as if saying openly, 'You are going to suffer battles and tribulations from your fellow-citizens, but accept them the more steadfastly in the [realization] that you are afflicted with them not so much out of hatred toward yourselves as out of zeal for the divine law'. Mindful of this advice, the blessed martyr Stephen, on bent knees, with a loving voice made supplication for those who were killing him, saying, *'Lord, do not hold this sin against them'.*[12] Those zealous for the law thought that they were doing a service to God when they were murdering the heralds of grace, but it was in vain that they were defending the law given by a servant when they refused to receive the grace the Son himself offered them; fruitlessly

7. Aug., *Tract. in Ioh.* 93, 4 (CC 36: 561, 24/28)
8. Si 2:1   9. Rm 10:2   10. Ac 26:9-10
11. Aug., *Tract in Ioh.* 93, 3-4 (CC 36: 559, 4 - 561, 24)
12. Ac 7:60

did they judge that they were pleasing God the Father when they were striving to disparage God's Son, nay even to persecute and blaspheme him. Hence there is properly added: *'And they will do these things because they have not known the Father nor me'*. Since the Son is in the Father and the Father is in the Son, and the one who sees the Son sees the Father too,[13] it is evident that all who resist belief in the Son with stubborn mind are proven not to know the Father. Hence the same John, teaching the truth of divine unity, says, *'No one who denies the Son has the Father;'*[14] and again, *'Every one who loves the parent loves the child'*.[15]

But because the disciples, who knew the Father and the Son well, were going to suffer many things for defending and speaking of their knowledge, the Lord added with prudent counsel: *'But I have said these things, that when their hour comes you may remember that I told you of them'*. His saying *'I told you of them'* we must ponder very seriously—'I who am going to die for the sake of your life and salvation, I who am going to redeem you with my blood, I who am going to aid you always in your tribulations, I who am going to give you eternal rewards after your tribulations'. He does indeed hold out great solace, and a great gift of consolation, to those engaged in strife, when he who is accustomed to aid his soldiers lest they be conquerable, and to requite them with an immortal palm [of victory] after their battles lest their victory be fruitless, recalls that he predicted their future strife. He who warned them ahead of time that the hour of persecution would come is the one who, a little later, pledged his help to his faithful in the persecution, saying, *'You will have distress in the world; but have confidence; I have overcome the world'*.[16] He elsewhere promised the crown of life to those who are sincerely engaged in strife, saying, *'Blessed are those who suffer persecution for the sake of justice, for theirs is the kingdom of heaven'*.[17]

I have completed this brief explanation of the reading from the gospel, dearly beloved brothers. Now I would like to say something more profound concerning the solemnity of

13. Jn 14:9-10   14. 1 Jn 2:23   15. 1 Jn 5:1
16. Jn 16:33   17. Mt 5:10

Pentecost[1]* which we are observing. Just as we celebrated
a forty-day observance of fasting as the Easter solemnity
was approaching, so now that it is over we carry out with
joyful devotion [the commemoration of] Pentecost, for the
sake of indicating a definite mystery. For since holy Church
in some of her members is still struggling on earth for eternal rest, but in others who have ended all their struggle she
now reigns with Christ in heaven, our forebears established
these twin solemnities of appropriate religious observance
as memorials of the two types of life. There are the forty
days [of Lent], with their affliction and fasting before the
period of commemoration of our Lord's resurrection and
the joy of Easter, that through them they might call us to
remember more often that it is through struggles and continence, through watchings and prayers, and through the
rest of *the armor of justice* which the Apostle mentions,[18] that
we must come into possession of the rewards of immortal
life.[19]

At the same time, [our forebears] wanted to begin the
commemoration of Pentecost with the day of the Lord's
resurrection, and they wanted it to be renowned for its joys
and praises rather than for fasting. Thus we might be
prompted in a pleasing way, by this annual festive celebration, to enkindle our desire always to obtain and hold fast
to festal times that are not annual but uninterrupted, not
earthly but heavenly. Our true bliss is to be sought not in
the present time of our mortality, but in the eternity of our
future incorruption—the solemnity where, after all our anguish has ceased, our life will be led totally in the vision
and praise of God, according to what the prophet, exult-
ing heart and flesh in the living God,[20] said, *'Blessed are they
who dwell in your house; they will praise you forever'!*[21]

Hence our custom is to chant 'Allelujah' more frequently
and happily during these fifty days in memory of this, our

18. 2 Co 6:4-7
19. Ambr., *Expos. euan. sec. Luc.* 8, 25-26 (CC 14: 306, 272 - 307, 302);
    Aug., *Ep.* 55, 15, 27-28 (CSEL 34: 200, 8 - 202, 14; *Serm.* 125, 2 (PL
    38: 695-696); *Serm.* 252, 9-12 (PL 38: 1176-1179); *Tract. in Ioh.* 17, 4-6
    (CC 36: 172, 27 - 173, 13)
20. Ps 84:2 (83:3)   21. Ps 84:4 (83:5)

most peaceful and blissful action. Allelujah is a Hebrew word, and in Latin it means 'praise the Lord'![22] Accordingly, where we chant in the psalms, 'Praise the Lord,' in place of this expression among the Jews 'Allelujah' is always chanted. In his book of Revelation, John the evangelist mentions that he had heard the throngs of heavenly virtues singing it.[23] And when the venerable father Tobit had understood from an angelic vision what the glory of the citizens on high is, [and] the great brightness of the heavenly Jerusalem, he said the following with mystical voice: *'All its streets are paved with precious and shining stones, and throughout all its districts 'Allelujah' will be sung'.*[24]

It is most proper and beautiful that a general custom has prevailed in holy Church of all the faithful throughout the world singing this word of praise in the Hebrew language, out of reverence for the primitive practice. This has come about so that, through the harmony of such a devotion, the whole Church may be admonished that now it ought to consist in one faith, confession and love of Christ, and in the future it ought to hurry to that fatherland in which there is no discord of minds, no disharmony of speech. For just as once in Jerusalem the heart and soul of the multitude of the believers was one, and all things were theirs in common,[25] so in the 'vision of supreme peace'[26] the heart and soul of the entire multitude of those who see God will be one, loving and praising him by whose grace they see that they have been saved. There everything will truly be theirs in common, for, as the Apostle says, *God will be all in all.*[27]

The last seven psalms, which are chanted specially in praise of the Lord, are prefixed with the title 'Allelujah' as an image of this time and of our praiseworthy rest. The seventh day was ordered in the law to be called and kept [as the day] of the sabbath,[28] that is 'of rest'.[29] And the Book of Psalms, after it has set forth such great ordinances of

22. Jer., *Nom.* (CC 72: 159, 13)   23. Rv 19:1
24. Tb 13:17-18 (13:22)   25. Ac 4:32
26. The meaning of 'Jerusalem' according to Jerome, *Nom.* (CC 72: 121, 9/10)
27. 1 Co 15:28   28. Gn 2:2; Ex 20:8-10; Dt 5:12-14
29. Jer., *Nom.* (CC 72: 77, 2)

heavenly commands, so many recitations of hidden spiritual mysteries, and such great utterances of salutary confession and most humble entreaties, is suitably ended by seven psalms with the title 'Allelujah'. Whatever good we do in this life, whatever we bring forward with exultant tongues in the service of our Redeemer, whatever we think of in our desire for the eternal fatherland—all these things will undoubtedly be taken into consideration with this reward in mind for us, that in undying rest we may be worthy to hear the voice of his praise[30] and to bless him ourselves together with his saints, and to tell of the glory of his kingdom and speak of the might of his power.[31]

For this reason many teachers in the Church have prescribed that the recitation of 'Allelujah' be suspended during the forty days [of Lent],[32] although divine praise is never discontinued in the Church: his gifts are daily chanted in other words which perfectly signify the same thing. This is so that the unfamiliar repetition [of Allelujah] may give to the celebration of Easter a greater and more pleasing respect and splendor. They also wished especially to point in this way to a mystery: that in our wandering during this time of exile, just as *we know in part and we prophesy in part,*[33] so also we praise the Lord in part, saying with the prophet, *How shall we sing a song to the Lord in a foreign land?*[34] But when we have deserved to enter into our fatherland, the land of the living, and the home of the heavenly kingdom once promised us by the Lord, then as we know him perfectly, so also will we be capable of praising him perfectly, according to what the psalmist says, *And in his temple all will say, 'Glory'!*[35] Hence he says elsewhere, *The heavens declare the glory of God!*[36] He is calling the citizens of the heavenly fatherland 'the heavens'. The earthborn are able to tell of the glory of God, but only the citizens of heaven are capable of 'declaring' it—the more nearly they see it, the more certainly they are able to express it.

---

30. Ps 26:7 (25:7)   31. Ps 145:11 (144:11)
32. E.g., Bened., *Reg.* 15:1-4 (*CSEL* 75²: 69, 1 - 70, 4)
33. 1 Co 13:9   34. Ps 137:4 (136:4)   35. Ps 29:9 (28:9)
36. Ps 19:1 (18:2)

The authority of our Lord and Savior himself, and not that of any human being, was decidedly the first to prescribe both of these solemnities for us, that is, both that of the forty days [of Lent] and that of the fifty days [between Easter and Pentecost]—the forty days inasmuch as he fasted for forty days and forty nights in the desert, and when he was victorious over the wiles of the tempter, he enjoyed the ministry of angels.[37] Here, by his example, he informed us of how we ought to avoid the deceits of our spiritual adversary and come to the company of the angels by the chastisement of the flesh. He also pointed out to us that we are to observe the joys of the fifty days [of Pentecost] since he presented *himself alive* to his disciples after his resurrection *by many proofs over a period of forty days, appearing to them, and speaking of the kingdom of God, and taking food with them,* as we read in the Acts [of the Apostles].[38] By the frequency of his visitations he caused this time to be regarded as one of joyfulness and festivity. But he did not take from them the delight of his earlier presence, even when he ascended into heaven; instead he increased this delight by the promised anointing with the Holy Spirit. Accordingly, after he promised them that they were to be baptized with the Holy Spirit before many days,[39] he blessed them, and ascended, and was borne into heaven on the fortieth day after his resurrection. They worshipped him and then went back with great joy to Jerusalem, and were continually in the temple, praising and blessing God.[40] [The apostles] taught us that we too must prolong the gladness of this solemnity with the [kind of] joy, praise and heavenly blessing with which they waited for the coming of the Holy Spirit up to the fiftieth day, which the Greeks name Pentecost.

At this point, dearly beloved brothers, we must look carefully at the fact that by keeping company during forty days with his disciples, not only did our Lord foreshadow the joys of the future age, which we will spend with him, but he also showed his indescribable feeling of benevolence

37. Mt 4:1-11   38. Ac 1:3-4   39. Ac 1:5
40. Lk 24:51-53

toward us. When he had already put off the weakness of his body, nay, had brought it to an end and altered it entirely by virtue of his resurrection into a glory that was heavenly, he nevertheless deigned to be still present at a feast with his disciples. This was so that he might be able to have them as his companions in heaven, [and] might set forth in a more enduring way, by his very intimacy, the precepts by which they might come to the kingdom of God. What, my brothers, is implied by this combination of words, in which it is said, *Appearing to them, and speaking of the kingdom of God, and taking food with them,*[41] unless it is being unmistakably shown that especially was he a companion at their banquet when he was speaking to them of the kingdom of God. Partaking of earthly food with them, by which he was revealing his heavenly body, he would bind them to him more firmly with bonds of charity, and strengthen their remembrance of the time he had foretold to them before his passion, by promising, *'As my Father has appointed a kingdom for me, so do I appoint for you* [a place] *to eat and drink at my table in my kingdom'.*[42] Rightly, therefore, during these most holy days, do we also give ourselves to more plentiful meals and heavenly hymns because of our reverence for the Lord's resurrection, because of the memory of the Lord's banquet with his disciples, and at the same time because of the hope of our future rest and immortal life. And according to custom we do not bend our knees in prayer, for bending of the knees is definitely an indication of repentance and mourning. Our forebears have also instructed [us] to observe [this] every Sunday on account of the mystery of the resurrection, either our Lord's or our own.

There have been many disagreements, however, among our forebears about the mystery of the numbers forty and fifty. Since I have already prolonged this sermon, it is enough now to speak briefly to you of the brotherhood to the effect that it is proper that the sacred usage of fasting should be observed for days that are forty in number, that

41. Ac 1:3-4   42. Lk 22:29-30

it may be suggested by this that we ought to labor through-out the entire period of this life in order to attain eternal life. Four times ten is forty, and the present life is fittingly prefigured by this number four, either because the whole of it alternates among the four seasons, or because the world itself in which we live is composed of four elements, namely fire, air, water and earth.

The blessedness of the future life is not inappropriately represented by the number ten. So it is that our Lord tells[43] that the workers in the vineyard were rewarded with a denarius.[2*] The workers in the vineyard are the laborers[44] in holy Church. The denarius designates the perfection of heavenly life, in which *surveying the glory of the Lord,* the supreme king, *we are transformed into the same image,*[45] not only from the fact that it bears the image and inscription of a king, but also from the fact that it is the equivalent of ten obols,[3*] which is a perfect number and the one from which it derives its name. Therefore, we rightly celebrate an annual fast of forty (that is, four times ten) days, so that by it we may be more specially admonished always to la-bor for the acquisition of the rewards of heaven as long as we live in the world. We also rightly venerate the state of our future blessedness under the image of the number of fifty days, namely by mitigating our fasts, by chanting 'Al-lelujah,' [and] by standing as we pray. All these things are most suitable foretastes of the everlasting rest of our resur-rection and time of praise. Seven times seven makes forty-nine, and it is as clear as light that rest is often indicated by the number seven. Seven multiplied by seven suggests the perfection of that rest which will never be brought to an end [or] marred by any blemish, but which will be made perfect by the more abundant gift of the reception of our bodies when the day of universal judgment and resurrec-tion arrives. One is added to seven-times-seven, (that is the day of Pentecost Sunday, on which the primitive Church received the Holy Spirit), and thus the number fifty is per-fectly completed. It shows that time of judgment and resur-

43. Mt 20:1-10   44. 'laborers' or 'worshippers' *(cultores)*
45. 2 Co 3:18

rection of all [people], when the rest of holy souls, which is now going on in that life,[4*] will be doubled by the reception of their immortal bodies, and that utterance of the Apostle will be fulfilled: *But if the Spirit of the one who restored Jesus to life from the dead dwells in you, he who restored Jesus to life from the dead will also bring to life your mortal bodies through his Spirit dwelling in you.*[46]

But let no one suppose that without suitable insight and a reason befitting the mystical meaning it has become the usual practice that we do not at once kneel down to pray when the celebration of Pentecost is over, but we still supplicate the Lord standing up during the week [that follows], and, although we resume our interrupted fasts, nevertheless we daily intone the Allelujah. Since the grace of the Holy Spirit is sevenfold,[47] the solemnity of his coming is rightfully honored for seven days, with the due praise of hymns, and likewise by the celebration of masses. Because the Church throughout the whole world is always accustomed, at the time of Pentecost, to add new people for God by the water of regeneration, rightly do we rejoice with them in their salvation until they put on white garments, and by the radiance of their dress they show forth the brilliance of their purified minds. We offer a hymn of devoted praise to God, according to the command of our most benevolent Pastor and Redeemer himself, in which he said, *'Rejoice with me, for I have found my sheep which was lost'.*[48] Rightly too do we then stand as we pray. This is to signify the liberation of these people, by which, through the gift of the Holy Spirit, they have been made worthy to be restored to life from the death of the soul, and to rise. We hope that by the gift of his grace we too will be clothed with the immortality of the flesh on the last day, and that we will be conducted to the joys of the blessed resurrection, according to what I taught a little while ago, with the Apostle as a witness.

But we must believe that the resumption of the chastisement of fasting at this time was taken over from the example

46. Rm 8:11   47. Is 11:2-3   48. Lk 15:6

of the apostles themselves. After they had received the Spirit, to the extent that they more perfectly enjoyed a new pleasantness in heavenly goods, they more thoroughly withdrew their minds from the memory of earthly delights. That time had now come concerning which our Lord had predicted that the disciples would not be able to fast as long as he was keeping company with them, but that they would fast after he had been taken from them. When *the disciples of John inquired of* [Jesus], *saying, 'Why do we and the Pharisees fast frequently, but your disciples do not fast'?* he asked them, *'Can the bridegroom's friends mourn as long as the bridegroom is with them? But the days will come when the bridegroom will be taken from them, and then they will fast'.*[49] It is true, then, that before the Lord's passion and after his resurrection they had been unable to mourn and fast on account of the Lord's presence, but after his departure they voluntarily subjected themselves to fasting. When they were renewed by the reception of the Holy Spirit, as they had turned their minds away from the rest of worldly allurements, so had they also done from their appetite for meals, rejoicing in nourishment for their souls rather than for their bodies, and devoting themselves to salutary prayers and tears as they remembered their heavenly fatherland. From the report of Luke concerning the three thousand men who believed on the very day of Pentecost, after Peter had preached, we acknowledge with what a frugal diet they were content, and what a sober and heavenly life they led on earth. [Luke] said: *They were persevering in the apostles' teaching, and in sharing in the breaking of bread, and in prayers;*[50] and a little further on: *Day by day, staying together in the temple, and breaking bread in their houses, they took food with exultation and simplicity of heart, praising God together,*[51] and other things of this sort.

We must model our lives and behavior carefully after their example, for the perfect instruction for our lives is always to imitate the actions of the primitive Church, and to keep up to the end that design of the spiritual edifice which was

49. Mt 9:14-15   50. Ac 2:42   51. Ac 2:46-47

clearly proposed to the apostles[52] themselves as the foundation of the faith. We must not doubt that we shall in the future reach the rewards of those in whose footsteps we now follow. And, indeed, my brothers, even in the present we carry out a most beautiful sketch of the future happiness which we have just now touched upon to some small extent; but we must live our lives in such a way that we keep with sincere heart before the eyes of the Searcher of hearts what we worship externally in imagery. Let us then persevere in the teaching of the saints, namely by learning from them, and let us carry out in our deeds what they teach; let us apply ourselves unremittingly to prayer; let us attempt to be of one heart by communion of the Lord's bread; let us remain in church at the canonical hours; let us reach out to a needy neighbor with bread, or whatever holy consolation we are able to give; let us gratify our bodies with food in such a way that the memory of living bread may instead bring gladness to the inner region of our mind; let us hold to simplicity of heart in everything—which is performing good works with the sole intention of retribution from on high.

And what is especially fitting on this present feast, let us intone a hymn of divine praise with our voices and minds in full accord. Only thus will our praise be agreeable to our God,[53] if we do not contradict in our work what we chant with our mouth, if we bring forth 'Allelujah' from our lips and keep our hearts chaste from base and evil thoughts. Nevertheless our praise will be sweet only for this reason, if we take delight not in perishable and base things, but in the Lord.[54] May he deign to endow us with this, who granted us such great and splendid assurances of his kindnesses through the paschal sacraments, Jesus Christ our Lord, who lives and reigns with the Father in the unity of the Holy Spirit throughout all ages. Amen.

---

52. var.: 'by the apostles'   53. Ps 147:1 (146:1)
54. Ps 37:4 (36:4)

NOTES

1. "Pentecost" = *quinquagesima*. More recently *quinquagesima* was used to designate the Sunday a nominal 'fifty days' before Easter. Bede used it of the fiftieth day after Easter, Pentecost Sunday, and it seemed best to avoid confusion by translating *quinquagesima* with the word 'Pentecost'. The Latin word is, of course, a translation of the Greek word meaning fifty.
2. The denarius was a silver Roman coin which was originally the equivalent of ten copper coins. Hence its name was derived from the Latin word *deni* meaning "ten altogether," related to the Latin word for ten, *decem*.
3. The obol was an ancient Greek coin, the equivalent of one-sixth of a drachma.
4. It was commonly believed by the early fathers of the Church that the souls of individuals who were saved were at rest after their death, awaiting the final judgment and the universal resurrection.

homily II.17

John 14:15-21   *Pentecost*

S ince we are celebrating today, dearly beloved brothers, the coming of the Holy Spirit, we ought ourselves to live in accord with the solemnity that we are honoring. Indeed we only worthily celebrate the joys of this festival if, with God's assistance, we render ourselves conformable to those to whom the Holy Spirit deigned to come and in whom he deigned to dwell. We ourselves are only suited to the coming and illumination of the Holy Spirit for this reason, that our hearts are filled with divine love, and our bodies are dedicated to the Lord's commands. Hence Truth says to his disciples at the commencement of this gospel reading, *'If you love me, keep my commandments, and I will ask the Father, and he will give you another Paraclete'*. Paraclete means 'consoler'.[1] The Holy Spirit is correctly called a Paraclete because, by producing a desire for the heavenly life, he raises up and restores the hearts of believers lest they falter amidst the adversities of this age. Hence, as holy Church increased, it was said in the Acts of the Apostles, *And it was being built up, walking in the fear of the Lord, and was filled with the consolation of the Holy Spirit.*[2]

1. Aug., *Tract. in Ioh.* 94, 2 (CC 36: 562, 1/4)
2. Ac 9:31

[The words], *'If you love me, keep my commandments, and I will ask the Father and he will give you another Paraclete,'* were brought to fulfillment in the disciples themselves. They were proven truly to have loved him, truly to have obeyed his commandments, on that day when all at once the Holy Spirit appeared to them in [tongues of] fire as they were praying in the upper room, and taught them, [putting] in their mouths a diversity of languages,[3] and made them strong in heart with the consolation of his love. Earlier, however, they possessed the Paraclete himself, namely our Lord sojourning with them in the flesh. By the sweetness of his miracles and the wealth of his preaching they were wont to be raised up and strengthened, so that they could not be scandalized at persecution by unbelievers. But since by ascending into heaven after his resurrection he had deserted them bodily, although the presence of his divine majesty was never absent from them, he rightly added concerning this Paraclete, that is, the Holy Spirit: *to abide with you forever.* He abides eternally with the saints, always illuminating them inwardly and invisibly in this life, and introducing them to the everlasting contemplation of the sight of his majesty in the future.

If we too, dearly beloved brothers, love Christ perfectly in such a way that we prove the genuineness of this love by our observance of his commandments, he will ask the Father on our behalf, and the Father will give us another Paraclete. He will ask the Father through his humanity, and will give [us another Paraclete] with the Father through his divinity. We must not suppose that it was only before his passion that he was asking on behalf of the Church, and that now, after his ascension, he is not also asking, since the Apostle says concerning him, *Who is at the right hand of God, who also intercedes for us.*[4]

We also have as our Paraclete our Lord Jesus Christ. Although we are unable to see him bodily, we recollect what he did and taught in the body, as written down in the gospels. If we commit ourselves with all care to hearing,

---

3. Ac 2:1-4   4. Rm 8:34

reading, conferring with one another, and preserving these [deeds and teachings] in heart and body, it is sure that we will easily overcome the hardships of this age—as if the Lord were sojourning with us forever and consoling us. If we love this Paraclete and keep his commandments, he will ask the Father, and he will give us another Paraclete—that is, he will in his clemency pour forth the grace of his Spirit into our hearts, and it will gladden us in the expectation of our heavenly homeland in the midst of the adversities of our present exile. Then we will be able to say with the prophet, *According to the multitude of my sorrows in my heart, your paraclesis, that is, your consolations, O Lord, have gladdened my soul.*[5]

Therefore [Jesus] said, '*He will give you another Paraclete, to abide with you forever,*' and added, '*The Spirit of truth, whom the world cannot receive*'. He is calling 'the world' the inhabitants of this world, who are given over to love of it.[6] In contrast, the saints who are aflame with desire for heavenly things are fittingly called 'the heavens,' as the psalmist says, *And the heavens will proclaim his justice to a people yet to be born,*[7] which is to say, 'And the most illustrious teachers will proclaim, with mind, voice, and action, his justice to a people, who, coming recently to the faith, desire to be born in him'. Thus, anyone searching for consolation outwardly, in the things of the world, is not capable of being reformed inwardly by the favor of divine consolation; whoever yearns after lowly delight cannot receive the Spirit of truth. The Spirit of truth flees from a heart it discerns is subject to vanity, and restores by the light of his coming only those it beholds carrying out the commandments of Truth out of love. Hence when he had said, '*Whom the world cannot receive*', he added next, '*because* [the world] *neither sees him nor knows him; but you recognize him, for he will dwell with you and be in you*'. Unbelievers too saw our Lord and Savior in the flesh before his passion, but only believers could know that he was the Son of God, that he was the Paraclete sent

5. Ps 94:19 (93:19)
6. Aug., *Tract in Ioh.* 74, 4, (CC 36: 514, 8/9)
7. Ps 22:31 (21:32)

by God into the world. Unbelievers were incapable of seeing the Holy Spirit with their eyes or recognizing him with
their minds, since he did not appear to the disciples clothed
with a human nature, but preferred to come to them, to
remain among them, in such a way as to consecrate for himself a most welcome abode in their very hearts. This is what
[the Lord] says, *'But you recognize him, for he will dwell with
you and be in you'.* The one who dwells with the elect invisibly in this life surely provides for them the grace of recognizing him invisibly.[8]

'I will not leave you orphans; I will come to you'. Our Lord
seemed to unbelievers to be leaving his disciples orphans
when he died on the cross. But he did not leave orphans
those *to whom he presented himself alive after his passion by many
proofs during forty days,*[9] and those to whom he granted the
anointing of the Holy Spirit from heaven ten days after his
assumption—that is, today. On this point no one who has
recognized the inseparable nature, power and working of
the holy Trinity disputes that Christ himself came to them.

Following up this matter more extensively, he gives notice of how greatly different their case is *from a nation that
is not holy:*[10] *'Yet a little while and the world no longer sees me.
You see me; because I live, you will live also'.* Since he said this
as he was about to go to his passion, it was but a little while
until the completion of his passion; from that time on, the
damned were never capable of seeing him again. Only the
just, who were saddened by his death, were worthy to see
the joy of his resurrection. Those who exulted at seeing him
dead had no [reason to] be glad at seeing his resurrection,
but they were disturbed and sorrowful on hearing of it, as
was fitting.

'You see me,' he said; *'because I live, you will live also'.* He
used a verb in the present tense, *'I live,'* and one in the future tense, *'you will live also,'* undoubtedly because he discerned [that his resurrection] was nigh. Therefore he spoke
of the hour in which he would rise to eternal life after destroying death as if it were present. He knew that their life

8. Aug., *Tract. in Ioh.* 74, 4 (CC 36: 515, 15/16)
9. Ac 1:3   10. Ps 43:1 (42:1)

was to be deferred into the future, for each one of them had to struggle up to the predetermined time of their deaths before they could enter everlasting life, and to wait until the end of the age for the resurrection of their bodies.[11] Therefore he said, *'Yet a little while and the world no longer sees me. You see me; because I live, you will live also,'* as if meaning, *'Yet a little while* and those who love the world will see me no more as a mortal; they will be unable to see me rising from the dead because they do not know that life whose glory only those who love my resurrection are worthy to contemplate. You will be capable of seeing me after this occurs, because *I live*, brought back from the dead; and you will be worthy to be comforted by the example of my resurrection, because you yourselves will come to everlasting life and the joys of a blessed resurrection'.

'On that day you will know that I am in my Father, and you in me, and I in you'. The apostles then knew that Christ was in the Father through his being united with the undivided divinity; they knew that they were in Christ through their reception of his faith and sacraments; they knew that Christ was in them through their love for him and their observances of his commandments. He himself said to them, *'If anyone loves me he will keep my word; and my Father loves him, and we will come to him and make our abode with him'.*[12] The apostles surely knew these things then because they had been imbued with them by Christ, and now the entire Church of Christ knows them, because she has been imbued with them by the writings of the apostles. But the just will undoubtedly begin to recognize them in a far more thorough way on that day when they begin truly to live, that is, on the day of [their] resurrection, when they begin to know more perfectly all the things that are to be known, to the extent that they endlessly look, from closer by, at the very font of knowledge. There is no doubt that this happens to some of the more perfect saints even before the time of their resurrection—to those, namely, who because of confidence in their good works are capable of saying with the

11. Aug., *Tract. in Ioh.* 75, 3 (CC 36:516, 1/20)
12. Jn 14:23

Apostle, *I long to die and be with Christ;* [13] and, *For me, to live is Christ and to die is gain.* [14]

Our Lord seems indeed to be saying all these things [as if they were intended] specially for his apostles; but so that we will not suppose that he is saying these things to them alone and not to us too, if we follow their example, he affixed after this statement an all-inclusive pledge of the happiness of divine knowledge, and he promises the same rewards of seeing and knowing him to all who love him, saying: *'He who has my commandments and keeps them, he it is who loves me; and he who loves me will be loved by my Father, and I will love him and manifest myself to him'.* Here we must consider with all our attention that truly to love Christ does not mean to avow this love with our lips, but that we ought to observe in our actions the commandments of Christ we have acquired through learning. Hence John counsels us and says, *My little children, let us not love in word or speech, but in deed and in truth.* [15] This we must embrace with all joy, because the reward for our true love will be that than which nothing can be greater—namely that we are loved by the Father and the Son, that the glory of God's Son is revealed so that we may contemplate it forever. We must not doubt that those to whom the glory of God's Son will be revealed will be permitted to be present at the sight of the Father and the Son and the Holy Spirit too, because certainly the vision of those whose divinity is one is also one and inseparable. Indeed thus he said, [16] *'One who sees me sees the Father too'.* [17]

And we must note that when he spoke using a verb in the present tense, *'And he who loves me,'* he continued in the future tense, *'will be loved by my Father, and I will love him and manifest myself to him'.* Even now the Son loves those who love him and the Father; but he loves them now for this reason, that they may live properly as a result of their faith which works through love; [18] then he will love them for this reason, that they may come to the vision of the

---

13. Ph 1:23   14. Ph 1:21   15. 1 Jn 3:18
16. 'he said' = *dicit,* a well-attested var. for *dicitur,* 'it is said'
17. Jn 14:9   18. Ga 5:6

truth of which they had had a taste through faith, and on behalf of which they had contended even to death. And it is not without effect that he makes this statement with the addition, *'And I will manifest myself to him,'* for he will manifest himself to all human beings, but he will manifest his very own being only to the elect. At the [final] judgment even the damned will see Christ, but as it is written, *They will see him whom they have pierced.*[19] Only the eyes of the just will see the king in all his beauty,[20] for, *'Blessed are the pure of heart, for they shall see God'.*[21]

I have spoken these things to you of the brotherhood in explanation of the gospel reading, dearly beloved, to the extent that the Lord has inspired me. It seems appropriate, however, still to discuss briefly the meaning of today's solemnity. First of all, we must be aware of the fact that this solemnity has been consecrated not only by the gospel anointings, but that it was also formerly foreshadowed by the mysteries of the law, and by the Lord's order it was observed each year with sacred ceremonies. Today, as we know, when the disciples were assembled in the upper room, there came all at once a sound from heaven and the Holy Spirit appeared in the guise of [tongues of] fire and passed on to them the knowledge of all languages.[22] When they had heard this sound, religious men from different countries, who had gathered at Jerusalem because of the feast of Passover, came together and were bewildered, wondering that each of them heard the apostles speaking of the wonders of God in his own language.[23] When the disciples explained that it was by the grace of the Holy Spirit that they saw that what was formerly promised by the words of the prophets was then being given by Christ's favor, three thousand of these men believed, were baptized, and themselves also received the gift of the Holy Spirit.[24]

Today is the annual celebration of this event; this is the always-welcome festivity of [the bestowal] of heavenly grace. In order to stamp the memory of this more firmly on the hearts of believers, a beautiful custom of holy Church

19. Jn 19:37   20. Is 33:17   21. Mt 5:8
22. Ac 2:1-4   23. Ac 2:5-6   24. Ac 2:14-41

has grown up, so that each year the mysteries of baptism are celebrated on this [day], and as a result a venerable temple is made ready for the coming of the Holy Spirit upon those who believe and are cleansed at the salvation-bearing baptismal font. In this way we celebrate not only the recollection of a former happening, but also a new coming in [the font] of the Holy Spirit upon new children by adoption.

Therefore, you dear ones, be attentive, to how the type and figure of the feast of the law is in agreement with our festivity. When the children of Israel had been freed from slavery in Egypt by the immolation of the paschal lamb, they went out through the desert so that they might come to the promised land, and they reached Mount Sinai.[25] On the fiftieth day after the Passover, the Lord descended upon the mountain in fire, accompanied by the sound of a trumpet and thunder and lightning, and with a clear voice he laid out for them the ten commandments of the law.[26] As a memorial of the law he had given, he established a sacrifice to himself from the first-fruits of that year, to be celebrated annually on that day, namely, two loaves of bread made from the new grain, which were to be brought to the altar.[27] It is obvious to all who read what the immolation of the paschal lamb and the escape from slavery in Egypt meant, for *Christ, our paschal Lamb has been immolated.*[28] He is the true Lamb who has taken away the sins of the world,[29] who has redeemed us from the slavery of sin at the price of his blood, and by the example of his resurrection has shown us the hope of life and everlasting liberty. The law was given on the fiftieth day after the slaying of the lamb,[30] when the Lord descended upon the mountain in fire; likewise on the fiftieth day after the resurrection of our Redeemer, which is today, the grace of the Holy Spirit was given to the disciples as they were assembled in the upper room. Appearing visibly and externally as fire, it shed rays of the light of knowledge invisibly on their inmost thoughts and kindled in them the inextinguishable ardor of charity.

25. Ex 12:2-19:1   26. Ex 19:16-20:17   27. Lv 23:15-17
28. 1 Co 5:7   29. Jn 1:29
30. Aug., *Ep.* 55, 16, 29-30 (*CSEL* 34: 203, 15 - 205, 14)

The elevation of the upper room in the one case, and the summit of the mountain in the other, indicate the sublimity of the commands and the gifts. Because no one who still clings to base desires can either comply with divine commands or be worthy of gifts from on high, in the one case, as a sign of greater perfection, all who received the Spirit were gathered in the upper room; in the other case, to indicate the hearts of the feeble hearers, the entire group of the people were standing at the foot of the mountain, and a few of the elders had gone partially up the mountain.[31] Moses alone ascended to its very top, where the divine majesty shone forth in fire and a dark cloud.[32] Only the more perfect know how to grasp and observe the deeper and most secret mysteries of the law; the carnal-minded people, content with the external aspects of the letter, and gathered apart, as it were, and below, stood to hear the words from heaven. But now that the grace of the Holy Spirit has been given more extensively, [for people] to understand more fully and fulfill more perfectly the words of the holy gospel, the hearts of the faithful are raised up higher.

There [on Sinai] the crashing of the thunder and the blasts of the trumpet resounded in the midst of flames of fire and flashes of lightning. Here [in the upper room], along with the vision of tongues of fire there *came down from heaven a sound as of a strong wind*.[33] But although in both bestowals, namely of the law and of grace, a sound was heard outwardly, yet here [in the upper room], by a more extensive miracle, when the sound was heard there was present the power of a heavenly gift, which would teach the hearts of the disciples inwardly without a sound. There [on Sinai], after all the legal decrees had been heard, the entire people answered with one voice, *'We will hear and do all the words which the Lord has spoken'*.[34] Here [in the upper room], after the assembly of the Church, which was being born, had received the enlightenment of the Spirit, they spoke of the wonders of God in the languages of all countries. Doubtlessly it was thanks to a certain discernment that the observ-

31. Ex 19:17, 22-24   32. Ex 19:20   33. Ac 2:2
34. Ex 24:3

ance of the law was given to only one nation, that of the
Jews, while the word of the gospel was to be proclaimed
to all nations throughout the world, and that the proclamations of the Christian faith were to be spoken in the languages of all peoples, fulfilling the prophecy that says, *From
the rising of the sun to its setting, praise the name of the Lord;
the Lord is high above all nations.*[35]

In addition, in veneration of the reception of the law, a
new sacrifice was ordered to be offered to the Lord annually on the day of Pentecost, from the time of the reception
of this grace; and it never stops being carried out spiritually,
also on this our festivity. Indeed the Church offers a new
sacrifice on this [day], when on the Saturday that marks
the beginning of the holy feast of Pentecost, she consecrates
to the Lord through baptism a new people of adoption, in
a rite that is truly most appropriate, as I noted above. Thus
not only is the memory of an ancient happening renewed
for the Christian people, but also a new sending of the
Paraclete from the Father upon a new progeny, those who
have been reborn, is celebrated. The apostles too, as soon
as they had received the gift of the Spirit, offered a new
sacrifice to the Lord on this [day]. After announcing the
good news to those who had come together, they converted many of them to the faith; and when they had been reborn in the font of baptism[36] and sanctified by the grace of
the Spirit, they offered them as living first-fruits of the New
Testament in communion at the Lord's altar. Two loaves
of bread made from the first-fruits of the new harvest were
rightly ordered to be offered,[37] for the Church gathers those
it can consecrate to its Redeemer as a new family from both
peoples, the Jews and the gentiles.

In this connection, in truth, we must carefully consider
that it was not without deep significance that the number
fifty was observed in the giving both of the law and of grace.
It was on the fiftieth day after Passover that the former was
given to the people on the mountain, and the latter to the
disciples in the upper room. By this number the long-lasting

35. Ps 113:3-4 (112:3-4)   36. Ac 2:41   37. Lv 23:17

quality of our future rest was surely being shown, since on this [fiftieth day] the ten commandments of the law were delivered, and the grace of the Holy Spirit was given to human beings. This was to point out clearly that all who carry out the commands of the divine law with the help of the grace of the Spirit are directing their course toward true rest. In the law, the fiftieth year was ordered to be called [the year] of jubilee,[38] that is, 'forgiving' or 'changed'.[39] During it the people were to remain at rest from all work, the debts of all were to be canceled, slaves were to go free, [and] the year itself was to be more notable than other years because of its greater solemnities and divine praises. Therefore, by this number is rightly indicated that tranquility of greatest peace when, as the Apostle says, at the sound of the last trumpet *the dead will rise and we shall be changed*[40] into glory. Then, when the labors and hardships of this age come to an end, and our debts, [that is] all our faults, have been forgiven, the entire people of the elect will rejoice eternally in the sole contemplation of the divine vision, and that most longed-for command of our Lord and Savior will be fulfilled: *Be still and see that I am God.*[41]

Since it is only by observance of the heavenly commands and the gift of the Holy Spirit that this stillness and vision of unchangeable Truth is reached, both the law of the ten commandments and the grace of the Spirit were given on that particular one of the days[42] which designates rest. Nor is it to be passed over that this number fifty is appropriate to signify inward tranquility, for it is arrived at by multiplying seven times seven and adding one.[43] Under the law the people were ordered to work for six days and to rest on the seventh,[44] [and] to plow and reap for six years and desist during the seventh,[45] because the Lord completed the creation of the world in six days and desisted from his work on the seventh.[46] Mystically speaking, we are counseled by

---

38. Lv 25:8-12   39. Jer., *Nom.* (CC 72: 67, 10)   40. 1 Co 15:52
41. Ps 46:10 (45:11)   42. *in ea dierum numero*
43. Aug., *Serm.* 259, 2 (*PL* 38: 1197-98); *Serm.* 268, 1 (*PL* 38: 1231-32); *Serm.* 270, 5-6 (*PL* 38:1242-43)
44. Ex 20:8-10   45. Ex 23:10-11   46. Gn 2:2

all this that those who in this age (which is comprised of six periods[47]), devote themselves to good works for the Lord's sake, are in future led by the Lord to a sabbath, that is, to eternal rest.

The fact that the seven days or years are multiplied by seven indicates the manifold abundance of this rest, in which there will be given to the elect that sublime reward concerning which the Apostle exclaims, *Eye has not seen, nor has ear heard, nor has it occurred to the heart of man what things God has prepared for those who love him.*[48] Since he bears witness that the knowledge of this reward cannot occur to the heart of man, that is, to those who still savor human things, he subsequently makes clear how it can be shown to those who love God: *But to us God has revealed* [it] *by his Spirit.*[49] The greatness, therefore, of the everlasting reward is revealed by the Spirit. When he inflames the hearts he fills with longing for invisible things, he manifests how splendid these invisible goods are, [and] how much they are to be preferred to all earthly things. Hence the grace of the same Spirit is well described by the prophet as being sevenfold,[50] since it is through his inspiration that one arrives at rest, and in the full partaking of and sight of him true rest is reached. Besides, this fiftieth day or year, which is over and above forty-nine and is more renowned than the others because of its greater solemnity, indicates the time of the future resurrection, when, to that rest which the souls of the elect now enjoy there will also be added the glory of the recovery of their bodies.

At this point we must look more carefully, my brothers, at the fact that the Holy Spirit not only bestows perfect tranquility in the future upon the just, but also very great [tranquility] in the present, when he enkindles their minds with the fire of heavenly charity. For the Apostle says, *Hope does not disappoint us, for God's charity has been poured forth in our hearts by the Holy Spirit, who has been given to us.*[51] And this is the true rest of souls—nay, this is [their] only rest in this life: to be filled with divine love, to despise the favorable

47. See *Hom.* I, 14.   48. 1 Co 2:9   49. 1 Co 2:10
50. Is 11:2-3   51. Rm 5:5

and adverse things of the world out of hope of retribution from on high, to root out earthly desires completely from oneself, to renounce earthly lusts, to rejoice in insults and persecutions that have been inflicted for the sake of Christ, and to be able to say with the Apostle, *Let us glory in our hope* [of sharing in] *the glory of God, but not only that, let us also glory in our tribulations.*[52] A person who trusts that he can find rest in the delights and abundance of earthly things is deceiving himself. By the frequent disorders of the world, and at last by its end, such a one is proven convincingly to have laid the foundation of his tranquility upon sand.[53] But all those who have been breathed upon by the Holy Spirit, and have taken upon themselves the very pleasant yoke of the Lord's love, and following his example, learned to be gentle and humble of heart,[54] enjoy even in the present some image of the future tranquility. Separated with their whole mind from the turmoil of worldly men, they rejoice always in remembering their Maker's countenance, and thirst after reaching perfect contemplation of him, saying to themselves with the apostle John, *We know that when he appears we shall be like him, for we shall see him as he is.*[55]

If we desire to arrive at the reward of this vision, dearly beloved brothers, we must demonstrate that, continually mindful of this gospel reading, we are not subservient to the allurements of the world. Thus we may be capable of becoming worthy to attain the grace of the Holy Spirit, which the world cannot receive. Let us love Christ, and let us observe, by persevering, his commandments, which we possess by beginning [to observe them]. It will come about as [our] just reward that, by loving him, we will be worthy to be more fully loved by the Father; and he himself may deign to present us with a more abundant gift of his love in the future. For, as a result of our loving him now, he grants to us to believe and hope in him, but then [he will grant us] to see him face to face,[56] and he will manifest himself to us,[57] that is, with that brilliance which he had with

52. Rm 5:2-3   53. Mt. 7:26; Lk 6:49   54. Mt 11:29
55. 1 Jn 3:2   56. 1 Co 13:12   57. Jn 14:21

his Father before the world began,[58] with whom he lives and reigns in the unity of the Holy Spirit, God throughout all ages. Amen.

58. Jn 17:5

homily II.18

John 3:1-16   *The Octave of Pentecost*

as you have heard from the reading of the holy gospel, dearly beloved brothers, a prominent man from among the Jews came to Jesus during the night. He longed to learn more fully, by speaking with him in secret, about the mysteries of the faith, the elementary stages of which he had already perceived to some extent by the clear disclosure of [Jesus'] signs. Since he had prudently taken care to understand what he saw being done by [Jesus], he deserved to explore more profoundly what he was seeking from him. *'Rabbi,'* he said, *'we know that you have come as a teacher from God. No one is able to do these signs which you are doing, unless God is with him'*. He thus confessed that Jesus had come from God to address his heavenly instruction to the world, [and] understood that God was with him because of the miracles that were being performed; nevertheless he did not yet recognize that he was God. But because he came eagerly to the one he knew to be the master of truth in order to be taught, when he had been perfectly taught, he arrived at the acceptance of his divinity. He perceived the hidden mysteries of both of his births— the divine and the human—as well as the hidden mysteries of his passion and ascension. He also learned about the way of second birth, and entry into the heavenly kingdom, and many other sacramental mysteries of the gospel teaching, as the Lord revealed these things to him.

Jesus answered and said to him, 'Amen, amen I say to you, unless a person be born anew, he cannot see the kingdom of God'. This statement shines forth all the more clearly in the sight of all the faithful, as it is obvious that without its light they cannot be faithful. Who indeed is capable of securing the forgiveness of sins, and of entering the kingdom of heaven, without the bath of regeneration? But Nicodemus, who came to Jesus by night, did not yet know how to grasp the mysteries of the light. Even the night during which he came indicates the ignorance by which he was oppressed.[1] He did not yet belong to the number of that fellowship to whom the Apostle says, *You were once darkness, but now you are light in the Lord,*[2] but rather he remained in the company of those to whom Isaiah speaks: *Arise, be enlightened, O Jerusalem, for your light has come, and the glory of the Lord has risen upon you.*[3]

Therefore he answered the Lord and said, *'How can a man be born when he is an old man? Can he enter into his mother's womb a second time and be born'?* Since he was persistent, though knowing nothing of a second birth, and was concerned about his salvation, he naturally asked whether the one birth with which he was acquainted could occur a second time, or in what way a regeneration could be accomplished lest by remaining ignorant about this he would be unable to be a sharer in the heavenly life. We should note, however, that what he said about physical generation should also be understood concerning spiritual generation, namely, that once it has happened it cannot be repeated. If any heretic or schismatic or wicked person baptizes in acknowledgment of the holy Trinity, the one who is so baptized cannot be rebaptized by good Catholics, lest it seem that the acknowledgment and invocation of so great a name was done in vain.[4]

1. Aug., *Tract. in Ioh.* 11, 4 (*CC* 36:111, 1 - 112, 10)
2. Eph 5:8   3. Is 60:1
4. Aug., *Tract in Ioh.* 12, 2 (*CC* 36: 120, 1 - 121, 15)

Since Nicodemus was so eager to inquire diligently how the Lord's first answer was to be understood, he now deserved to be instructed more fully, and to hear that the second birth was not fleshly but spiritual. *Jesus answered* him, *'Amen, amen I say to you, unless a man be born again of water and the Holy Spirit, he cannot enter into the kingdom of God'*.

Subsequently explaining the manner of this birth, and further distinguishing it from a fleshly one, he said, *'What is born of the flesh is flesh, and what is born of the Spirit is spirit'*. By its nature spirit is invisible; flesh is visible, and so fleshly generation is carried out in visible stages—one who is born in the flesh develops through moments of time. Spiritual generation is carried out entirely invisibly. We see the one being baptized descend into the font, we see him being immersed, we see him come up out of the water; but what is done in that washing of regeneration cannot be seen. Only the piety of the faithful knows that a sinner descends into the font, and a purified person comes up; that a child of death[1]* descends, and a child of the resurrection comes up; that a child of original sin[5] descends, and a child of reconciliation comes up; that a child of wrath descends, and a child of mercy comes up; that a child of the devil descends, and a child of God comes up. Only the Church, a mother who gives birth, knows these things; otherwise, to the eyes of the foolish, the person seems to come forth from the font just as he went in, and the entire action seems to be a game. In the end, those groaning in torment will say as they see the glory of the saints, *These are they whom we once held in contempt and like persons to be despised; how then are they counted among the sons of God?*[6] And the apostle John says, *Dearly beloved, we are now children of God, and it has not yet appeared what we shall be.*[7] What is born of the Spirit is spirit, because the person who is regenerated invisibly of water and the Spirit is changed into a new human being, and from being fleshly he becomes spiritual.[8] Rightly then is he called not only spiritual but even 'spirit,' because just as the substance of a spirit is invisible to our sight, so the one who is invis-

5. *praeuaricationis*   6. Ws 5:4-5 (5:3, 5)   7. 1 Jn 3:2
8. Aug., *Tract. in Ioh.* 12, 5 (CC 36: 123, 14/16)

ibly renewed by the grace of God becomes spiritual and a child of God, although he appears visibly to all as flesh and the child of a human being.

There follows: *'Do not marvel that I have said to you that you must be born anew. The Spirit breathes where he wills, and you hear his voice but you do not know whence he comes and whither he goes. So it is with everyone who is born of the Spirit'.* *'The Spirit breathes where he wills'* because he has in his power [to choose the] heart he will enlighten by the grace of his visitation. *'And you hear his voice'* when one who is filled with the Holy Spirit speaks in your presence. *'But you do not know whence he comes and whither he goes'* because even if the Spirit fills someone in your presence for the moment, [you] cannot see how he makes his entry into him or how he departs, since by nature he is invisible. *'So it is with everyone who is born of the Spirit'.* By the Spirit acting invisibly he begins to be what he was not, so that unbelievers do not know *whence he comes and whither he goes*—that is, [they do not know] that the grace of regeneration *comes*, bringing about adoption as sons of God, and *goes*, bringing about the reception of the heavenly kingdom.

As Nicodemus was still asking how these things could come about, the Lord added, *'Are you a teacher in Israel, and ignorant of these things'?*—not as if he wanted to scoff at him for being a teacher in Israel and yet ignorant of the heavenly mysteries; he was stirring him up toward the way of humility, without which the gate of heaven cannot be found.[9]

'If I have told you earthly things and you do not believe, how will you believe if I tell you heavenly things'? He told them earthly things when, as we have found in a previous reading,[10] he spoke of the passion and resurrection of his body, which he had taken from the earth, saying, *'Destroy this temple, and within three days I will raise it up'.*[11] Yet they did not believe the words he spoke; they were not capable of understanding that he was speaking of no other temple than that of his body. Therefore, since they did not grasp earthly things when they heard about them, how much less capable

9. Aug., *Tract. in Ioh.* 12, 6 (CC 36: 123, 5/10)
10. In *Hom.* II.1   11. Jn 2:19

would they be of grasping heavenly mysteries—that is, mysteries of his divine generation?

Our Lord, however, still continued to instruct the one he saw was wisely and diligently attentive to what he was hearing about both heavenly mysteries and earthly ones. His ascension to eternal life is a heavenly [mystery]; his being lifted up to temporal death is an earthly one. He says of the heavenly [mystery], *'And no one has ascended into heaven except the one who descended from heaven, the Son of man who is in heaven'.* He adds about the earthly [mystery], *'And just as Moses lifted up the serpent in the desert, so must the Son of man be lifted up'.*

We must ask how the Son of man can be said both to have descended from heaven, and still to be in heaven while he was speaking these things on earth. We are familiar with the article of the Catholic faith [which says] that the Son of God descended from heaven and became Son of man in the Virgin's womb, and that once the divinely-arranged plan of his passion was brought to fulfillment, he was raised from the dead and taken up into heaven. Therefore it was not Christ's flesh that descended from heaven, nor was it in heaven before the time of his ascension. And for what reason is it said, '[And no one has ascended into heaven] *except the one who descended from heaven, the Son of man who is in heaven,'* except that the person of Christ is one, existing in two natures? And so it is rightly said of the Son of man that he descended from heaven, and that before his passion he was in heaven, because what he could not possess in his own nature he possessed as God's Son, by whom [his human nature] was assumed.[12] On account of the single personality of Christ, which comprises two natures, the Apostle says, *The Holy Spirit has made you overseers to govern the Church of God, which he obtained by his own blood.*[13] It was not in his own substance but in the human nature he assumed that God possessed the blood he poured forth on behalf of the Church. So it is that the psalmist says, *God ascends with a shout of joy!*[14] How could God ascend except

12. Aug., *Tract. in Ioh.* 12, 8 (CC 36: 125, 1/20)
13. Ac 20:28   14. Ps 47:5 (46:6)

in his human nature, since he is always present everywhere in the nature of his [divine] majesty?

This too we must ask, why was it said, *'And no one has ascended into heaven except the one who descended from heaven'*? All the elect are truly confident that they will ascend into heaven,[15] according to the Lord's promise that *'Where I am, there will my servant be also'*.[16] Yet a very clear argument unties the knot of this question—namely *that The Mediator between God and human beings, the human being Jesus Christ,*[17] is the head of all the elect; likewise all the elect are members of this head, as the Apostle says, *And he made him head over everything for the Church;*[18] and again, *For you are the body of Christ, member for member.*[19] *'No one, then, has ascended into heaven except the one who descended from heaven, the Son of man who is in heaven'. No one* [that is] *has ascended into heaven except* Christ in his [human] body, which is the Church.[20] He first of all ascended in his own being, in the sight of the apostles, his most eminent members; after that, by ascending daily in his [other] members, he gathers himself [together] in heaven. So it is that his body, entangled in the adversities of the present age, glories and says, *But now he has exalted my head above my enemies,*[21] as if it were saying, 'I hope that he who restored Christ, who is my head, to life from the dead after he was killed by the Jews, and so brought to naught all the plots of his enemies by raising him up into heaven, will rescue me too from my present dangers and join me to my head in his kingdom'.

Since *'No one has ascended into heaven except the one who descended from heaven,'* let anyone who desires to ascend into heaven join himself, in a true unity of faith and love, to him who descended from heaven, clearly understanding that in no other way can he ascend into heaven except through him who descended from heaven. Hence he himself says elsewhere, *'No one comes to the Father except through me'.*[22] Those things were said to Nicodemus, and they are said

15. Aug., *Tract. in Ioh.* 12, 9 (CC 36: 125, 1/12)
16. Jn 12:26   17. 1 Tm 2:5   18. Eph 1:22
19. 1 Co 12:27   20. Col 1:24   21. Ps 27:6 (26:6)
22. Jn 14:6

to all catechumens, so that they may learn to be incorpo-
rated by being born again into the members of him, through
whom they may be able to ascend into the kingdom of God.

Since ascension and entry into the kingdom cannot happen without faith and the sacraments of the Lord's passion,
there is added: *'And just as Moses lifted up the serpent in the
desert, so must the Son of man be lifted up, so that everyone who
believes in him may not perish but have eternal life'.* With the
wonderful skill of heavenly teaching, the Lord directs our
attention to the teacher of the Mosaic law, and to the
spiritual meaning of this law, by recalling some of the
ancient history and explaining that it happened as a figure
of his own passion and of human salvation. The Book of
Numbers tells that the people of Israel were wearied in the
desert from their long journeying and exertion, and mur-
mured against the Lord and Moses, and so the Lord sent
fiery serpents in among them. When they cried out to Moses
because of their wounds and the death of many of them,
and he prayed for them, the Lord ordered him to make a
bronze serpent and set it up as a sign.[23] He said, *'Whoever
is bitten and looks at it will live,'*[24] and so it happened.

The wounds caused by the fiery serpent are the poisonous enticements of the vices, which afflict the soul and bring
about its spiritual death. The people murmuring against the
Lord, and stricken by the serpents' bites, provide an excellent instance of how one may recognize from the results
of an external scourge what a great calamity a person might
suffer inwardly by murmuring. The raising up of the bronze
serpent (when those who were stricken beheld it, they were
cured) is our Redeemer's suffering on the cross, for only
by faith in him is the kingdom of death and sin overcome.
The sins which drag down soul and body to destruction at
the same time are appropriately represented by the serpents,
not only because they were fiery and poisonous [and] art-
ful at bringing about death, but also because our first parents were led into sin by a serpent,[25] and from being
immortal they became mortal by sinning. The Lord is aptly

23. Nb 21: 5-8   24. Nb 21: 9   25. Gn 3: 1-13

made known by the bronze serpent, since he came in the likeness of sinful flesh.[26] Just as the bronze serpent had the likeness of a fiery serpent, but had absolutely none of the strength of harmful poison in its members—rather by being lifted up it cured those who had been stricken by the [live] serpents—so the Redeemer of the human race did not clothe himself in sinful flesh, but in the likeness of sinful flesh, in order that by suffering death on the cross in [this likeness] he might free those who believed in him from all sin and even from death itself.

'Just as Moses lifted up the serpent in the desert', he says, *'so must the Son of man be lifted up'*. Just as those who looked at the bronze serpent which had been lifted up as a sign were cured at that time from temporal death and the wounds which the serpents' bites had caused, so too those who look at the mystery of the Lord's passion by believing, confessing, [and] sincerely imitating it are saved forever from every death they have incurred by sinning in mind and body.

Hence there is added: *'That everyone who believes in him may not perish but may have eternal life'*. The meaning of this sentence is evident: one who believes in Christ not only escapes the perdition incurred as a penalty, but also attains eternal life. But there is this difference between the figure and the truth—through the former, temporal life was [only] prolonged, [but] through the latter, a life is granted which will continue without end.[27] But we must zealously take care that worthy works complete what our understanding comprehends well, so that the confession of our right faith may deservedly bring us, by a pious and sober way of life, to the perfection of the life that has been promised us.

But these things were said about the Son of man, who could be lifted up on the cross and suffer death. So that Nicodemus would not suppose it was solely from the Son of man that everlasting life was to be looked for, our Lord took care to disclose to him as well the mystery of his divinity, and to show that the Son of God and the Son of man

26. Rm 8:3
27. Aug., *Tract. in Ioh.* 12, 11 (CC 36: 126, 1 - 127, 46)

were one and the same Savior of the world, for there follows: 'For God so loved the world that he gave his only-begotten Son, that everyone who believes in him may not perish but have eternal life'.

At this point we must note that John repeats of the Son of God what he had mentioned earlier of the Son of man lifted up on the cross:[28] 'That everyone who believes in him may not perish but have eternal life'.[29] Our Redeemer and Maker, who was Son of God before the ages, became Son of man at the end of the ages. Thus the one who, through the power of his divinity, had created us to enjoy the happiness of everlasting life, might himself restore us, through the weakness of our humanity, to recover the life we had lost. Hence we must attempt in return to repay the acts of his divine kindness by loving God the Father with our whole heart, our whole soul [and] our whole strength.[30] He first loved us with so great a love that *he did not spare his own Son but handed him over for us all.*[31] Let us love the Son, who, *though he was in the form of God,* for the sake of our liberty and life *took the form of a slave and was made obedient even to death, death on a cross.*[32] As the apostle John says of him, *He it is who loved us and washed away our sins by his blood.*[33] Let us love the Holy Spirit of the Father and Son, for by his grace we are reborn, by his anointing we are signed[34] unto the day of redemption; he breathes where he wills, and wherever he breathes he immediately enkindles the flame of divine love. Let us believe that the Father himself and the Son and the Holy Spirit are one God and our Lord, and *let us exalt his name together.*[35] His is the glory, sovereignty and power before all ages of ages. Amen.

---

28. Jn 3:14-15   29. Jn 3:16   30. Mk 12:30
31. Rm 8:32   32. Ph 2:6-8   33. Rv 1:5
34. Eph 1:13, 1 Jn 2:20   35. Ps 34:3 (33:4)

NOTE

1. 'Child of death'—a typical Hebrew manner of expression. A person who is destined for a particular fate is referred to as being a child of that lot, hence 'child of death' means one who is sure to die, either physically or spiritually. Here the latter is meant, and so with the similar expressions that immediately follow.

homily II.19

Luke 1:5-17   *Vigil of the Nativity of John the Baptist*

When our Lord and Redeemer was about to come in the flesh, he sent on ahead many witnesses and heralds of his divinely-arranged plan. Though they arose at different times and from different tribes of the people of Israel, they were to foretell by their prophecies the mystery of his incarnation, not differing in their faith, but with one and the same meaning in all its details. The last of them and a kind of dividing line between law and gospel, figure and truth, was John [the Baptist]. He appeared as the Lord attested, saying, *'The law and the prophets* [were] *until John; since then the good news of the kingdom of God is proclaimed'*.[1] Hence [John] was said to be more than a prophet,[2] because he was the first to express by his prophecy that [Christ] was going to come, and also to point him out, showing him when he came, whereas the others only foretold [his coming] by prophesying long before.[3]

Thanks to the certain, divinely-arranged plan, [John] is declared to have been born to parents who were not only just, but who also arose from high-priestly stock. For, as we heard in the gospel reading, *There was a priest named*

1. Aug., *Serm.* 293, 2 (*PL* 38:1328); Lk 16:16   2. Mt 11:9
3. Jer., *In Matth.* 11, 9 (*CC* 77: 79, 70/72)

Zechariah, of the priestly division of Abijah, and he had a wife of the daughters of Aaron, whose name was Elizabeth; and they were both just in the sight of God. He was begotten of just parents so that he might more confidently give to the people the commands of justice, not simply as novelties which he had recently learned, but as things which he had received by hereditary right from his forebears and which he was himself observing.[4] He arose from priestly lineage so that he could more powerfully proclaim a change in the priesthood as it was apparent that he himself belonged to the priestly class. Just as our Redeemer, when he appeared in the flesh, deigned to become like a king to us by bestowing a heavenly kingdom, so too did he become a high priest by offering himself for us as a sacrifice to God with an odor of sweetness.[5] Hence it is written: *The Lord has sworn and will not repent; you are a priest for ever according to the order of Melchizedek.*[6] Melchizedek, as we read, was a priest of the most high God long before the time of the priesthood of the law, and he offered bread and wine to the Lord.[7] Our Redeemer is said to be a priest *according to the order of Melchizedek,* because he put aside the sacrificial victims [stipulated] by the law, and instituted the same type of sacrifice to be offered in the New Covenant in the Mystery of his own body and blood.

Who could more fittingly prophesy the transference of the priesthood of the law and its replacement by the priesthood [instituted] in the gospel than the son of a high priest under the law? Even though it would seem that [John] could have been a high priest according to the law, by reason of the inward and unchangeable teaching of the truth he preferred being a herald of the new priesthood rather than continuing as a successor and heir of the old. Taught by the Spirit, he preferred preaching the mysteries of the New Covenant to a people called out into the desert, to officiating for those coming to him in the temple as a member of the glorious office of the old priesthood existing at that time. He elected the long-lasting thirst and hunger of solitude in

4. Ambr., *Expos. evang. sec. Luc.* 1, 16 (*CC* 14: 14, 254/59)
5. Eph 5:2   6. Ps 110:4 (109:4)   7. Gn 14:18, Heb 7:1

preference to the continual solemn sacrificial offerings [in the temple]. He esteemed the high priestly garment woven of gold cloth of less value than a garment made of camel's hair, girded with a leather belt.[8] Why was this, my brothers? Was it not that he who, by reason of a more perfect justice, had received for himself authority to preach, might show, even by the neglect of his ancestral right to the high priesthood, how certainly he was the herald and precursor of a better high priesthood?

But if you of the brotherhood would take delight in hearing who that Abijah was from whose priestly division it is said that Zechariah derived his rank, he was the high priest during the time of King David.[9] By the Lord's order, Aaron was the first single high priest[1*] appointed by Moses under the law; after his death his son, Eleazar, received the gift of the [high] priesthood.[10] When he too had died, his son, Phinehas, became his successor as [high] priest.[11] Thus up to the time of [King] David, over a period of about four hundred and seventy years, one after the other became heir of the high priesthood. When [King] David, burning with great zeal for religion, wanted to fashion a temple for the Lord, the Lord willed this to be carried out by his son Solomon instead. David himself nevertheless was concerned carefully to make ready everything which pertained to the future construction and reverent [ceremonies] of this temple.[12] He also arranged for singers[13] to chant the psalms daily at the time of sacrifice, to the tune of musical instruments. This was to arouse the minds of the people in attendance to remembrance and love of heavenly matters, not only by the sublimity of the words which were sung, but also by the sweetness of the sounds by which they were sung. Desiring that, as the worship and magnificence of the temple increased, the graceful exercise of the ministry and the assembly of those ministering might also increase, [David] called together all the descendants of the sons of Aaron,[14]

8. Mk 1:6   9. 1 Ch 24:10
10. Ex 28:1; Nb 3:2-4; 20:25-28; Dt 10:6   11. Jos 24:33; Jg 20:28
12. 2 S 7:4-13; 1 Ch 22:1-10; Josephus, *Ant. Iud.* 7, 13, 4; 14, 12
13. 1 Ch 23:5, 30-31   14. 1 Ch 24:1-19

those descending from the stock of Eleazar and those from the stock of Ithamar, and he divided them into twenty-four sections, choosing individuals from each section as high priests; the rest, who were in the sections of the lower priesthood (which is now called that of priest[15]), he ordered to exercise their offices with this provision, namely that when any one of the high priests departed this life, whoever was considered the best in his section should succeed him in the high priesthood.

[David] set up these sections in such a way that the individual high priests, along with the priests who were under them, should minister for eight successive days, that is, from sabbath to sabbath.[16] And although all in the priestly class were equal, yet one of them who seemed to be more worthy of special reverence and more outstanding and in power was to have the name of 'high priest'. As to the order which was to be observed among these sections, it was determined by the casting of lots in the presence of King David and the leading persons of the priestly and levitical families. In this distribution of lots, it is found that Abijah, from whose priestly division and generation Zechariah sprang, occupied the eighth place.[17] It was fitting that the herald of the New Covenant, in which the glory of the resurrection was declared to the world, was born in the place of the eighth lot, both because our Lord rose from the dead on the day after the sabbath, which is the eighth day following [the seven days of] creation, and because we are promised at the end [of time] an eighth age of everlasting resurrection, following the six ages of this world and a seventh of tranquility for souls, which comes in the next life.

They were both just before God, walking in all the commandments and ordinances of the Lord, without reproach. It often happens that those who are judged already perfect in the estimation of their fellow human beings still have some imperfection in the sight of the Searcher of hearts.[18] And again it often happens that some people, by being overly zealous

15. *presbyteratus*   16. 2 Ch 23:8; Josephus, *Ant. Iud.* 7, 14, 7
17. 1 Ch 24:10
18. Ambr., *Expos. evang. sec. Luc.* 1, 18-19, (CC 14: 15, 286 - 16, 325)

in the pursuit of certain virtuous works (since they are eager to please God, but without awareness), are offensive in the sight of their neighbors. The parents of blessed John are declared to have been free on each count when it is said, *They were both just,* and immediately there is added, *before God;* and when it continues, *walking in all the commandments and ordinances of the Lord,* there is next brought in, *without reproach,* as if it was clearly being said: 'They conducted themselves discreetly in their actions and in their thoughts, so that they were pleasing both to the divine gaze in secret, and to human judgment outwardly, according to that [saying] of the Apostle, *For we direct our endeavor toward what is good not only in God's sight but also in that of human beings'.*[19]

But they had no son, because Elizabeth was barren and they were both advanced in years. It was an act of divine decision that John should be born of a mother who was barren and of parents who were both of an advanced age, so that it would be evident even by the miracle of his origin that the one born would be a man of great virtue. Where all enjoyment of fleshly concupiscence had ceased, it would be obvious that there was no consideration of sensual pleasure in his conception but only the grace of a spiritual offspring. Thus Isaac, the son of the promise,[20] who as a figure of our Redeemer *became obedient* to his father *even unto death,*[21] was born of parents who were old, and he had a mother who had long been barren.[22] Thus Jacob,[23] the patriarch Joseph,[24] Samson, [who was] the bravest of the chieftains,[25] and Samuel, [who was] the most distinguished of the prophets,[26] [all] had as their progenitors [mothers who were] for a long time barren in body but always fruitful in virtues. In this way their dignity would be known from the miraculous nativity of those who were born, and it might be proven that they would be famous in their lives, since at the very outset of their lives they transcended the norms of the human condition.

As to what follows, *It happened that when he was serving as priest in the order of his priestly division, according to the*

19. 2 Co 8:21 20. Gn 18:10 21. Gn 22:9; Ph 2:8
22. Gn 18:11 23. Gn 25:20-21 24. Gn 30:22-24
25. Jg 13:2, 24 26. 1 S 1:2, 20

custom of the priesthood, he came forward by lot to enter the temple of the Lord to offer incense, it is apparent to everyone that, as the weekly turn of the priestly division which had fallen to his lot as a member of the priestly division of Abijah now came round, he entered the temple in order to exercise his ministry. But perhaps it is unintelligible to some that the scriptures seem to be silent about the time of year in which these events took place. They are to be told that the scriptures did not overlook this, but implied it indirectly in what is added in the assertion, *And the whole multitude of the people were praying outside at the hour of incense.* Indeed there was only one solemnity during the year during which, when the high priest entered the Holy of Holies to pray, no other person was permitted to remain inside the doors of the temple, but all were ordered to pray outside at the time of the offering. This was the solemnity that had been established in the seventh month after Passover, on the tenth day of the month. It was called the day of propitiation or expiation,²* because the blood of the victims offered on the altar of holocaust was brought into the Holy of Holies in order to bring expiation [from sin]. Not only was the blood sprinkled there, but incense was burned—Zechariah is recalled in the present reading as having done this. The Lord said to Moses of this solemnity, *In the seventh month, on the tenth day of the month, you shall afflict your souls and do no work.*[27] *And the high priest shall expiate the sanctuary and the tabernacle of testimony, together with the altar, the priests also, and the entire people; and this will be for you an everlasting statute, that you should pray for the children of Israel and for all their sins once during the year.*[28] And a little earlier, when he was teaching about this rite of expiation, he said among other things, *Let there be no person in the tabernacle when the high priest enters the sanctuary to pray on behalf of himself and his household and for the entire assembly of Israel, until he comes out.*[29]

It would take a long time to enumerate the testimonies from the scriptures concerning the particular ceremonies of this day, and an even longer time to explain sufficiently how

---

27. Lv 16:29   28. Lv 16:33-34   29. Lv 16:17

they are now carried out in a spiritual way in the Church. Hence I am especially pleased to tell you of the brotherhood how appropriate was the choice of the time in which the birthday of the Lord's precursor and his future virtue were declared. The seventh month, and the tenth day of it, were dedicated to this most sacred announcement because it was being foretold that he was about to be born who would proclaim the consummation of the law's observance and the beginning of the gospel's grace. His origin was being pointed out, who first of all would show that the Lord and Saviour was both coming, and was already at hand, of whom it was written, *For the end of the law is Christ*, [who is the means] *of righteousness for everyone who believes.* [30] Now the fulfillment of the law is prefigured both by the number seven, on account of the sabbath, and by the number ten, on account of the ten commandments of the law. This was a day of propitiation and expiation, on which the whole people was commanded to be free of work, and to be afflicted and chastised through prayers and abstinence. This was very appropriate to both the life and the preaching of blessed John. He was free from earthly work and gave his mind solely to heavenly pursuits and desires; and when the crowds gathered round him, he taught them to abstain from evil works, to be expiated through penance and faith, and to be consecrated to Christ, [31] because the time of divine propitiation was already upon them, when the entry into the heavenly kingdom would be open to all who piously sought it.

As to the fact that on this day the high priest was commanded to expiate the sanctuary and the tabernacle of testimony, together with the altar, the priests as well, and the entire people—John himself showed clearly who that high priest was, and what the expiation was, when, as [Christ] was coming to his baptism, he spoke, saying, *'Behold the Lamb of God, who takes away the sins of the world'.* [32] This expiation had been established to be celebrated once during the year, because, as the Apostle says, *Christ, having been*

---

30. Rm 10:4   31. Mt 3:1-8   32. Jn 1:29

offered once to bear the sins of many, will appear a second time without sin to those awaiting him for salvation.[33] As for the fact that after the high priest went into the sanctuary to make intercession, no other person was permitted to be in the tabernacle until after he came out—this indicates the weakness of holy Church, which was not yet fit to suffer for her faith in him. This was made evident in the case of the apostles themselves, who, when his passion had begun, *all abandoned him and fled.*[34] When the expiation was completed, the high priest came forth so that an opportunity might be given to others to go into the tabernacle: when the sacrifice of his passion was over, Christ appeared to his disciples; by giving them the grace of the Holy Spirit he strengthened their hearts further for offering to God sacrificial offerings, not only of devoted works and prayer, but also of his own blood. I have explained these details about the observance of this festivity under the law so fully in order that you, dear ones, may acknowledge how appropriately the proclamations of new grace took their starting-point from it, in which, in so many ways, the working out of this grace and the redemption of the whole world is expressed.

And there appeared to Zechariah as he was praying an angel standing on the right side of the altar of incense. We must note that [the angel] bore witness to the grace about which he had come to give the good news, not only by the power of the words which he brought forward, but also by the point in time and the location of the place in which he appeared. He appeared at the time when the priest was making an offering to express the fact that he was proclaiming the coming of the true and eternal high priest, who would be the true sacrificial offering for the salvation of the world. He stood beside the altar of incense to teach that he had come as the herald of a New Covenant. There were two altars in the temple,[35] which expressed the two covenants in the Church. The first, the altar of burnt offerings, which was plated with bronze and was situated in front of the doors of the temple,[36] was for the offering up of victims and

33. Heb 9:28   34. Mt 26:56   35. Ex 27:1; 30:1
36. Ex 27:2; 1 K 8:64; 2 Ch 8:12

sacrifices; it signified the fleshly-minded worshipers of the
Old Covenant. And then there was the altar of incense,
which was covered with gold[37] and set near the entrance
of Holy of Holies, and was to burn fragrant gums on; this
signified the interior and more perfect grace of the New Covenant and its worshipers. [The angel] stood on the right side
of this altar to point out that he was not promising humankind earthly and lowly things, but the joys of heavenly and
everlasting happiness (which are commonly indicated by
the right hand). [He was promising these things] especially
to those who through their purity of heart can themselves
become an altar of gold, those who are able to abide with
attentive thought near the entrance of the heavenly kingdom, who are able to burn the sweet fragrances of their
prayers with the fire of their love for God, [and] who can
say with the prophet, *Let my prayer be directed like incense in
your sight.*[38]

As far as the statement to Zechariah is concerned, *For your
entreaty has been heard, and your wife Elizabeth will bear you
a son,* we must not be of the opinion that the high priest,
who had gone in to pray for the people, suddenly changed
his mind [and prayed] for his own private concerns; that
he began to ask especially for children, when he had completely abandoned hope of begetting any, inasmuch as he
was an old and infirm man—he would not believe, even
at the promise of an angel, that a son could be born to him.[39]
But of this we must definitely be aware, that he was asking
for the salvation of his people. He knew that they were troubled by a very great burden of sin, and that in addition they
were oppressed by the domination of a foreign king. Hence
from the angel's account he recognized that he had been
heard, and learned in what manner the salvation which he
had been seeking would come: there would be born to him
a son who would be a prophet and outstanding teacher;
and [his son] would turn this people to the way of truth
and the hope of meriting salvation; and that soon after this

37. Ex 30:3   38. Ps 141:2 (140:2)
39. Aug., *Serm.* 291, 3 (*PL* 38: 1317-18)

there would follow the Savior himself, who would endow them with the gifts of the heavenly kingdom.

'*And you will call his name John,*' he said, '*and he will be a cause of joy and exultation to you, and many people will rejoice at his birth*'. Whenever in the scriptures a name is imposed, or changed for people, by God, it is indicative of great praise and virtue. It was good that our Redeemer's precursor was ordered to be called John. The name John means 'the grace of the Lord,' or 'in whom there is grace'.[40] He received a special grace beyond other saints, that of being [Christ's] precursor, and he came to proclaim a heretofore unheard of grace to the world, that of entry into heaven. Therefore he who was full of grace himself, and who brought the good news of God's grace to the rest [of humankind], expressed even by his name a proclamation of grace. It was rightly foretold that there was to be cause for exultation for many persons at his birth, since it was through him that the Author of their regeneration was manifested to the world.

'*He will be great in the sight of the Lord*'. We should note that there was the same proclamation of praise for John by the angel as that declared by the evangelist for his parents. It was testified that they were just before God,[41] and that [John] was great in the sight of the Lord. How great he was in the sight of the Lord, the Lord himself suggested, since he alone granted him the virtue of his greatness and knew [of it] as well, saying, '*Among those born of women there has risen none greater than John the Baptist*'.[42]

The angel subsequently explained his manifold greatness in the sight of the Lord by saying, '*And he will drink no wine or strong liquor, and he will be filled with the Holy Spirit while he is still in his mother's womb; and he will turn many of the children of Israel to the Lord their God*'. Inasmuch as [the angel] alleged that [John] would practice temperance in regard to wine and strong drink, that is, from everything which can cause drunkenness, he indicated that he was going to be exempt from all the vices and allurements of the world

40. Jer., *Nom.* (CC 72: 146, 16/17)   41. Lk 1:6
42. Mt. 11:11

that tend to cause one's state of mind to waver. Inasmuch as [the angel] recounted that [John] was to be filled with the Holy Spirit while he was still in his mother's womb, he showed that once he was born into the world he would become illustrious for all the fruits of the virtues. What virtue could be lacking to one living among other human beings and keeping company with them, who, although as a human being he was conceived in iniquity,[43] yet, contrary to what is usual in the human condition, was given birth to by his mother not in the moral fault of [original] sin,[44] but in the gift of pardon? We must not doubt that the Holy Spirit, with whom he was filled, absolved him from all sin. It is the truly spoken opinion of the Fathers that the gift of the Holy Spirit is not bound by any legal restrictions. For this reason [the one who] consecrated Cornelius and his household by his grace before their reception of baptism[45] was surely the very one who infused John with the gift of the same grace, not only before his circumcision, but even before his birth. This was so that by already manifesting joy while he was still in the womb, he might perform his office of being the Lord's precursor, even though he could not yet do so by speaking. [This is shown] when, as the following section of the holy gospel bears witness, the blessed mother of God entered [the house] and greeted Elizabeth, the infant in her womb leaped with joy.[46]

As to the affirmation that [John] would turn many of the children of Israel to the Lord their God, the angel here indicated the extent of his greatness in the sight of God, and declared that he would go through life in the best way of conducting himself. What way of life can be more lofty, as far as other human beings are concerned, or more acceptable to God, than that of those who refuse to assent to vices, who bring their minds under the sway of the virtues, and who in addition also strive to turn others to the grace of their Creator by their daily practices, and always to increase the joy of the heavenly homeland by their frequent recruiting of faithful souls?

43. Ps 51:5 (50:7)
45. Ac 10:44-47
44. *non in delictis praeuaricationis*
46. Lk 1:40-41

'*And he will go before him in the spirit and power of Elijah*'. John is said to go before the Lord in the spirit and power of Elijah, because just as Elijah will precede his second coming with great power of the Spirit, so John, gifted with no less might of the Spirit, preceded his first coming; and just as Elijah is going to be his precursor as Judge, so John became his precursor as Redeemer.

Nor did John precede the Lord's first coming in the spirit and power of Elijah in time only, but also by the similarity of his teaching, for as the angel continued concerning John, '*That he may turn the hearts of fathers toward their children and the incredulous to the prudence of the just*'. The Lord too brought forward, through the prophet, a statement regarding the preaching of Elijah which was not very different: *Behold, I shall send you Elijah the prophet before the great and horrible day of the Lord comes, so that he may turn the hearts of fathers toward their children and the hearts of children toward their fathers.*[47] Thus the work of both is one and the same—by their preaching, to pour into the minds of children the faith and the understanding which the fathers had. Now the holy [and] ancient fathers were also called 'just' when the Savior said to his disciples about them, '*Many prophets and just persons have longed to see what you see, and did not see it*'.[48] People of that age were called 'children' and 'incredulous' at the time when Elijah was going to preach, and when John was actually preaching. John turned the hearts of fathers toward their children because, by teaching the children to believe and rejoice that Christ had come in the flesh, he transferred to them the wisdom which their fathers, who believed in and desired Christ's coming in the flesh, had possessed; he turned the incredulous to the prudence of the just, because those whom he found to be without faith in Christ, vainly glorying in the works of the law, he taught to believe in Christ, to submit themselves with their whole concentration to his grace, and to imitate the prudence of the just ones who had preceded them. They were striving to observe the law most diligently, and nevertheless they

47. Ml 3:23-24 (4:5-6)   48. Mt 13:17

had learned to hope for salvation from the gift of the Lord Jesus and not from the justice of their own works. So it is that one of them said, *The just person lives from faith.*[49]

Hence there is added: *'To prepare for the Lord a perfect people'*. Indeed this is the most noble perfection of the Lord's people—which John was preparing during his time by his preaching, and which now the Lord himself fulfills more completely by giving it throughout the world—when, educated by the words of the gospel and imbued with its mysteries, we learn to possess the same faith and love which our fathers, taught by the commandments of the law, are shown to have possessed. This is the most perfect beauty of holy Church—when we long for the joys of heavenly peace which they have surely entered into, and exert ourselves to practice a heavenly life on earth so that we may deserve to enter into these joys; when, following their example, we ascribe none of the good deeds which we perform or see being performed to our own deserts, but in all things we regard them [as having been brought about] by the grace of our Creator.

We are taught by their testimonies that *It is God himself and not we ourselves who made us*[50]—not only to be human beings, but also to be holy and blessed human beings. If by the gift of his grace we pursue him eagerly, always with a pure and untiring heart, he will be propitious toward all our iniquities, according to the promises made to those same fathers of ours; he will satisfy our desire with good things; he will crown us unto eternal life not as a reward for the works of justice which we have done of ourselves, but in the compassion and mercy[51] which he has given us, for he lives and reigns in the unity of the Holy Spirit, throughout all ages. Amen.

49. Hab 2:4; Rm 1:17   50. Ps 100:3 (99:3)
51. Ps 103:3-5 (102:3-5)

NOTES

1. Here and elsewhere in this homily, Bede seems to use *pontifex* and *summus sacerdos* merely as stylistic variants for 'high priest'.
2. This is the solemn day known by its Hebrew title of Yom Kippur, and still celebrated by the Jewish people during the autumn.

homily II.20

Luke 1:57–68   *Nativity of John the Baptist*

The earthly birthday of the Lord's precursor, as the most holy history of the gospel reading puts it forth, shines brightly with the great sublimity of its miraculous happenings. Surely it was right that, since no one greater than he has arisen from among those born of women, [John] should, from the very moment of his birth, stand out above the rest of the saints in the brilliance of his virtues.[1] His old and long barren parents exulted at the gift of a most celebrated offspring; the mouth and tongue of his father, whose incredulity had rendered him mute,[2] were opened to greet the herald of a new [gift of] grace. Nor was it only his ability to bless God that was restored, but he was also blessed with the power of prophesying concerning him. Roused by the report of this happening, all the neighbors were struck with wonder and apprehension, and the hearts of all who heard of it all around were made ready for the coming of a new prophet.

Hence holy Church, which throughout the world solemnizes the victories of so many of the blessed martyrs by which they deserved to enter into the kingdom of heaven,

---

1. Mt 11:11; Lk 7:28   2. Lk 1:20-22

has rightly been accustomed to celebrate even the earthly birthday of this man, [and] only his besides that of our Lord.[3] We must believe that this arose as a custom in no other wise than from apostolic authority, and we must most attentively bear in mind that, just as at the birth of our Lord one of the angels, who appeared to the shepherds, said, *Behold, I bring you good news of a great joy which will be for all people: for to us is born today a Savior who is Christ the Lord,*[4] so also the angel who proclaimed to Zechariah that John would be born said, *He will be* [a cause for] *joy and exultation to you, and many will rejoice at his birth; for he will be great in the Lord's sight.*[5] The earthly birthdays of both [Christ and John] are rightfully celebrated with festal devotion, but, inasmuch as Christ was the Lord's anointed, the Savior of the world, the Son of almighty God, [and] *the sun of righteousness,*[6] on his [earthly birthday] the good news of joy was brought to all people; at the birth of [John], inasmuch as he was coming as our Lord's precursor, an extraordinary servant of God, and *a lamp burning and shining,*[7] it is [simply] recounted that many were to rejoice.

It is told of the latter that he would be great in the Lord's sight; of the former the prophet bore witness that *Great is the Lord and highly to be praised, and his greatness is unlimited.*[8] The latter avoided the company of sinners and abstained from everything that might cause drunkenness;[9] the former lived his life among sinners and remained free from all sin. The latter was filled with the Holy Spirit from the time [when he was still in] his mother's womb; in the former, *All the fullness of divinity dwelt bodily,*[10] for by giving her his Spirit he consecrated for himself a place in the Virgin's womb, in which he was to take on [human] flesh. The latter, by his preaching, turned many of the children of Israel to the Lord during his time [upon earth]; the former, by illumining them inwardly, does not cease to turn many people daily from all countries throughout the world to faith

3. Aug., *Serm.* 287, 1 (*PL* 38: 1301); *Serm.* 292, 1, 1 - 2, 2 (*PL* 38: 1319-21)
4. Lk 2:10-11   5. Lk 1:14-15   6. Ml 4:2
7. Jn 5:35   8. Ps 145: 3 (144:3)   9. Lk 1:15; 7:33
10. Col 2:9

and charity in him. The latter *went before him in the spirit and power of Elijah,* [11] so that by baptizing his people with water he could teach a perfect [people] to receive him when he appeared; the former came after him in the spirit and power of God the Father, so that by baptizing his people *with the Holy Spirit and with fire* [12] he could grant them the perfect vision of his Father's face. When John was born, his mother's *relatives and neighbors wished her joy because the Lord had magnified his mercy upon her;* [13] when our Lord was born the angelic spirits, who are the Church's *neighbors and relatives, wished* [the Church] *joy* because *the time had come to have mercy upon her;* [14] they are citizens of the same heavenly fatherland which she herself awaits, and by chanting a hymn of glory to God [15] they were the first to suggest from heaven what she was to do throughout the world.

We are thus right to celebrate the earthly birthday of one whose power was of such greatness that he was next to our Lord in his works. We are right to observe the solemnity of the coming of one whose loftiness of life was so great that whoever is more lofty than he no doubt already surpasses the nature of a human being. And indeed when our Lord had said that there was no one from among those born of women greater than [John], he went on to say, *'Yet he who is of lowest rank in the kingdom of heaven is greater than he'.* [16] He is suggesting that he himself, who was later than John in his human birth, still surpassed him because he is the highest in the heavenly kingdom.

Not without mystical meaning is it recounted that the earthly birthday of John occurred when the [length of the] day started to lessen, but that of our Lord occurred when the [length of the] day started to increase. [17] The crowd believed that [John] was the Christ because of the greatness of his power, while some people supposed that our Lord was not the Christ but a prophet because of the weakness of his flesh. John himself revealed the secret meaning of

11. Lk 1:17   12. Mt 3:11; Lk 3:16   13. Lk 1:58
14. Ps 102:13 (101:14)   15. Lk 2:13-14   16. Mt 11:11
17. Aug., *Serm.* 190, 1 (*PL* 38: 1007); *Serm.* 194, 2 (*PL* 38: 1016); *Serm.* 287, 3, 4 (*PL* 38: 1302); *Serm.* 293, 1, (*PL* 38: 1328)

this difference [of time] when he said, *'He must increase, but I must decrease'*.[18] Our Lord increased because it became known to believers throughout the entire world that he who was believed to be a prophet was the Christ; John diminished and decreased because it became apparent that he who was judged to be the Christ was not himself the Christ but the herald of the Christ. And so when John was born, the daylight rightly began to decrease, since his reputation for being someone divine was about to cease, and his baptism was shortly to come to an end. And when our Lord was born, the shortened days began to increase in light because he had appeared who would disclose the light of knowledge of himself to all nations, when formerly only Judaea, and that only partially, possessed it, and would spread the warmth of his love into the whole wide world.

We should note, however, that this earthly birthday of blessed John had some similarity to our Lord's coming and to the grace which he came to preach. It is highly fitting that the one to whom all the earlier prophets and patriarchs bore witness, by their earthly births, or deaths, or ways of life, or preaching, was much more fully represented by his precursor, who was more than a prophet, not only in his life and his suffering, but in his earthly birth. For what is the meaning of John's being born to elderly parents? Was it not to indicate the earthly birth of the one who was soon to follow, since by bringing forward the hidden spiritual mysteries of the New Covenant, he would teach that the fleshly observance of the law and the priesthood of the Old Covenant were now to be brought to an end? For *that which belongs to former times and is growing old has almost reached the point of destruction.*[19] And what does it mean that our Lord's precursor came from a father who was mute, a leader of the priests of that time? Is it not that by the time our Lord appeared, the tongue of the ancient priesthood had to a large extent become mute as regards the spiritual sense of the [law's] teaching, since the scribes and those learned in the law were only concerned with teaching the keeping of

18. Jn 3:30   19. Heb 8:13

the letter [of the law]; moreover in a number of instances they were even falsifying the letter [of the law] by [substituting] their own traditions, as is proven by our Lord's having rebuked them more than once in the gospels?[20] And what does it mean that he was born to a barren mother? Is it not that the law, which was ordered to beget spiritual issue for God with the help of the priestly office, led no one to perfection,[21] undoubtedly because it was unable to open up the gates of the kingdom to its followers? The author of the law himself, born under the law,[22] took away from the law the opprobrium of its barrenness, for he pointed out that it was to be understood spiritually; and he taught that in it was formerly prefigured, and as it were conceived, the gift of happiness from on high which now shines out clearly in the gospel.

And it came about that on the eighth day they came to circumcise the child, and they called him by his father's name, Zechariah. But his mother answered and said, 'Not so; he will be called John'. John means 'the grace of God,' or, 'in whom there is grace'.[23] By this name [are expressed] the entire extent of the grace of the gospel dispensation which he was to proclaim, and especially the Lord himself, through whom this grace was to be granted to the world. Those who were determined that the new-born child was to be called by the name of his father, Zechariah, rather than John, surely prefigure those people who, when our Lord was declaring the new gift of grace, wanted him to preach instead the accustomed statutes of the ancient priesthood. Hence it is right that the name Zechariah means 'the memory of the Lord,'[24] for it figuratively denotes the memory of the ancient observances which were given by the Lord.

Those who had come together there were discussing what was to be the name of the prophet who had been born, and they were attempting to have him called Zechariah; but against this, his mother by words, and his father by writing, insisted strongly that he should be called John instead.

---

20. Mt 15:3; Mk 7:7-8   21. Heb 7:19   22. Ga 4:4
23. Jer., *Nom.* (CC 72: 146, 16/17)
24. Jer., *Nom.* (CC 72: 138, 16)

Since there were some less well-versed in the heavenly mysteries, who, at the beginning of the gospel's shining forth were determined that the fleshly injunctions of the still-existing priesthood of the law should be observed as well, it was as though Elizabeth emboldened them by the teaching of the law concerning the reception of the grace of Christ, when she said in a lively voice of the name John (quoting from the lawgiver [Moses]), *'The Lord has raised up for you a prophet from among your brothers; you should listen to him as to me in regard to everything which he speaks to you'.*[25] As regards the legal priesthood, Zechariah too bore witness to the grace that was being born, but kept silent about the meaning of its ceremonies as types, as though they were mute figures of the literal [observance]. We are not to believe that anything in all the observances of the ancient priesthood was done or said which did not represent the grace of the gospel, if they are properly understood. As to his subsequent declaration and confirmation of the name of John, and the opening of Zechariah's mouth and his speaking, blessing God, it is surely evident that once the grace of the New Covenant was manifested by the apostles, a large number of priests also became obedient to the faith and, after abandoning their harmful silence, submitted themselves devoutly to confessing, praising and preaching the gifts of their Redeemer.

On the day of John's circumcision, when he also received his name, *Fear came upon all their neighbors, and all these words were spread abroad throughout the mountain country of Judaea.* Furthermore, at the time of our Lord's resurrection, when the Spirit had been sent down from above and the glory of his name was made known to the world by the apostles, a most salutary fear immediately struck the hearts, not only of the Jews, who were of the neighborhood either by their physical location or by their knowledge of the law, but also those of foreign nations, even to the ends of the earth. And John's reputation for virtue exceeded not only the whole mountain country of Judaea, but also all the heights of

25. Dt 18:15; Ac 3:22

worldly kingdoms and worldly wisdom, so that everywhere
[people] left behind their former way of life and flocked together to attain the sacramental mysteries of his faith.

[John's] circumcision clearly set forth an image of the
Lord's resurrection because it too occurred on the eighth
day, that is, on the day after the sabbath. And just as the
former was wont to release people from the punishable state
of everlasting death, so the latter displayed the perfect newness of immortal life in our Creator, and revealed that it
is to be hoped for in us. That Zechariah was filled with the
Holy Spirit as all this was in progress, and prophesied concerning our Redeemer and our redemption, this signifies
mystically that many of the priestly stock, who for a long
time had kept silent and refrained from confessing Christ,
would later be filled with the power of the Holy Spirit
through receiving faith in him, would be lifted up by the
gift of prophecy, and would be set over the people in the
office of pastoral instruction. But we should believe that
Zechariah's reception of the Spirit and prophecy are a figure of this too: that the time was then at hand when it would
be announced to the faithful that all the rites and ceremonies of the priesthood of the law abounded inwardly with
spiritual knowledge and prophetic mysteries. These bore
testimony to the dispensation in time, or to the eternal divinity, of the Mediator between God and humankind, the
man Jesus Christ.[26] This accords with what he himself said,
when he was rebuking the hardness [of heart] of the Jews,
*'If you would believe Moses, perhaps you would believe me also,
for he wrote about me'.*[27]

But let us hear what Zechariah, prophesying and blessing God said: *'Blessed be the Lord God of Israel, because he has
visited and wrought redemption for his people'.* We must note
in these words that blessed Zechariah was telling by way
of prophecy, as if it had already come to pass, what he had
foreseen in spirit had begun and would soon come to pass.
By his appearance in the flesh our Lord visited us when
we were, in a certain way, drawing farther away from him,

26. 1 Tm 2:5   27. Jn 5:46

and he took care to seek out and justify us when we were lying in sins. He visited us as a physician does a patient who is ill, and, in order to cure the ingrained sickness of our pride, he provided for us the unheard-of example of his own humility. He brought about the redemption of his people by giving us freedom, at the price of his own blood— we who had been sold into the slavery of sin and were held bound to serving the ancient enemy. Hence the Apostle does well to exhort us, saying, *For you have been purchased at a great price; glorify and carry God in your bodies.*[28]

When [Zechariah] says, *'for his people,'* he surely does not mean that he found them his people at his arrival, but that he made them his by visiting and redeeming them. Do you want to hear, my brothers, in what condition he found this people, and what he made of them? The end of this canticle (because it is so familiar, and also so long, I have considered it too protracted to treat of in detail, and to explain in its totality, to you, dear ones) clearly makes this evident by saying, *The daystar from on high has visited us, to enlighten those who sit in darkness and in the shadow of death, to guide our feet into the way of peace.*[29] He found us sitting in darkness and in the shadow of death, weighed down, that is, by the long-standing blindness of sins and ignorance, beguiled by the deception and besieged by the errors of the ancient enemy. He is rightly called death and a lie,[30] just as on the contrary our Lord is called truth and life.[31] [Our Lord] brought us the true light of recognition of himself, and having taken away the darkness of errors, opened up for us a sure way to the heavenly fatherland. He guided the course of our works so that we may be able to advance in the way of truth, which he pointed out to us, and enter into the dwelling of perpetual peace, which he promised us.

Since we possess these gifts of the divine goodness, dearly beloved brothers, these promises of eternal goods, let us bless the Lord at all times,[32] because *he has visited and wrought redemption for his people.* Let his praise be continually in our mouth;[33] let us retain the memory of him, and tell one

28. 1 Co 6:20   29. Lk 1:78-79   30. Jn 8:44
31. Jn 14:6   32. Ps 34:1 (33:2)   33. *Ibid.*

another of the virtues of him *who has called you out of darkness into his own wonderful light.*[34] Let us constantly plead
for his help, that he may preserve the light of knowledge
which he has conferred upon us and bring us all the way
to perfect day. And that we may be worthy of being heard
as we make our entreaty, let us cast off the works of darkness and clothe ourselves with the armor of light.[35] Indeed
it is by thus making supplication that we will rapidly receive what we desire, because undoubtedly the labor of pious work aids the words of devout prayer.

And since we are celebrating today the earthly birthday
of the [Lord's] blessed precursor, it is fitting that we seek
in our prayers the aid also of the one we have received as
the herald of eternal salvation. Accordingly, by making intercession to him, let us ask to have our request granted,
that we may deserve to come to that light, life and truth[36]
to which he bore witness, Jesus Christ, our God and Lord,
who lives and reigns with the Father in the unity of the Holy
Spirit throughout all ages. Amen.

---

34. 1 P 2:9   35. Rm 13:12   36. Jn 14:6

homily̅ II.21

Matthew 20:20-23   *Saints John and Paul (or St James)*

Our Lord, our Creator and Redeemer, desiring to cure the wounds of our pride, *though he was in the form of God,* having received a human form *humbled himself and became obedient even to death.*[1] Us too he commanded, if we wish to reach the summit of the truly sublime, to take the path of humility, [and] if we long to see true life, to bear patiently the adversities of the present age as well as death itself. He promised us the gifts of glory, but premised the struggles of the battle. By way of promise he told us, *Your reward will be great and you will be children of the Most High;* by way of command he charged us, *'Love your enemies, and do good and lend, hoping for nothing in return'.*[2] Thus, he promised rewards to his elect, that showing in advance what meritorious deeds were worthy of these rewards he might thus grant eternal life [and] decree that it was to be through the narrow gate and difficult way[3] that we were to come to this [life]. Hence he said, *Hasten to enter through the narrow gate.*[4] Indeed there is need of no little haste if one wishes to ascend to the heights. Now since we climb to the heights of mountains with such great effort, how great is the effort

1. Ph 2:6-8   2. Lk 6:35   3. Mt 7:14
4. Lk 13:24

required for us to endeavor to be worthy of having our way
of life in heaven,[5] of resting on the holy mountain of the
Lord, of which the psalmist chants?[6] Hence in today's reading from the holy gospel, when the sons of Zebedee were
seeking from [Jesus] seats in his kingdom, he immediately
called them to drink of his chalice, that is, to imitate the
struggle of his passion. Thus they were to remember that
they were to seek the heavenly heights only through the
despised and harsh realities of earthly existence.

*The mother of the sons of Zebedee approached him with her two
sons, adoring and seeking something from him. He said to her,
'What do you want'? She replied to him, 'Say that these two sons
of mine may sit, one at your right hand and one at your left hand,
in your kingdom'.* No one should suppose that the mother
sought this for her sons without their consent and concurrence, but instead let us understand that it was with the
unanimous agreement of all of them that it had been arranged that the disciples should disclose their desire through
their mother, since they knew that she was especially beloved by our Lord. Hence in reporting this incident, the
evangelist Mark kept silent about the intervention of their
mother, and made mention only of the craving of the disciples' hearts, of which he was aware: *James and John,* he
says, *the sons of Zebedee, approached him, saying, 'Master, we
want you to do for us whatever we ask'. And he said to them,
'What do you want me to do for you'? And they said, 'Grant us
that one may sit at your right hand and the other at your left
hand in your glory'.*[7] [Mark] alleged that they alone approached our Lord and asked him, since he saw that in making their request their wills were the more prominent, and
he knew that their mother had been spurred on to ask at
their incitement.

We must believe, however, that the special cause that
stirred up either the womanly affection of the mother[8] or
the still carnal minds of the disciples to implore this was
their remembering the utterance of our Lord in which he

5. Ph 3:20   6. Ps 15:1 (14:1)   7. Mk 10:35-37
8. Jer., *In Matth.* 20, 21 (CC 77: 177, 1054/55)

said, *When the Son of man sits on the seat of his majesty, you also shall sit on twelve thrones, judging the twelve tribes of Israel.*[9] They knew that among the disciples they were more specially loved by our Lord, that together with blessed Peter they had often been informed of hidden mysteries of which the rest were ignorant, as the text of the holy gospel frequently indicates. Thus a new name was given to them by [Jesus], just as it was to Peter, so that as he who was formerly called Simon merited the name of Peter on account of the strength and firmness of his unassailable faith,[10] so they were called Boanerges, that is, sons of thunder,[11] because they heard,[12] along with Peter, the voice of the Father honoring the Lord,[13] and they recognized the secrets of the mysteries more than the rest of the disciples; and what is more important, they sensed that they clung to our Lord with their whole heart and embraced him with the greatest love. So they did not disbelieve that it was possible that they would be sitting closely on either side of him in the kingdom, particularly when they saw that John, for his singular purity of mind and body, was held in such great love that he rested on his breast at supper.[14]

But let us hear what the One who recognizes merits and bestows thrones answered them, as they were seeking the dignity of the [highest] thrones: *In answer Jesus said, 'You do not know what you are seeking'.* Indeed they did not know what they were seeking, since they supposed that there would be someone sitting at Christ's left hand in the heavenly kingdom, when we read that in the separation at the final judgment all the elect will come to the right hand of the most high King and Judge.[15] That life has nothing to do with the left hand; eternal bliss embraces nothing that is condemned; everlasting peace accepts nothing that is destined to perish.

When the left hand of Christ is interpreted as referring to something good, the present life of holy Church is understood. Hence it is written: *Length of days is in her right*

---

9. Mt 19:28   10. Mk 3:16   11. Mk 3:17
12. Some MSS add: 'on the mountain'
13. Mt 17:5   14. Jn 13:23   15. Mt 25:33

hand, in her left riches and glory.[16] Length of days in her right hand [refers to] our Redeemer's wisdom because in the fatherland of the dwelling on high unfailing light is granted to the elect of both angels and human beings. Riches and glory are in her left hand, because we are restored during [our time of] exile in our journey [on this earth] by both the riches of the virtues and the glory of our faith, until we come to our eternal [resting place]. Of this glory the Apostle says, *And we glory in our hope of the glory of the children of God, and not only this, but we also glory in our tribulations;* [17] and of these riches he says, *Because in everything you have become rich in him, with all speech and knowledge.*[18]

They did not know what they were seeking because they maintained that it was possible to choose ahead of time, by human opinion, what thrones each one would be granted in the future as his recompense, and they were not rather entreating the Lord that they could prolong even to the end the firm confidence and glory of the hope they possessed by deserving well, knowing that he would reward whatever good they performed with a priceless prize. The holy simplicity of those who earnestly asked, with the confidence of a devout mind, to sit at the Lord's side in the kingdom is worthy of praise, but much more worthy of being praised is the prudent humility of the one who, conscious of his own frailty, said, *I have chosen to be a castaway in the house of God rather than to dwell in the tents of the wicked.*[19]

They did not know what they were seeking when they asked for the loftiness of rewards from the Lord rather than the perfection of [good] works. But the heavenly master, suggesting what they were first of all to ask, called them back to the way of hardship, by which they might be able to reach the palm of victory: *'Are you able to drink of the chalice of which I am going to drink'*? he asked. In speaking of his chalice he was referring to the bitterness of suffering which is frequently offered to the righteous by the hostility of unbelievers. All who humbly, patiently and joyfully receive it for Christ's sake rightly will reign[20] on high. There-

16. Pr 3:16   17. Rm 5:2-3   18. I Co 1:5
19. Ps 84:10 (83:11)   20. Some MSS add: 'with him'

fore because the sons of Zebedee desired to sit with him, he first advised them to follow the example of his suffering, and only then to try to reach the summit of the longed-for majesty. The Apostle teaches that this manner of living is to be followed by all the faithful when he says, *For if we have been buried with him in the likeness of his death, we shall at the same time* [be sharers] *in his resurrection.*[21]

They said to him, 'We can'. They were simply making known their frame of mind and their devotion to our Lord, such as it was at the time, when they testified that they could drink of his chalice. Later on they showed unmistakably how great their weakness was when, as the time came for their Lord to drink of this chalice, they along with the rest of the disciples *abandoned him and fled.*[22] But their fear of drinking of his chalice did not long oppress their hearts, for although they fled as their Lord was about to suffer, they returned very quickly when he rose. They had been terrified when the storm of his passion frightened them, [but] they amended their ways when the triumph of his resurrection shone forth; and once they had received the grace of the Spirit, from then on they kept a firm resolve to drink of the Lord's chalice.

Then they began to be invincible in suffering and dying for their Lord, and his promise, in which he said that they would drink of his chalice, was fulfilled, for there follows: *He said to them, 'Indeed you shall drink of my chalice'*; and also what follows: *'As for sitting at my right or left hand, this is not mine to give you, but* [it is] *for those for whom it has been prepared by my Father'*. A person gladdened by the sight of him present in [the state of] happiness on high sits at the the Savior's right hand; a person who in his position as a priestly ruler presides over his holy Church during this time of pilgrimage sits at his left hand.

But we must look very carefully at how it was that the true master could say to his disciples' request, *'This is not mine to give you, but* [it is] *for those for whom it has been prepared by my Father,'* when he himself said elsewhere, *'All*

---

21. Rm 6:5   22. Mt 26:56

things have been handed over to me by my Father'.[23] It is certain that whatever gifts the Father has given or prepared
for those who believe in him, these also the Son prepares
and gives together with him. Again, our Lord says of his
Father, *'For whatever he does, these things the Son also does likewise'.*[24] If *the Son also does likewise* everything that the Father does, how is it that the Son says, *'This is not mine to
give you, but* [it is] *for those for whom it has been prepared by
my Father,'* unless the Son is both God and a human being? Thus throughout his gospels he sometimes speaks with
the voice of the divine majesty, by which he is equal to the
Father, and at other times with the voice of his assumed
humanity, in which he became equal to us.

In this reading, because he was about to offer an example of humility to human beings, he spoke everything especially from the viewpoint of his assumed human nature.
At the outset, when the mother came with her sons to him
to make her request, he asked her what she wanted [of him],
questioning her like a human being, like a person unaware
of things hidden from him, like a person ignorant of the
future—although in the eternity of his divine power he knew
everything before it came to pass. In her entreaty she provided a reminder of his humanity rather than of his divinity,
as she implored for her sons thrones at his right hand and
left hand. In his bodily form, to be sure, he had a right hand
and a left hand, but in his divine majesty he was made up
of no arrangement of [bodily] parts. Consequently he was
silent concerning the glory of his divine nature, which was
incapable of suffering, and brought forth publicly a reminder
of the suffering which he was going to undergo as a human being. This he set before the disciples [as an example]
to be imitated, when he confirmed their devout response
by his own affirmation, saying, *'Indeed you shall drink of my
chalice,'* appropriately adding, *'As for sitting at my right or
left hand, this is not mine to give you, but* [it is] *for those for
whom it has been prepared by my Father',* as if he were clearly
saying: 'You are indeed to follow me in suffering the passion

23. Mt 11:27   24. Jn 5:19

which I am about to undergo in my human flesh, but it is not for me, according to the substance of my human weakness,[25] to give you the favors of heavenly gifts which have been prepared by my Father for all who are worthy of them to receive, even though I, being an equal sharer in this divinity, prepare and give them, for everything which he does I myself do likewise by being united with his divine power'.

Because these sons of Zebedee showed a ready spirit for drinking of the Lord's chalice, it is sure that they, along with the rest of the apostles, did receive the dignity of the thrones they were seeking, yet not with the distinction which they sought, that one of them should sit at his right hand and the other at his left in the kingdom. In accord with what I have explained above, both of them first deserved to sit temporarily at his left hand, and now they have deserved to sit forever at his right hand. They sat at Christ's left hand when, governing in this life by apostolic right, they presided over the faithful people, in that kingdom about which he said, *'The kingdom of God is within you'*.[26] Now they are sitting at his right hand in that life which knows no death, as judges with him of the world, since the Son himself, together with his Father, prepared both thrones for them. The lavishing of gifts cannot be separated in those whose unity of nature remains always inseparable, as the Son bore witness when he said, *'The Father and I are one'*.[27]

And we should not pass over without due consideration how our Lord said that the sons of Zebedee without distinction would drink of his chalice, when we know that one of them, James, ended his life by shedding his blood, but the other, John, died during a period of peace for the Church. Concerning the martyrdom of James it is clearly pointed out by Luke that *Herod put forth his hands to afflict some* [members] *of the Church; he killed James, the brother of John, by the sword.*[28] Church history also records a detail about his suffering which is worthy of being remembered. It says: *The person who had brought James before the judge to*

25. Some MSS add: 'in which I suffer'   26. Lk 17:21
27. Jn 10:30   28. Ac 12:1-2

be martyred was himself moved to admit that he was a Christian.
*They were both brought together to punishment. And when they
were being led* [to death], *he asked James on the way to give him
pardon. James, after considering it for a little while, said, 'Peace
be with you,' and he kissed him. And so both of them were beheaded at the same time.*[29]

Concerning John, trustworthy histories tell that when he
was aware that the day of his death was near, he called his
disciples together at Ephesus. Declaring Christ by many
proofs and signs, he let himself down into the place that
had been hollowed out for his burial, and when he had
made his prayer he was gathered to his fathers, as free from
the sorrow of death as he was a stranger to corruption of
the flesh.[30] How, then, is he said to have drunk of the Lord's
chalice, since it is sure that he did not depart this body by
a death caused by suffering? Is it not because this chalice
is drunk in two ways: one when death inflicted by a persecutor is patiently endured, the other when the mind is held
ready for suffering, when a life is led that is worthy of martyrdom?

John himself taught how prepared he was to drink of[31]
the chalice of death for the Lord's sake when he bore prison
and beating with the rest of the apostles with a joyful mind,
as we read in their acts;[32] when he was exiled to the island
of Patmos on account of [his speaking] the word of God
and on account of [his bearing] witness to Jesus;[33] when,
as Church history tells, he was cast into a pot of boiling oil
by the emperor Domitian: by the Lord's favor he emerged
from it as unscathed and clean as he had been chaste in
mind and body—just as when he was in exile, by [the
Lord's] favorable disposition, the more he seemed to be
deprived of human solace, the more abundantly did he merit
to be consoled by the company of citizens from on high.[34]
Hence he too is truly understood to have drunk of the

29. Eusebius/Rufinus, *Hist. Eccl.* (*GCS* 9: 125, 19/24)
30. Bede, *Hom.* I.9 (*CC* 122: 64, 137/43)
31. 'drink of' (*potandum*); var.: 'choose' (*optandum*)
32. Ac 4:3; 5:18, 40-41   33. Rv 1:9
34. Bede, *Hom.* I.9 (*CC* 122: 63, 125/32)

Lord's chalice, along with his brother James who was killed by the sword, for one who underwent such great [torments] for the sake of the truth showed how ready he was to accept even death, if it were offered him.

But we too, dearly beloved brothers, even if we endure nothing of this sort—if we do not put up with chains, beating, prison, other bodily punishments, persecution at the hands of our fellow human beings for righteousness' sake[35]—nevertheless we are capable of receiving the Savior's chalice[36] and obtaining the palm of martyrdom if we take care to chastise our bodies and subdue them;[37] if we accustom ourselves to supplicating the Lord *in the spirit of humility and with a contrite heart,*[38] if we attempt to accept with a calm mind insults inflicted by our neighbor; if we rejoice in loving[39] even those who hate us, who inflict injustice upon us, and in doing good to them[40] and praying earnestly for their lives and safety; if we exert ourselves to be adorned with the virtue of patience and also with the fruits of good works. Indeed if we live our lives in this way and, according to the Apostle's words, display our bodies as a living sacrificial offering, holy [and] pleasing to God,[41] he will with heavenly condescension deign[42] to see to it that we are rewarded with the same glory as those who have given their bodies up to death for the Lord's sake. Just as their death is precious in the sight of the Lord,[43] so will our lives become precious [in his sight], and once the chains of the flesh have been broken, we too will be worthy to enter into the courts of the city on high, and, together with the chorus of the blessed martyrs, to render our prayers of thanksgiving to our Redeemer, who lives and reigns with the Father in the unity of the Holy Spirit, God throughout all ages of ages. Amen.

35. Mt 5:10
36. Ps 116:13 (115:13), *calicem saluatoris;* some MSS have the Vulgate reading, *calicem salutaris*
37. 1 Co 9:27   38. Dn 3:39   39. var.: 'strive to love'
40. Mt 5:44   41. Rm 12:1
42. var.: 'we will be given by divine condescension'
43. Ps 116:15 (115:15)

homily̆ ΙΙ.22

John 21:15-19   *Saints Peter and Paul*

The present reading from the holy gospel commends to us the virtue of perfect love. Perfect love is that by which we are ordered to love the Lord with our whole heart, our whole soul and our whole strength, and our neighbor as ourselves.[1] Neither of these [two kinds of] love is capable of being perfect without the other, because God cannot be loved apart from our neighbor, nor our neighbor apart from God.[1*] Hence as many times as Peter was asked [by our Lord] if he loved him, and answered that he was a witness that he loved him, the Lord added at the end of each inquiry, *'Feed my sheep,'* or *'Feed my lambs,'* as if he were clearly saying: 'There is only one true proof of whole-hearted love of God—if you strive to exercise care by laboring solicitously on behalf of your brothers'. Now whoever neglects to commit himself [to practicing] the work of piety toward his brother to the extent of his ability shows that he loves his Maker less than he should, for he is scorning [Christ's] commandment concerning support of his neighbor in his time of need.

1. Mk 12:30-31

Our Lord is suggesting in a sort of implicit way that this [perfect] charity cannot be possessed in any way other than by the grace of divine inspiration, when, as he inquired of Peter concerning it he gave him the name *'Simon, son of John,'* something he never does elsewhere. [Jesus] asked, *'Simon, son of John, do you love me more than these* [others]'? Although we can understand this as merely a simple mention of [Peter's] earthly father, yet there is a possibility, if one so wishes, of taking [the use of] the name John as a mystical indication of the source of his supernatural birth. The apostle John bears witness to this when he admonishes, *Dearly beloved, let us love one another, for charity is of God; and everyone who loves is born of God and recognizes God.*[2] Now Simon means 'obeying,' and John means 'the grace of God'.[3] And on this account the first among the apostles, when he was asked about his love, was properly called *'Simon, son of John'*, that is, 'one who is obedient to the grace of God', to make clear to everyone that when one obeys the injunctions of the Lord more eagerly than others, and embraces him in charity more ardently, it is the result not of human merit, but of divine favor. Hence the apostle Paul, when he was comforted by this grace, said that *the charity of God is poured forth into our hearts through the Holy Spirit who has been given to us.*[4] Therefore, one who is proven to love the Lord more warmly than others deserves the name *'son of John'* because undoubtedly it is only by the grace of the Spirit that the virtue of this kind of love is attained.

Nevertheless we must note how cautiously and circumspectly he gave testimony to his love. When the Lord sought to know whether he loved him more than the rest, he did not presume to answer, 'You know that I love you more than they do,' but [gave] the restrained and simple reply: *'Yes, Lord, you know that I love you'*. This is clearly to say: 'I know, as you know even better than I do, that I love you wholeheartedly; as to whether the others love you, that is something that is unknown to me, but you know all things'. His cautious answer is a model of speaking and of

2. 1 Jn 4:7   3. Jer., *Nom.* (*CC* 72: 148,4; 146, 16/17)
4. Rm 5:5

thinking for us. Let us learn from his example to presume less about the purity of our own consciences [and] to judge less rashly concerning the secret matters of our brothers' consciences, especially in affairs that are dubious, and those we are unable to look into as regards the intention or necessity with which they were done. Concerning the open faults of our brothers, we have not only the power but also the precept of judging, that they may be corrected. Our Lord says, *'If your brother commits a sin, rebuke him, and if he repents, forgive him'*.[5] With regard to their doubtful deeds, and those which can be interpreted in one way or another, we are ordered to reserve these rather for divine judgment. The Apostle says, *Do not pass judgment ahead of time, until the Lord comes; he will bring to light matters hidden in darkness, and disclose the counsels of* [people's] *hearts*.[6]

Peter restrained himself in this inquiry of our Lord's by answering cautiously for this reason too, that he remembered that earlier on, when [Christ's] passion was drawing near, he had attributed greater constancy to himself than he possessed. He avowed that he was prepared to go with him to prison and to death,[7] when he was not yet capable even of admitting under pressure of danger that he knew him,[8] and that he had once been with him.[9] He had learned by experience, from that former time of danger, to speak more carefully with the Lord. He well realized that [Christ] knew the state of a human conscience better than that conscience was competent to know itself. He did not, indeed, presume to set forth anything at all concerning the secrets of his brothers' hearts, but concerning the whole-heartedness of his own love, he laid bare the testimony, not only his own, but also of the Lord who was questioning him, saying, *'Lord, you know that I love you'*. Oh, how blissful and pure was the conscience which did not feel apprehensive about saying to its Maker, to whose eyes everything is open and clear,[10] *'Lord, you know that I love you'*! How chaste and holy was the soul which did not hesitate to lay open its own thoughts to our Lord, and was well aware that it was thinking nothing else than what our Lord approved of!

5. Lk 17:3 6. 1 Co 4:5 7. Lk 22:33
8. Lk 22:57 9. Lk 22: 59-60 10. Heb 4:13

Hence in the Apocalypse the hearts of the saints are validly compared to golden bowls, as John says, *And they each had a harp and golden bowls full of incense, which are the prayers of the saints.* [11] The elect do indeed have golden bowls, for every utterance of theirs [and] every thing about them that reaches the notice of their neighbors, as report of it is spread abroad, appears to be gilded with the light of pure love. They have golden bowls (which are open vessels, extensive in width) because when they sense more truly than usual that their hearts are resplendent with the fire of that love, they rejoice that these lie open to the divine sight.

Hence it is rightly added, [that the bowls are] *full of incense, which are the prayers of the saints.* Golden bowls are filled to overflowing with incense when the inmost hearts of the righteous, gleaming with charity, become known to their neighbors, because of their reputation for spiritual virtues. John himself, who realized all this, went on beautifully to add by way of interpretation, *which are the prayers of the saints.* The incense in the bowls is indeed the prayers of the saints, because whatever good work those who are zealous in their service of God perform or speak about with unfeigned intention fills for them the place of prayer, when it directs the devotion of their minds to the divine presence. We are not otherwise capable of carrying out the command of the Apostle wherein he says, *Pray without ceasing,* [12] unless we direct all our actions, utterances, thoughts, [and] even our silence, by God's gift, in such a way that each of these may be carried out with regard to fear of him, so that all of them may be rendered profitable for our eternal salvation.

It was with benevolent foresight that our Lord inquired three times of Peter as to whether he loved him, so that by this triple confession [Christ] might free him from the chains which bound him as a result of his threefold denial. [13] As often as he had denied that he knew [Christ], when he was terrified during his passion, so often was he to bear witness that he loved him with his whole heart when he had

11. Rv 5:8   12. 1 Th 5:17
13. Mt 26:70-75; Aug., *Tract. in Ioh.* 123, 5 (*CC* 36: 678, 1/42)

been renewed by his resurrection. By his provident divinely-arranged plan, [Christ] three times commended his sheep for feeding [to Peter] as [Peter] was confessing his love three times. It was fitting that as often as he had wavered in his shepherd's trust, so often should he be ordered to take care of the shepherd's members when his shepherd's trust had been restored.

What [Christ] said to [Peter] at this point, *'Feed my sheep,'* was surely the same thing that he had said to him more clearly before his passion, *'But I have asked on your behalf that your faith may not fail you, and once you have recovered, strengthen your brothers'*.[14] To feed Christ's sheep is to strengthen those who believe in Christ, lest their faith fail them, and to devote oneself ceaselessly [to seeing to it] that they may make greater and greater progress in their faith. However, we must look carefully at the fact that this feeding of the Lord's flock is not to be carried out with a single but with many-sided solicitude. A director must diligently see to it that earthly necessities are not lacking to his subjects, and also be solicitous in providing them with examples of virtues along with words of preaching. If he detects any opposing their spiritual, or even their general interests, he should, as far as he is capable, withstand these uncalled-for attacks. When those who are under his care may perhaps themselves have fallen into error, *he as a righteous person should,* according to the word of the psalmist, *accuse them mercifully and rebuke them,*[15] but he should not soothe their hearts with the oil of harmful approval. This too is one of the obligations of a pious shepherd.

Under what pretext does a [shepherd] who neglects to correct the errors of those under his care, and to cure the wounds of their sins, as much as he can, presume to count himself among the shepherds of Christ's flock? And a shepherd must keep this also firmly in mind: let him remember to treat those of whom he has charge not as his own flock but as his Lord's, according to what was said to Peter, 'If you love me, *feed my sheep'*. 'My [sheep],' he said, not

14. Lk 22:32   15. Ps 141:5 (140:5)

'yours'. 'Know that my [sheep] have been commended [to you], and rule them as mine if you love me perfectly; recall that what you should be seeking in them is my glory, my authority [over them], my profit and not your own'. There are those who feed the sheep of Christ not out of love for Christ, but for the sake of their own glory or authority or gain. Sorrowing over the large number of these, the apostle Paul said to the [Christians] at Philippi, *I hope in the Lord Jesus to send Timothy to you soon, for I have no one else who is so in harmony* [with me and] *who will be solicitous for you with sincere affection. They all seek their own interests, not those of Jesus Christ.*[16] In the gospel the Lord calls such as these 'hired hands' instead of 'shepherds,' saying that when a wolf comes, *'The hired hand flees because he is a hired hand and has no concern for the sheep'.*[17] It is an obvious and special characteristic of a true shepherd, whose concern for the sheep is sincere, that he shows himself ready not only to be deprived of all the advantages of this temporal life, but even to lay down his life for Christ's flock.

Hence now, after [Christ] committed his sheep to Peter to be pastured, that is, after he committed his people [to him] to be taught and governed, he subsequently added, *'Truly, truly I say to you, when you were younger, you girded yourself and walked where you would; but when you are old, you will extend your hands and another will gird you and lead you where you do not wish* [to go]'. By the extension of hands he suggested the position of his members by which he would be fastened to the cross;[18] by another's girding him he expressed the fastening of the chains with which he would be restricted by his persecutor; by the leading where he did not wish [to go] he indicated the anguish of his suffering and death, from which his bodily weakness shrank; but in the firmness of his spiritual soul he was glad to suffer even every adversity for the Lord's sake. He did not seek his own will, but the will of him who sent him,[19] Christ.

Having first mentioned the feeding of his sheep, the Lord next added to the chief shepherd the triumph of his suffer-

16. Ph 2:19-21   17. Jn 10:12-13
18. Aug., *Tract. in Ioh.* 123, 5 (CC 36:679, 72 - 680, 101)
19. Jn 5:30

ing by saying, '*You will extend your hands and another person will gird you and lead you where you do not wish* [to go],' as if he were unmistakably saying: 'By the greatness of the charity with which you love me, you will clearly prove that since by your striving you will come even to death for the life of my little ones, so that they can be saved in body and in mind, you will tolerate with steadfast constancy of mind all of the torments of the body that your enemies please to inflict'.

The evangelist himself subsequently suggests this, when he says: *He said this signifying by what kind of death he would glorify God.* Peter glorified God by his death when by this evidence he showed everyone how much God was to be worshipped and loved. He himself, when offered an alternative, preferred to undergo the torment of the cross rather than discontinue his preaching of the heavenly word. We should note that he glorified God not only by his death, but also by his life and by the sufferings that preceded his death. He glorified God by his life, since in everything he did he sought not his own will but the will and praises of his Maker. He glorified [God] by his sufferings too, since no oppression from those who were persecuting him was capable of turning him away from the goal of divine love that he had set for himself.

But since along with the memorial of blessed Peter, we are today celebrating the heavenly birthday of his fellow apostle Paul, let us see, dearly beloved brothers, whether he too glorified the Lord by his life, his sufferings and his death. Surely he too did so. The evangelist Luke, who completed his book on the Acts of the Apostles largely by describing [Paul's] struggles and labors on Christ's behalf, bears witness to this. He permeated the corpus of his writings, which is made up of fourteen letters, with the aroma of Christ alone, if I may speak in this way. Whatever you read there either reveals the hidden mysteries of the faith, or shows the results of good works, or promises the joys of the heavenly kingdom, or lays bare the tribulations he sustained in preaching these things, or relates the divine consolation he received in the midst of his tribulations, or suggests by a general exhortation that all *those who wish to live a good life in Christ*[20] will not lack persecutions. He bears witness to how much he glorified God by his life when, cast into chains and drawing near to his passion, he proposes to Timothy in a letter the example of his own work, saying, *I have fought a good fight, I have finished my course, I have kept the faith.*[21] He showed by what kind of death he was to glorify God when he set forth, *I am being sacrificed even now, and the time of my dissolution is at hand.*[22] Oh, how precious in the sight of the Lord was the death of this saint of his![23] He knew most clearly, and foretold with an unrestrained voice that his being killed for the Lord's sake was nothing else but a most acceptable and pure sacrificial offering made to the Lord. Therefore Paul too glorified God, as did the rest of the apostles, for they too loved Christ with a pure heart and took care of Christ's sheep with a sincere intent.

What was said to Peter, *'Feed my sheep,'* was said to all [the apostles]. *The other* apostles *were Peter's equals, but the first place was granted to Peter,*[24] so that the unity of the Church might be set forth. *All are shepherds, but one flock is revealed.* Then *it was fed by all the apostles with* harmonious *agreement,*[25] and ever since it is fed by their successors with joint concern; many of these [successors] are proven to have glorified their Maker by their deaths, and all of them by their lives. Not only these great luminaries of the Church, but the rest of the throng of the elect as well, each in his own time, glorifies God by his life or by his death.

We too must follow in their footsteps in our own time, my brothers, by directing our lives after the example of those who are good, and by persisting even to death in our proposed righteousness of life. Then, as companions of their way of life, we may deserve to be made companions also of their recompense. We shall accomplish this if, according to the content of this most sacred reading, we hold fast to our Redeemer with due affection, and if we watch out

20. 2 Tm 3:12   21. 2 Tm 4:7   22. 2 Tm 4:6
23. Ps 116:15 (115:15)   24. Mt 16:18-19
25. Cyprian, *De unitate* 4 (CC 3: 251, 79 - 252, 96)

with brotherly solicitude for the salvation of our neighbor. He assists us who orders us to do these things, and promises that he will repay us for what we have done, Jesus Christ our Lord, who lives and reigns with the Father in the unity of the Holy Spirit, God throughout all ages of ages. Amen.

NOTE

1. In this homily Bede varies constantly between two words for 'love,' *dilectio* and *amor* (and the related verbs *diligo* and *amo*). The variation appears to be merely for the sake of variety, rather than reflecting a semantic distinction. 'Love' is therefore used throughout in the translation because there is no true synonym in English, 'like' and 'affection' implying a distinction in intensity that Bede does not seem to have in mind. Note, however, that in this discussion Bede also uses a third term, *caritas*, which has been translated 'charity'.

homily̛ II.23

Matthew 14:1–12   *The Beheading of John the Baptist*

a s we celebrate the heavenly birthday of blessed John, dearly beloved brothers, we must not only recall with pious devotion his steadfastness in suffering, but also turn into weapons of salvation the malice of those at whose hands he suffered. Then indeed do we usefully direct our minds to the sacred scriptures, when we put before [us] as a motive for doing good not only the virtues and the rewards of the just, but also the vices and punishment of the damned. We are taught this by our Lord's own example. To shatter the pride of human beings, and to put on us the exalted yoke of humility, not only did he suggest the model of his own humility for us to follow, saying, *'Learn of me, for I am meek and humble of heart,'*[1] but he also called our attention to the casting down of the angels through pride (which we must guard against), saying, *'I saw Satan falling like lightning from heaven'.*[2] This was to enkindle in us the practice of the highest virtues, not only by the example of his own divine goodness, but also by that of the devil's depravity.

1. Mt 11:29   2. Lk 10:18

Herod the tetrarch heard of the fame of Jesus, and said to his servants, 'This is John the Baptist; he has risen from the dead, and that is why these powers are working through him'. He understood clearly that a dead man could be raised from the dead; he had a good understanding of the glory of the resurrection, since he discerned that the just would possess greater power after their resurrection than [their] human weakness held. But he was utterly mistaken in refusing completely to believe of the God-man what he could believe an ordinary being [accomplished] by his own power, [even though] so many miracles bore witness to [him], and the many great declarations of preachers were in agreement. Why was this, dearly beloved brothers? Was it not that we might clearly understand that the miracle of the resurrection was not unbelievable, but, because their sinfulness stood in their way, the minds of the evil were kept back from the gift of belief? Let us give great thanks to him, who, by removing the veil of error from our hearts, has deigned to open them up to the light of truth!

For Herod had seized John and bound him and put him in prison, because of Herodias, his brother's wife; for John had said to him, 'It is not lawful for you to have her'. We see fulfilled here in John's case what the angel had foretold to Zechariah concerning him before he was born—that he would go before the Lord in the spirit and power of Elijah.[3] Both [Elijah and John] lived in continence, both wore rough dress, both spent their lives in the wilderness, both were heralds of the truth, both underwent persecution for justice's sake at the hands of a king and queen—the former at the hands of Ahab and Jezebel,[4] the latter at the hands of Herod and Herodias.[5] The former, lest he be killed by the wicked, was carried up to heaven in a fiery chariot;[6] the latter, lest he be overcome by the wicked, sought the heavenly kingdom by his martyrdom, which was accomplished in spiritual combat. Surely he was transported by the help of angels, of whom it is written, *The chariots of God* [are accompanied by] *ten thousand* [angels], *numberless thousands of those who are glad: the Lord*

3. Lk 1:17
5. Jer., *In Matth.* 14, 4 (CC 77: 117, 1125/27)
4. 1 K 19:1-3
6. 2 K 2:11

is among them;[7] and again, *He makes his spirits angels, and his ministers a burning fire.*[8]

But perhaps someone is asking who Herod was, and who his brother, and who Herodias, with whom the reading is concerned? This Herod, who had John the Baptist beheaded, and who was in agreement with Pilate during our Redeemer's passion,[9] was the son of the Herod during whose reign our Lord was born.[10] [The elder Herod] ruled for a brief time after our Lord's birth (as the gospel history testifies); his son Archelaus succeeded him in his kingdom.[11] When [Archelaus] had been ruler for barely ten years the Jews accused him of tyranny, and he was expelled from his kingdom by [the Roman emperor] Augustus, and condemned to exile for life.[12] Then Augustus, in order to lessen the power of the Jewish kingdom, divided the province into four parts and appointed Archelaus's four brothers to rule over it.[13] Each of them, for his headship over a fourth part, was called a tetrarch in the Greek language.[1*] [One] of these [tetrarchs], Philip, took as wife Herodias, the daughter of King Aretas of Arabia;[14] later Aretas took her away from him and gave her to Herod, because he had greater power and a higher reputation. Thus there came about a public adultery.

As this was a cause of ruin for the faithless, so was it an opportunity for the most faithful herald of our redemption to triumph. By prohibiting the crime of the unrighteous king, he merited to be punished by an undeserved death; but after he had tasted death, he received from the King of righteousness, to whom he had borne testimony, the righteous crown of everlasting life.

For John had said to him, 'It is not lawful for you to have her'. And [Herod] *wanted to have him put to death, but he feared the people, because they regarded* [John] *as a prophet.* Not only the people but even Herod himself regarded John as a prophet, as the evangelist Mark testifies, saying, *For Herod was afraid*

7. Ps 68:17 (67:18)
9. Lk 23:7-11
11. Mt 2:22
13. Lk 3:1
8. Ps 104:4 (103:4)
10. Mt 2:1
12. Joseph. *Ant. Iud.* 17, 13, 2
14. Joseph. *Ant. Iud.* 18, 5, 1

of John, knowing that he was a just and holy man, and kept him safe. When he heard him, he did many things, and heard him willingly.[15] But his love for the woman prevailed, and she forced him to lay his hands upon a man whom he knew to be holy and just. Since he was unwilling to restrain his lust, he incurred the guilt of homicide; what was a lesser sin for him became the cause of a greater sin. By God's strict judgment it happened to him that, as a result of his craving for the adulteress whom he knew he ought to reject, he caused the shedding of the blood of the prophet, who he knew was pleasing to God. Now this is [an illustration of] the divine dispensation of judgment, of which it is said, *'Let the evildoer still do evil, and the filthy still be filthy'.*[16] But what follows, *'Let the holy still be holy,'*[17] is appropriate to the person of blessed John. Already holy, he became more holy still when, through his office of spreading the good news, he reached the palm of martyrdom.

On Herod's birthday the daughter of Herodias danced before the company, and pleased Herod. Hence he promised with an oath to give her whatever she asked of him. We hear at the same time of three evil deeds [done by] wicked people: the inauspicious celebration of a birthday, the lewd dancing of a girl, and the rash oath of a king. We should be instructed by each of these against doing such things. We ought not to call to mind the day of our birth with a feast, nor ought we to indulge at any time in alluring bodily amusements, but instead we ought to anticipate the day of our death with tears and prayers and frequent fasts. It is indeed for this reason that the wise man admonishes us, saying, *In all your works remember your final end, and you will never sin.*[18] Nor is it proper to surrender the members of our [body], which have now been consecrated to the Lord, to trifling and unsuitable movements. The Apostle says, *Do you not know that your bodies are members of Christ? Shall I therefore take the members of Christ and make them members of a harlot? May it not be so!*[19] He entreats us elsewhere by the mercy of God to display our bodies *as a living sacrificial offering, holy* [and] *pleasing to God.*[20]

15. Mk 6:20	16. Rv 22:11	17. *Ibid.*
18. Si 7:36 (7:40)	19. 1 Co 6:15	20. Rm 12:1

Like the Lord in the gospel,[21] James in his letter teaches how strictly we ought to avoid the rashness of swearing, saying, *Above all, my brothers, do not swear, either by heaven or by earth or with any oath whatsoever; but let your yes be yes, and your no be no, that you may not be liable to judgment.*[22] This is the judgment to which Herod fell victim, so that he found he had either to break his oath or, to avoid breaking his oath, to commit another shameful act. If it should perhaps happen that we swear carelessly to something which, if carried out, would have most unfortunate consequences, we should know that we should willingly change it [in accord with] more salutary counsel. There is an urgent necessity for us to break our oath, rather than turn to another more serious crime in order to avoid breaking our oath. David swore by the Lord to kill Nabal, a stupid and wicked man, and to destroy all his possessions; but at the first entreaty of the prudent woman Abigail, he quickly took back his threats, put back his sword into its scabbard, and did not feel that he had contracted any guilt by thus breaking his oath in this way.[23] Herod swore that he would give the dancing girl whatever she asked of him, and, to avoid being accused of breaking his oath by those who were at his banquet, he defiled the banquet with blood when he made the reward for her dancing the death of a prophet. And not only in swearing, but in everything that we do, this is the rule[24] we should carefully observe: that if we should perhaps fall into the snares of a wily enemy from which we cannot escape without some taint of sin, we should rather seek that way out in which we discern that we will suffer less danger. We should follow the example of those shut up within enemy walls: they are desirous of finding a way out, but consider that access to every gate is closed to them—out of necessity they choose a place where the wall is lower from which to jump down, so that when they fall they incur the least danger.

There follows: *But she, on the advice of her mother, said, 'Give me the head of John the Baptist here on a platter'. And the king*

21. Mt 5:34-37   22. Jm 5:12
23. 1 S 25:2-35; Aug., *Serm.* 308, 1, 1 - 3, 3, (*PL* 38: 1408-09)
24. *moderatio*

was sorry. The king's sorrow is not absolution from his wicked deed, but a confession of it. This indeed is [characteristic of] the justice of the judgment from on high: the damned often recognize and admit that they have done wrong, and manifest a certain regret for their wrongdoing, yet do not cease their wrongdoing. By their confession and [false] repentance they give testimony against themselves that they have not transgressed out of ignorance when they refuse to stop the action of which they disapprove. They thereby perish the more justly, inasmuch as they have neglected to turn away from the pit of perdition which they were able to foresee.

Herod's sorrow was indeed similar to the repentance of Pharaoh[25] and Judas.[26] Each of them, after he had unwillingly admitted his offense because his conscience accused him, foolishly made it worse. Herod, when asked for the head of John, simulated sorrow on his countenance, but by doing so he condemned himself by showing everyone clearly that he knew that the person whom he was about to give over to be slaughtered was guiltless and holy.[27] If we inspect the heart of this detestable man more attentively, [we find that] he was secretly happy at being asked for something that he had all along in mind to do, if he could find an excuse for doing it. If he had been asked for the head of Herodias, no one can doubt that he would have been truly sorrowful as he refused.

But because of his oath and those who were at table with him, he ordered that it be given; and he sent and had John beheaded in prison, and his head was brought in on a platter. The king provided an unworthy spectacle on his birthday. He brought forward the head of the man who had been killed on a platter, to be gazed on by the rulers, tribunes and leaders of his nation, who had been invited to the meal. The invited guests were equally unworthy, or rather as bad as their host. None of them was found to object to a man being punished at a festival dinner, to a just man being punished by adulterers, to the judge being beheaded by the guilty. Parti-

25. Ex 9:27; 10:16   26. Mt 27:3-4
27. Jer., *In Matth.* 14, 9 (CC 77: 118, 1157/58)

cularly when the king was protesting, by his pretended appearance of sadness, that he was doing this under compulsion, it would have been appropriate to the occasion that he should have been released from his promised wicked deed at the urging of the diners, if they recognized that he had not arranged this intentionally. Moreover, a love of this wicked deed would involve them [in it] too.

But the blessed precursor of our Lord's nativity, preaching, and death showed in his own struggle strength that was worthy of divine regard. As scripture says, *Even if he suffered torments in the sight of men, his hope was full of immortality.*[28] It is right that year after year we commemorate with festive celebration his heavenly birthday. He caused it to be a solemnity for us by his own passion; he adorned it by the rosy brightness of his blood. Rightly do we venerate his memory with spiritual joy, since he closed the testimony he had shown to our Lord by the seal of his own martyrdom. We must have no doubt that blessed John underwent imprisonment and chains to give testimony to our Lord, and he gave up his life for him of whom he was the precursor. Yet he was not ordered by his persecutor to deny Christ, but to conceal the truth. Still he met his death for Christ's sake: since Christ himself said, *'I am the truth,'*[29] it was for Christ that [John] shed his blood, because [he shed it] for truth.

And just as by his own earlier birth, preaching, and baptizing, [John] bore testimony to the one who was going to be born, to preach, and to baptize, so he indicated by suffering first that [Christ] also was to suffer. Nevertheless, by the sure plan of divine Providence,[30] it was decreed that their passions be carried out in different ways: our Redeemer would be lifted up on a cross outside the city's gate with the entire populace standing round, while his precursor would be beheaded in secrecy, in prison, with the magistrates and nobles from among the people gathered in the house at a feast, and the executioner sent in secret. It might seem fitting that John would have prefigured the mystery

28. Ws 3:4   29. Jn 14:6
30. *certa supernae prouisionis dispensatione*

of the Lord's cross by being crucified [himself]. However, in bearing witness to the Lord, John said, *'He must increase, and I must decrease'*[31] (that is, 'he whom you marvel at as a great prophet must be understood to be the Christ, true Lord and God, whereas though you are of the opinion that I am the Christ, it will be evident that I am not the Christ, but a prophet'). Therefore the different manner of their passions suggests the different status of each, [and this] was not determined by the power of their slayers, but foreseen by heavenly reason. Again, John says, *'One who is from the earth belongs to the earth and speaks of earthly matters; one who comes from heaven is above all'*.[32] The beheading in prison of the one from the earth, and [the fact that] his decapitation was carried out in private indicates the aforesaid decreasing of importance. The lifting up on the cross, which was carried out in public, in the sight of the entire populace, clearly denotes the increase in importance of the one who comes from heaven and is above all. When lifted up on the cross, he held his head up toward heaven and stretched out his hands over [all] lands, toward the north and south, so that by the very posture of his body he might figuratively show that he was Lord of heaven and of the whole earth, and that all the heavenly powers were subject to his authority. The bottom of the cross went down into the hidden depths of the earth to signify that the kingdom of the lower world was pierced and destroyed in his passion. The bystanders, Jews, Greeks and Romans,[33] read from an inscription written on the cross that this was the King of all who believed, so that it might appear that his sovereignty was to be extended to all nations. The Apostle includes all this briefly in one sentence, saying, *He became obedient even to death, death on a cross. Therefore God has exalted him, and given him the name that is above every name, so that at the name of Jesus every knee should bend of those in heaven, on the earth, and in the lower world, and every tongue confess that the Lord Jesus Christ is in the glory of God the Father.*[34]

31. Jn 3:30   32. Jn 3:31   33. Lk 23:38; Jn 19:20
34. Ph 2:8-11

After John was beheaded, and his head had been brought on a platter, there follows: *And it was given to the girl, and she brought it to her mother. And* [John's] *disciples came and took his body and buried it.* This is also related to the decrease of the Lord's precursor, that his body was given burial without its head. His body was buried in a city of Samaria which is now called Sebaste, and his head in Jerusalem, as we find [written] in the ecclesiastical histories;[35] he was beheaded, however, in a certain fortress of Arabia, to which they give the name Machaerus.[36] In these histories we also discover this, that his most holy head, a long time after the beheading, was disclosed by [John] himself to two Eastern monks who had come to Jerusalem to pray, and from there it was taken to the Phoenician city of Emessa, for due homage to be paid to it by the faithful. His bones were transferred from Samaria to Jerusalem after a period of time, and still later they were sent to Alexandria, where they are now preserved in a church consecrated in honor of his name. It is obvious that this was done by divine Providence, so that with the relics of the blessed martyr spread to more places there would be more tokens of his virtues, and through recollection of his teaching and his life more people might be brought to the faith and love of him whom he preached.

At this point we might consider and commit more actively to memory how almighty God allows his chosen ones and beloved servants, those he has predestined to life and his eternal kingdom, to be so stricken in this life by the persecution of the wicked, [and] to be wasted by so many kinds and such fierce punishments and deaths. This is so that when we have viewed the sufferings of perfect men, we may grieve less over the adversities that perhaps have happened to us, and learn instead to esteem it complete joy when we fall into various kinds of temptations,[37] keeping in mind that *The Lord chastises the one he loves, and scourges every child whom he receives.*[38] Now although the principle stands[39] that *We all offend in many ways,*[40] which of us would

---

35. Eusebius/Rufinus, *Hist. Eccl.* (*GCS* 9: 1033, 20 - 1034, 1)
36. Eusebius/Rufinus, *Hist. Eccl.* (*GCS* 9: 79, 16/17)
37. Jm 1:2   38. Heb 12:6   39. *principalis sententia constat*
40. Jm 3:2

dare to say that blessed John sinned in act or word or dress
or food, when the gospel history praises the harshness of
his clothing and the frugality of his meals;[41] when everything he said either rendered testimony to the truth or
refuted those who spoke against him; when even those who
did not like him held in veneration his works of justice?
What place could there have been in his inmost heart for
sin, when the coming of the Holy Spirit consecrated him
even before his birth, when not even in comparison with
the ordinary way of human life could he be turned aside
from the path of virtue, who from his boyhood on led an
entirely solitary life?[42] And yet a man of this sort, one who
was so preeminent, reached the end of his earthly life by
shedding his blood after a long period of affliction in chains.
He who brought the good news of the freedom of heavenly peace was thrust into chains by wicked people; he who
came to bear testimony to the light,[43] and who merited to
be called a burning and shining lamp[44] by the very light
which is Christ, was shut up in the darkness of prison; he
than whom no one from among those born of women was
greater[45] was punished by being beheaded at the request
of the basest of women; and he to whom it was granted
to baptize the world's Redeemer, to hear the Father's voice
above him, and to see the grace of the Holy Spirit descending upon him, was baptized in his own blood.[46]

But it was not burdensome for such as these.[2*] Rather it
was bearable and desirable to suffer temporary torments
for the sake of the truth, since they knew that they were
going to be rewarded with perpetual joys. They regarded
death, which by natural necessity was inevitable, as something desirable, along with the palm of eternal life, when
they had confessed Christ's name. Hence the Apostle does
well to say, *To you has it been given by Christ not only to believe in him but also suffer for his sake.*[47] He says that it is
Christ's gift that the elect should suffer for his sake, because
as he also says, *The sufferings of this time are not comparable*

41. Mt 3:4   42. Lk 1:80   43. Jn 1:7
44. Jn 5:35   45. Lk 7:28   46. Mt 3:13-17
47. Ph 1:29

to the glory which will come upon us and will be revealed in us. [48]
When, therefore, we see such extraordinary heirs of the
heavenly kingdom suffering such great [torments] during
the time of their mortal exile, what remains for us to do under these circumstances, dearly beloved brothers, except to
humble ourselves the more in the sight of our benevolent
Maker and Redeemer, the more clearly we become aware
that we are unable to follow them either by imitating their
lives or their deaths? As a result, according to the words
of the first shepherd, *Let us become humble beneath the powerful hand of God, so that he may exalt us at the time of his visitation;* [49] let us become humble with John, and fast, and make
our entreaties unceasingly; [50] let us exult at decreasing in
the sight of human beings; let us be tested, and for a short
while let our spirit fail us—that is, our fleshly and proud
[spirit], which tends to be puffed up—so that by advancing in good deeds we may be capable of growing in his sight,
and of being exalted with him, who deigned to come from
heaven to earth to raise us who are of the earth to heaven,
Jesus Christ our Lord, who lives and reigns with the Father in the unity of the Holy Spirit, God throughout all ages
of ages. Amen.

48. Rm 8:18   49. 1 P 5:6   50. Lk 5:33

NOTES

1. The Greek word for 'four' is *tessares,* and from this is derived *tetrarcha,* one who has rule over a fourth part.
2. 'Such as these' = *talibus,* presumably the 'chosen ones and beloved servants' mentioned at the beginning of the preceding paragraph. One manuscript reads *tali uiro,* 'such a man,' that is, John the Baptist, and the following verbs are made singular to agree with this reading.

homily˘ II.24

John 10:22-30   *Dedication of a Church*

We have heard in the gospel reading, dearly beloved brothers, that *The feast of the dedication took place at Jerusalem.*[1] This 'feast of the dedication,' referred to the solemn observance of the dedication of the temple,[2] which God's people used to celebrate each year according to the ancient tradition of their ancestors. Following in their footsteps and in accord with the practice of the Christian world, we today take pains to observe with divine praises and vigils the annual solemn observance of the dedication of our church.[1*] And it is fitting that we celebrate this festival day with great devotion, in that we recognize that [such a feast] was so agreeable to our Redeemer that he deigned on it to enter the temple and deliver a discourse to the people, and to make known to them the mysteries of his divinity.

The feast of the dedication took place at Jerusalem, and it was winter, and Jesus was walking in the temple, in Solomon's portico. If he chose to walk in the temple, where the flesh and

---

1. *encaenia*, from the Greek word meaning 'renewal,' referring particularly to the rededication in 165 B.C. of the temple at the time of Judas Maccabeus.
2. Aug., *Tract. in Ioh.* 48, 2 (CC 36: 413, 2-4)

241

blood of brute animals used to be offered, much more will we rejoice to visit our house of prayer, where the sacrament of his own body and blood is celebrated. If he did not disdain to walk round the portico where a mortal and earthly king, albeit the most powerful and wisest one, was once accustomed to stand and pray, how much more greatly does he desire to inspect and enlighten the innermost recesses[3] of our hearts—if he regards them as equivalent to the portico of Solomon, that is, if he regards them as having the fear of him which is the beginning of wisdom.[4] We must not suppose that only the building in which we come together to pray and celebrate the mysteries[5] is the Lord's temple, and that we ourselves, who come together in the Lord's name, are not more fully his temple and are not so named, since the Apostle clearly says, *You are the temple of the living God; as God says, 'I will live in them and walk among them'.*[6]

If we are the temple of God, let us take great care and busy ourselves with good deeds, so that he may deign to come more often into this temple of his, and to make his dwelling place there. Let us avoid winter's image, lest the Lord, on coming into our hearts, find them numb from [lack of] charity's ardor, and so, since he has been turned away, quickly leave them. For why did the evangelist trouble to record that it was winter time, except that he wished to indicate by the harshness of winter winds and storms the hardness of the Jews' unbelief, and that his utterance was appropriate for many of those he found then in the temple, whom he told, *because iniquity will abound, the charity of many grows cold.*[7]

[John] subsequently intimates this clearly, saying: *The Jews gathered round him and said, 'How long do you cause perplexity in our minds? If you are the Christ, tell us openly'.* They did

---

3. *penetralia*, a word also used to refer to the central portion of a shrine or temple.
4. Ps 111:10 (110:10), Si 1:16
5. *mysteria*, a Latin word for the eucharistic celebration.
6. 2 Co 6:16
7. Mt 24:12. Several MSS have the Vulgate reading for the tense of both verbs: 'because iniquity has abounded, the charity of many will grow cold'.

not say this as seeking the truth of the faith but as laying
snares for him whom they were questioning, and as con-
triving a false accusation. They believed that the Christ,
whom orthodox faith confesses to be true God and true
man, would be only a man, not God. They were mindful
that the Lord swore to David concerning [Christ's] humanity
that the fruit of [David's] body would sit upon his throne,[8]
but they forgot what [the Lord] chanted concerning
[Christ's] divinity through the [mouth of] David, saying,
The Lord said to me, 'You are my Son'.[9] They therefore believed that the Christ would be born of the stock of David
and would come as a king surpassing every other. [They
believed this] with the same lack of sense that their descendants possess even at the present time, and they will not
cease to err until at length they accept the antichrist in place
of Christ. If the Lord Jesus answered that he was the Christ,
they had in mind to hand him over to the power of the
[Roman] procurator to be punished as one rebelling against
[Caesar] Augustus and usurping for himself unlawful sovereignty.[10] But he, with regard for our salvation, on whose
account these things were to be written, qualified his answer so as to stop the mouth of his calumniators, and to
divulge with a clear voice to those who believed in him that
he was the Christ. They were inquiring about Christ's humanity, but he told them openly about the mysteries of his
divinity, in which he is equal to the Father.

Let us too gather round him, dearly beloved, not trying
to entrap him like the Jews, but by preparing a restful place
for him within ourselves like the most faithful [members
of his] house. Of them it is rightly said, *The most high has
sanctified his tabernacle; God is within, it shall not be shaken.*[11]
Let us make our request of him, not by raging madly against
him, *'How long do you cause perplexity in our minds? If you are
the Christ, tell us openly,'* for what is madder than their com-
plaining that the teacher of truth was causing perplexity in
their minds, because he did not clearly unlock to them the

8. Ps 132:11 (131:11)   9. Ps 2:7
10. Aug., *Tract. in Ioh.* 48, 3-4 (CC 36: 414, 16/4)
11. Ps 46:4-5 (45:5-6)

hidden mysteries of his majesty, when they were incredulous and they were speaking against him? But, as
scripture advises us, let us have a goodly feeling about him
and seek him in sincerity of heart, *since he is found by those
who do not put him to the test; he shows himself to those who
have faith in him.*[12] Let us say to him in supplication, 'You
are the Christ; we acknowledge that you, the only-begotten
Son of God, are coeternal and consubstantial with the Father and the Holy Spirit in their divinity, [and] that you have
become a sharer of our substance in time. Grant that what
we at present venerate with devout faith we may contemplate with full vision in the future. This indeed is the only
health and life of our soul—to discern your countenance,
your light, forever'.

We must not doubt that he hears us asking when we ask
what he himself commanded us [to ask, and] we request
with attentive minds what he desires to give [us]. How can
we believe that he would deny to his servants who devoutly
supplicate him the gifts he did not refuse to disclose even
to his opponents beyond the measure that they requested?
When they inquired of him as to whether he as a human
being was the Christ, he was not reluctant [to reveal] to them
that he was not only a human being but also the Christ,
God and Son of God. For he answered them, saying, *'If
I tell*[13] *you, you do not believe. The works which I do in my
Father's name bear testimony concerning me; but you do not believe because you are not of my sheep'.* Therefore he who testifies that he is performing his works in the Father's name
implies that they should believe that he is God's Son. They
are held to be guilty on a double charge: they could not be
attracted to faith either by the words he spoke, or by the
deeds he added to give force to the truth of his words. It
is rightly said that they are not of his sheep, because they
were concerned not with following the good Shepherd with
the sincerity of sheep, but rather with persecuting him with
the ferocity of wild beasts.

---

12. Ws 1:1-2
13. 'If I tell' = *Loquar*; some MSS have the Vulgate reading *Loquor*, 'I tell'.

Since there are some who keep the faith in word only, and cover their brutish hearts under the guise of sheep, the Shepherd himself subsequently teaches them what the life of his sheep is, and what their reward: *'My sheep hear my voice, and I know them, and they follow me, and I give them eternal life, and they will not perish for ever'*. Everyone, then, who desires to avoid eternal destruction and to see everlasting life must follow [the Shepherd's] voice not only by hearing and believing, but also by living uprightly. What he says about his recognizing his sheep surely signifies that he chooses them and predestines them for his heavenly kingdom. Hence Solomon said,²* *The Lord knows the ways which are at his right hand,*¹⁴ and on the other hand, the Apostle said of the condemned, *One who does not know* [him] *will not be known* [by him].¹⁵

[Christ] said beautifully of those who hear his voice and follow him, *'And I give them eternal life, and they will not perish for ever'*. Now in the eyes of the ignorant the martyrs seemed to die;¹⁶ they seemed to perish when, after undergoing various kinds of torments, they lost their mortal lives. But they will not perish for ever; they will not see death for ever.¹⁷ As soon as they are released from the prison of the flesh, they will be allotted the reward which is theirs for their contest.

The text continues fittingly of such as these: *'No one will snatch them out of my hand'*. Wicked persecutors strove to snatch Christ's holy confessors from his hand when they forced them by torture to deny their faith in order to estrange their souls from Christ; or, in the case of those who died victorious, when they cast their lifeless bodies into water to be dissolved or into the fire to be burned, in order to take from Christ, so to speak, the possibility of raising them up. But no one will snatch them out of his hand—as he says elsewhere, *'Everything has been delivered to me by my Father'*.¹⁸ He helps those who are struggling that they may be victorious, and crowns those who are victors that they may reign forever; and in his own time he makes the flesh

14. Pr 4:27
17. Jn 8:51

15. 1 Co 14:38
18. Mt 11:27

16. Ws 3:2

in which they have struggled immortal. By these words he also confuted the rashness of those preparing the trap of death for him. He clearly implied that it was very foolish of them to plan treacherously for his destruction, since he could give immortal life which no one would snatch away from any of those whom he had known as his own before the ages.

But lest by speaking in this way he might seem to be seeking his own glory, he refers all his power to the glory of the Father when he adds, *'What my Father has given me is greater than everything'*. What the Father gave to the Mediator between God and men, the man Jesus Christ,[19] is greater than everything: that [Christ] is his only-begotten Son, in no way unlike him in nature, or inferior in power, or later in time than his begetter.[20] Our Lord possessed this equality of divinity with the Father before the world began,[21] but he received his human nature from the time of his incarnation.

'And no one is able to snatch [them] *out of my Father's hand'*. Previously he had said about his sheep, *'No one will snatch them out of my hand,'* and now he adds, *'And no one is able to snatch* [them] *out of my Father's hand,'* clearly giving it to be understood that his hand, that is, his power, is one and the same with that of his Father.[22] So we must believe him to be the Christ, not like others sanctified by grace in time, but always existing as the true Son of God.

He makes this notion clearer than light by saying openly in the following sentence, *'I and the Father are one'*. 'We are one,' he says—'We have one substance, one divinity, one eternity, one perfect equality, no dissimilarity'. By these words he explicated not only the question at hand, in which the Jews were inquiring whether he was the Christ, but also pointed out how much we should abhor heretics' lack of faith, which he foresaw for the future. Photinus says, 'Christ is only a human being; he is not God': but since he himself

19. 1 Tm 2:5
20. Aug., *Tract in Ioh.* 48, 6 (CC 36: 415, 25 - 416, 32)
21. Jn 17:5
22. Aug., *Tract in Ioh.* 48, 7 (CC 36: 416, 3/6)

says, '*I and the Father are one,*' it is openly shown that a person who is only a human being cannot be of one substance with God the Father. Because Christ is of the same [substance] with the Father, we must eschew the heresy of Photinus, which prohibits believing him to be God. Arius says that Christ was created by God and was not born of God, and so must be believed to be lower than the Father. Again [Christ] himself contradicts this by saying, '*I and the Father are one*'. Who does not easily see that no created being can be one by nature with him who created everything? And since Christ is by nature one with the Father, the perversity of Arius must be condemned, because he affirms that [Christ] is a created being. In turn, Sabellius says that the Father and Son are not to be confessed to be two distinct persons, but that the Father is the Father when he wishes and the Son when he wishes, and that they are one and the same person.[23] The Son himself condemns this in the already mentioned [statement]. It is sure that '*I and the Father are one*' cannot be said of one person; it is not logical that, '*I are,*' be said of one person. Wherefore, having rejected the error of Sabellius along with the others, we must follow the apostolic faith of blessed Peter, wherein he confessed [his faith in] the Lord and said, '*You are the Christ, the Son of the living God*'.[24]

I have completed, with God's help, the explanation of the gospel reading. But I would still like to discuss with this fraternal gathering more fully the solemnity of the dedication, which was being celebrated then at Jerusalem, and which we are celebrating today. First of all, we should note that the dedication about which we have learned in the gospel reading refers not to that of the first temple, but to that of the last one. This is easily inferred from the fact that it is reported that it took place during the winter. The first dedication of the temple, by Solomon, occurred during the autumn;[25] the second one, by Zerubbabel and Jeshua the priest, occurred during the spring;[26] and the last one, by

23. Bede, Hom I.8 (CC 122: 53, 46/49)   24. Mt 16:16
25. 1 K 6:38; 8:63; 2 Ch 7:5-10
26. Ezr 6:15-19; Joseph., *Ant. Iud.* 11, 4, 7

Judas Maccabeus, occurred during the winter time.[27] Then, as we read, it was specially established that the dedication should be recalled each year as a memorial, with solemn observances. Accordingly, when the gospel was just now read, we heard that this had been done until the time of our Lord's incarnation.

This was the reason for the second and third dedications: Solomon completed the work on the temple which he built to the Lord after seven years, and during the eighth year, on the tenth day of the seventh month, which by us is named October, he dedicated it with great glory.[28] Formerly, under the law,[29] this day was decreed a solemn one, so that on it each year the entire tabernacle had to be cleansed by greater sacrificial offerings.[30] When Zechariah, the father of blessed John the Baptist, was performing his service at the altar in these cleansing rites, an angel came and instructed him about the mystery of our Lord's incarnation and the joy of human salvation.[31]

After the passage of four hundred and thirty years, the Chaldeans burnt [Solomon's] temple, and after destroying the city, they led the people captive into Babylon. Seventy years later, when the Persians were ruling, [the Jewish people] were led back to their homeland, and the temple was rebuilt over a period of forty-six years.[32] This work was brought to completion on the third day of the twelfth month,[33] which we call March. Zerubbabel, of royal rank, and Jeshua the high priest, as I have said, were the most zealous leaders of the people, and they were in charge of the work; the prophets Haggai and Zechariah assisted them,[34] strengthening the hearts of the people against the plots of the enemies impeding the work.

Then, after about three hundred and fifty-six years, the most detestable king of the Greeks, Antiochus, took Jerusalem by deception. He profaned the temple with the filth of idols, removing from it and breaking into pieces the altar

27. 1 M 4:52-59   28. Joseph., *Ant. Iud.* 8, 4, 1
29. Lv 16:29-34   30. Bede, *Hom.* II.19 (CC 122: 322, 144/50)
31. Lk 1:8-14   32. Jn 2:20
33. Ezr 6:15   34. Ezr 5:1-2

of the Lord, the golden table [of the loaves] of proposition, the candelabrum which provided light, and all the other golden vessels of the temple which he could find. He set up in the temple a statue of Jupiter, and by torture forced the people to offer sacrifice to the idols.[35] During this persecution many of the people were slaughtered for keeping the divine law, among whom was that rightly-renowned mother of seven sons, who along with her sons merited the most noble crown of martyrdom for the Lord's sake.[36] Judas Maccabeus, since he was of the priestly rank, gathered an army of the just [to fight] against the chieftains of Antiochus; he took away their arms, drove them out of Judaea, put an end to this most cruel persecution, and thoroughly cleansed the temple of idolatrous images. Again making new altars and other implements and ornaments and putting them back in the temple, he dedicated them together with the temple, which he had purified and restored, on the twenty-fifth day of the ninth month, which among us is called December. No one can doubt that this relates to the winter time.[37] As I have said, he issued a decree that each year the day of dedication (the day of the renewal and rededication of the temple) should be celebrated with festal devotion.

All these things, as the Apostle teaches, *were done as an example for us,*[38] and were written down for us, and so we must scrutinize them carefully for their spiritual meaning. King Solomon, whose name means 'peaceful,'[39] typologically designates our Redeemer himself, of whom Isaiah says, *His sovereignty will be increased, and there will be no end of peace.*[40] The temple which he built is his catholic Church, which he gathers into the one structure of his faith and charity from all the believers throughout the world, as it were from living stones.[41] That the temple was built in seven years[42] signifies that the building up of holy Church never stops increasing throughout the whole period of this age,

35. 1 M 1:11-58   36. 2 M 5:21-7:41   37. 2 M 8:1-10:6
38. 1 Co 10:6   39. Jer, *Nom.* (CC 72: 138, 5)   40. Is 9:7
41. 1 P 2:5; cf. the 6-7 cent. hymn, '*Urbs Jerusalem beata,*' formerly sung
    at Vespers of the Dedication of a Church
42. 1 K 5:38

which proceeds [through periods of] seven days. That it was dedicated in the eighth year, and that this most renowned solemnity was handed down by King Solomon to all the children of Israel at the time of the completion of its dedication, mystically implies that when the number of the elect is completed at the end of the world, a festivity of long-desired immortality will follow; and that once the miracle of universal resurrection has been accomplished, all who belong to the kingdom of the peaceful King[43] (the true Solomon) will enter at once with him into the eternal joys of the heavenly fatherland. Now, since our Lord willed to be raised from death on the eighth day, that is, [on the day] after the seventh day of the week [Saturday], the number eight also symbolizes the coming festival of our own resurrection. That the temple was rebuilt by the mercy of God after it had been burned by [Israel's] enemies, and that it was cleansed again with the help of benevolence from on high after it had been polluted with idols suggests the various events which happen to holy Church: at one time she is overwhelmed by the persecution of unbelievers; at another she is freed from persecutions and serves her Lord peacefully; at another she is endangered in certain of her members by the snares of the ancient enemy; at another because of the meticulous concern of her faithful teachers, she recovers those whom for a while she seemed to have lost, chastised by repentance. That the temple was built for a second time during a period of forty-six years looks especially for its significance to our Lord's body, which he took from the Virgin. Of it he said to the Jews, 'Destroy this temple, and within three days I will raise it up'.[44] On the third day he restored to life his own body which had been destroyed during his passion. It is claimed that the body of a human being is articulated into its separate members on the forty-sixth day after the start of its conception,[45] and so it did not happen by chance, but was divinely arranged, that the temple was built during the same number of years as the days required for the Lord's body, which was prefigured by the

43. 1 Ch 22:9   44. Jn 2:19
45. Bede, *Hom.* II.1 (*CC* 122: 189, 190/94)

temple, to be developed in the Virgin's womb. That the temple's dedication was appointed to be celebrated yearly prompts us always to keep in mind the memory of our Lord's resurrection, which we believe has already taken place, and of our own, which we hope will occur, and to conduct ourselves in such a way that we may merit to rise not to judgment but to life, as our Lord promised to those who have done good.[46]

Nor should we pass over without comment the fact that during the dedication of the temple, when Solomon had finished praying, fire came down from heaven and consumed the burnt offerings and the sacrificial victims.[47] Now we are the burnt offerings and victims of the true Solomon; all his elect are the burnt offerings and victims of the most high King, of whom the apostle Peter says, *Christ died once for our sins, the just for the unjust, so that he might offer us to God, having been put to death in the flesh but made alive in the spirit.*[48] The heavenly fire is the flame of extraordinary love, with which the citizens of the heavenly fatherland rejoice always to burn as they behold one another's happiness and their Maker's glory. Thus it is that a certain choir of the heavenly powers, which from their unique nearness to their Maker burn with immeasurable love, are called by the special name 'Seraphim,' that is, 'burning,' or 'on fire'.[49] When the dedication of the temple was completed, fire came down from heaven and consumed the sacrificial offerings made to the Lord. When the time of our resurrection comes, and faithful servants have entered into the joy of their Lord,[50] the flame of true love with which the angelic powers now burn will engulf their minds also, as they behold the vision of their Redeemer. We cannot doubt that most of the elect are even now fully engulfed by this flame of love in that city on high, but undoubtedly this will be more perfectly fulfilled at the time when they have recovered their immortal bodies, and have received into the same happiness all their fellow servants and brothers whom they have seen still

46. Jn 5:29   47. 2 Ch 7:1   48. 1 P 3:18
49. Jer, *Nom.* (CC 72: 121, 24 - 122, 25)
50. Mt 25:21

struggling on earth. They will have nothing further toward which to cast the eyes of their thoughts outwardly, even a little, since they have God with them inwardly. They rejoice at having an undying vision of him, and rejoice with their neighbors' everlasting felicity. Then will be brought to full perfection that first and greatest commandment of the Lord, to the fulfillment of which all the just in this life are bound with all their strength, *'You shall love the Lord your God with all your heart and with all your soul and with all your mind; and you shall love your neighbor as yourself'.*[51] The more closely they discern the presence of the Lord's countenance, the more ardently do they give themselves totally to love of him; the more they recognize that all their neighbors are among the elect of God and loved by him, and realize that their neighbors' hearts are overflowing with sincere love no less than their own, the more they take delight in the fact that these love him no less than they themselves do.

But we should note this too: having explained the dedication and subsequent festival, scripture concludes: *And Solomon dismissed the people, who blessed the king* [and] *set out for their own dwellings joyfully and glad of heart for all the goodness the Lord had done for David his servant and for his people Israel.*[52] When he has brought to completion the gift of resurrection, our Lord dismisses his elect joyfully to their eternal dwelling places. Surely he does not move them farther away from his presence, but lets them pass into the dwelling place of the heavenly fatherland after the division at the [final] judgment (which, according to the saying of the Apostle, we know will take place in the air[53]), so that each may receive his promised seat in the kingdom in proportion to his deserts. What is said here, that the people set out for their own dwellings, [refers to] the setting-out of which our Lord speaks in the gospel, *'In my Father's house are many mansions'.*[54]

And it is well said that [the people] set out for their own dwellings while blessing the king, because this is the single supremely tranquil and joyful action of the heavenly

51. Mt 22:37, 39   52. 1 K 8:66   53. 1 Th 4:17
54. Jn 14:2

citizens, singing hymns of thanksgiving to their Maker. Thus is it written: *Happy are they who dwell in your house; they will praise you forever.*[55] Thus the same prophet [David] has filled the final seven psalms[56] with the sweetness of the divine praises; moreover in the eighth psalm before the end of the psalter,[57] he commemorates by blessing the Lord his victory in the fight in which he slew the giant [Goliath]. In this he clearly indicates that all who triumph in their contests against the malignant enemy here below will sing the praises of their Maker and Helper there, where they will have true rest.

They blessed the king [and] *set out for their own dwellings joyfully and glad of heart for all the goodness the Lord had done for David his servant and for his people Israel.* The just do indeed go into the dwellings of the heavenly mansions joyfully because of the goodness they have received from the Lord. Although the labors of this age are burdensome and prolonged, whatever ends in eternal blessedness seems short-lived and trifling. Hence each one of us, dearly-beloved, must press on with his devout actions by exerting himself to the extent of his ability by encouraging, entreating [and] rebuking[58] in the building up of the house of God, lest, if the heavenly King catches sight of anyone slothful now in the work [of building] his temple, he may make him an outcast from his great solemn celebration at the time of the dedication. Let us busy ourselves with the mutual help of charity, so that finding all of us with cheerful hearts and tireless in [the performance of] the good works which he has commanded us [to do], Jesus Christ our Lord may bring us all to the reward of the perpetual vision [of him] which he has promised, for he lives and reigns with the Father in the unity of the Holy Spirit, God throughout all ages of ages. Amen.

55. Ps 84:4 (83:5)
57. Ps 144 (143)
56. Ps 145-147:11, 147:12-150 (144-150)
58. 2 Tm 4:2

NOTES

1. The dedication stone for the monastery church of St Paul at Jarrow still exists, embedded over the chancel-arch of the building which now serves as a parish church for the area of Jarrow, across the river, to the south-east of Newcastle-upon-Tyne in northeastern England. It indicates that the church was dedicated on 23 April, 685, when Bede was a boy of twelve. The anniversary of this dedication would have been celebrated each year on this date.
2. This part of Pr 4:27 is omitted in many of the manuscripts of the Latin Vulgate. It is, however, found in the *Codex Amiatinus,* a copy of the Vulgate written at the monasteries of Wearmouth/Jarrow in northeastern England during the seventh/eighth centuries, and preserved now in the Laurentian Library at Florence.

homily II.25

Luke 6:43–48   *Dedication of a Church*

Since by divine beneficence we are celebrating the solemn feast of the dedication of the church, dearly beloved brothers, we ought to be in accord with the solemnity of the feast which we are celebrating. Just as we traditionally spend the night vigil joyfully singing additional psalms and [hearing] a larger number of lessons, in a church where many lights are burning and the walls are adorned more lavishly than usual, so should we always embellish the innermost recesses[1] of our hearts with the indispensable adornments of good works; the flame of divine as well as of fraternal charity should always increase within us; remembrance of the heavenly commands and the holy sweetness of evangelical praise should always resound in the sanctuary of our breast. These are the fruits of the good tree, these are the treasures of the good heart, these are the foundations of the good architect which today's reading from the holy gospel commends to us—not only the outward appearance of piety, but rather its power.

The mystical [meaning of the] history of the Old Covenant also earnestly suggests this, both when Moses fash-

---

1. *penetralia*

ioned the tabernacle for the Lord, and when Solomon fashioned the temple as a type of holy Church. Both structures
are reported to have had firm foundations—the tabernacle
because it had walls [made of] wooden frames set upon silver supports,[2] the temple because it was built upon a foundation of squared stones.[3] The wood, from which the entire
tabernacle was constructed, and with which the temple,
adorned within and covered above, gleamed, was imperish-
able.[4] The finest gold was brought from a large store, and
the walls of the tabernacle were covered within and without; not only the walls, but also the ceiling panels, rafters,
door posts and the floor of the temple were gilded. The vessels and utensils of both dwellings were almost all made
of gold, and only the purest gold was permitted in making
them.[5] It was commanded that the fruit of the trees to be
offered in the house of the Lord be most pure and choice,
that is, [the fruit] of the vine, the olive, incense, myrrh and
cinnamon, and others of this sort.[6]

If we understand all these things spiritually, they denote
true sincerity in our faith and works. Each of these dwellings, as I have said, show us beforehand an image of the
universal Church. No one should think it incongruous that
two dwellings of the Lord were constructed as symbols,[7]
when no one would dispute that the Church is the one
dwelling of Christ. Two dwellings were fashioned to signify the two peoples who were to come together in the same
faith, the Jews and the gentiles. Hence it was well [done]
that the Hebrew people alone fashioned the tabernacle in
the desert, but the proselytes, that is, newcomers from the
[pagan] nations, as many as could then be found among
the people of Israel, completed the structure of the temple
with devout faith. The powerful King of Tyre was contracted
by Solomon, and he helped him by gladly lending him
workmen and wood,[8] for before our Lord's incarnation God
was known only in Judaea.[9] But afterwards, in the flesh in

---

2. Ex 26:15-19   3. 1 K 5:17   4. 1 K 5:8; 6:14-15
5. Ex 26:29, 37; 30:3-5; 2 Ch 4:7-22; Joseph., *Ant. Iud.* 8, 3, 2
6. Ex 30:23-24, 34   7. *in mysterio*   8. 1 K 5:1-10
9. Ps 76: 1 (75:2)

which he was born and suffered, was raised from the dead and exalted as God above the heavens,[10] immediately he shone forth over the whole earth by the glory of his name, and the entire world joyfully hastened to the building up of his dwelling, having received from him the promise of heavenly gifts.

Let us hear, then, what our Maker and Redeemer himself said, in the reading which was just now recited to us, concerning the construction of his dwelling—which we are: *'No good tree bears bad fruit, nor does a bad tree bear good fruit'.* The wise king is seeking good trees and their good fruit in the construction and ministry of his temple. In truth he is the same one who teaches elsewhere what the end of a bad tree is, saying, *'Every tree which does not bear fruit will be cut down and cast into the fire'.*[11] Now he is referring to human beings as trees, and to their works as the fruit. Do you want to know which are the bad trees, and what are the bad fruits? The Apostle teaches us this, saying, *The works of the flesh are manifest: they are fornication, impurity, self-indulgence, idolatry, sorcery, rancor, strife, jealousy, anger, quarrels, dissensions, factions, envy, murder, drunkenness, carousing, and things of this sort.*[12] Do you want to hear whether trees which bring forth fruits such as these belong in the heavenly temple of the eternal King? The Apostle continues, saying, *I warn you, as I warned you before, that those who do such things will not attain the kingdom of God.*[13] He subsequently lists the fruits of a good tree when he says, *The fruit, however, of the Spirit is charity, joy, peace, patience, goodness, kindness, faith, gentleness, self-control.*[14] Concerning these [fruits], counseling us in another place he says, *Walk as children of light: the fruit of light is in all goodness and justice and truth.*[15] These fruits, together with the trees from which they come, truly pertain both to the dwelling-place of faith here below and to the abode of blessedness on high there [in heaven].

Let us listen to a good tree rejoicing in its increase in good fruit: *But I, like a fruitful olive-tree in the house of God, have trusted in the mercy of my God forever and unto all ages.*[16] The

---

10. Ps 57:5 (56:6) 11. Mt 3:10 12. Ga 5:19-21
13. *Ibid.* 14. Ga 5:22-23 15. Eph 5:8-9
16. Ps 52:8 (51:10)

fruit of the olive-tree is the light-producing work of mercy, and therefore one who now in God's present house shines with the grace of mercy rightfully trusts in God's mercy in the temple of eternity. Rightfully is such a one assured that he belongs in the temple of the great King, saying elsewhere, *And his mercy shall follow me all the days of my life, so that I may dwell in the house of the Lord forever.*[17]

But let us see what kind of fruits a bad tree produces, and let us avoid bearing such fruits. The prophet Jeremiah says, *Cursed is the one who puts his trust in human beings, and makes his flesh his support, and whose heart turns away from the Lord; such a person will be like a tamarisk in the desert.*[18] The tamarisk is an unfruitful and low-growing tree, very bitter to the taste, and in a word utterly unworthy of human cultivation; therefore it grows in the desert.[19] A person who turns away from fear and love of God, who hopes for a kingdom and riches from human beings, is rightly compared to this kind of tree. How far we must judge a person like this to be exiled from the beauty of God's house the prophet tells us as he continues, *And he shall not see any good when he comes, but shall dwell in a dry place in the desert, in a salt and uninhabitable land.*[20] Therefore, my brothers, let no one secretly living in a bad way flatter himself because of his reputation among ordinary people as if he were good. Although he may yield beautiful leaves, his words, or sweet-smelling blossoms, his fame, *no good tree bears bad fruit.* Let no one who does the good of which he is capable with an upright heart despair of his salvation, because *no bad tree bears good fruit.*

'Each tree is recognized by its own fruit'. We must take this recognition to refer only to the clearly-perceived vices or virtues that I have recorded above from the Apostle's statement. There are some actions of which [our] neighbors do not know with what intention[21] they are performed; hence they can be judged in either way [as being good or bad]. But all doubtful actions are more rightly judged as good by those who love what is good, that the Apostle's words may be fulfilled: *Do not pass judgment ahead of time.*[22]

17. Ps 23:6 (22:6)   18. Jr 17:5-6   19. Isid., *Etymol.* 17, 7, 49
20. Jr 17:6   21. *quo animo*   22. 1 Co 4:5

'For people do not pluck figs from thorn-bushes, nor do they gather grapes from a bramble-bush'. Thorns and brambles are bushes full of briers. They represent the hearts of those disfigured by the prickliness of self-indulgence, envy, concupiscence, and by the sharpness of irascibility, calumny, hatred, pride and bitterness—persons who are disagreeable toward their neighbors and as it were intractable. The fig signifies the sweet memory of the heavenly kingdom, and the grape the ardor of love of the Lord. Therefore, *'people do not pluck figs from thorn-bushes nor do they gather grapes from a bramble-bush,'* for all those who are still encumbered with the briers of the vices are unworthy to be examples or to administer the teaching of the virtues to their neighbors.

'The good man produces good from the good treasure in his heart, and the evil man produces evil from the evil [treasure]'. The treasure in one's heart is the intention of the thought, from which the Searcher of hearts[23] judges the outcome. Hence it quite frequently occurs that some persons perform good deeds of lesser importance with a resultant greater reward of heavenly grace: this is because of the intention in their heart to accomplish greater good if they could; others, though they display greater works of virtue, are allotted smaller rewards by the Lord on account of the indifference in their lukewarm hearts. The deed of the widow who contributed two copper coins to the temple was preferred to the large contributions of those who were rich by the one who weighs what is within peoples' hearts.[24]

'For it is out of the abundance of the heart that the mouth speaks'. Human judgment is often deceived, because a neighbor's heart is not able to weigh [what is done] except from what is said or carried out,[25] whereas the Lord ponders carefully both our works and our utterances from their root in the heart. The mouth speaks out of the abundance of the heart in the case of one who is not ignorant of the intention with which his words are uttered.

[Christ] subsequently adds force [to his pronouncement] by clearly showing that good speech without the additional

---

23. *internus arbiter*   24. Mk 12:42-44   25. *ex ore et opere*

attestation of deeds is of no advantage at all.[26] He asks, *'And why do you call me, "Lord, Lord," and not do what I say'*? To call the Lord seems to be the gift of a good treasure, the fruit of a good tree. For everyone who calls upon the name of the Lord will be saved.[27] But if anyone who calls upon the name of the Lord resists the Lord's commands by living perversely, it is evident that the good which the tongue has spoken has not been brought out of the good treasure in his heart; it was not the root of a fig-tree but that of a thorn-bush which produced the fruit of such a confession—a conscience, that is, bristling with vices, and not one filled with the sweetness of the love of the Lord.

But the Lord indicates what the true distinction between good and bad fruits is by continuing under another figure [of speech], *'Everyone who comes to me and listens to my words and does them, I will show you who he is like: he is like a man building a house'*. Now this man building a house is the *Mediator between God and men, the man Christ Jesus*,[28] who deigned to build and consecrate a beloved and holy house for himself, namely the Church, in which to remain forever.

'He dug deep, and laid the foundation upon rock,' for he strove to root out completely whatever base drives[29] he found in the hearts of his faithful, so that when the traces of earlier habits and unnecessary thoughts had been cast out, he could have a firm and unshakable dwelling place in them. He himself is the rock upon which he laid the foundation for a house of this sort. Just as in building a house nothing is to be preferred to the rock on which the foundation is laid, so holy Church has its rock, namely Christ, concealed in the depths of her heart. She puts nothing ahead of her faith and love of him, because he was not reluctant even to suffer death for her. Because the prince of the Church clung firmly to this rock, from it he received his name when he heard, *'For you are Peter, and I shall build my Church upon this rock'*.[30]

---

26. Jer., *In Matth.* 7, 21 (*CC* 77: 45, 982/83)
27. Jl 2:32; Ac 2:21; Rm 10:13   28. 1 Tm 2:5
29. *terrenae intentionis*   30. Mt 16:18 ('rock' = *petra*)

'When a flood came the stream was dashed against that house
and could not shake it, for it had been founded upon the rock'.
The explanation is obvious: the Church is often struck by
distressful situations, but is not overthrown. If any believers
are overcome by evils and yield, they surely did not belong
to this house. If they had taken a stand founded upon the
rock of faith instead of upon the sand of faithlessness and
inconstancy, they would have been absolutely incapable of
ever being shaken.

We should note that this flood of temptations assails the
Church in three ways: *one is tempted, drawn on and lured by
one's own concupiscence,*[31] or is worn down by the depravity
of false brothers, or is assaulted by the more open[32] snares
of those outside [the Church]. In another place the Lord
calls these temptations 'the gates of the lower world,' and
rightly so, for if victorious they drag us down to eternal destruction. He says, *'I shall build my Church upon this rock,
and the gates of the lower world shall not prevail against her'.*[33]
Although the gates of the devil strike against her, yet they
do not overthrow Christ's Church; although the flood of
faithlessness inundates her, it does not undermine the house
of faith. For she[34] is able to say truthfully to her helper, *When
my heart was disquieted, you raised me up upon a rock.*[35] She
is not vanquished by external forces because, by suffering
and acquiring the crown of martyrdom, she triumphs over
the ferocity of the unbelievers who persecute her. She is
not corrupted by false brothers because she refutes the dog-
mas of heretics by believing properly, and she avoids the
vicious example of some Catholics by living soberly and justly and piously.[36] She is not blinded by the smoke of private greed because she is inwardly aflame with the ardor
of the Lord's charity alone.

The elect, each in his own degree, are likened to this man
[who was the builder] (that is, to our Redeemer, who joined
the universal Church to himself with unconquerable

31. Jm 1:14   32. *apertioribus;* var.: 'more fitting' (*aptioribus*)
33. Mt 16:18
34. Both 'Church' and 'house' are of the feminine gender in Latin.
35. Ps 61:2 (60:3)   36. Tt 2:12

strength of mind) when they take special care to carry out
as individuals in their hearts what he does generally
throughout the whole Church. By digging deep, as it were,
they attentively examine their consciences lest anything
sordid lie lurking within them; they meticulously search out
from the depths of their hearts all the hiding places of use-
less thoughts; they draw these out by the labor of painstaking discernment, so that they may make ready within
themselves a firm and peaceful resting place for that strong-
est rock, that is, Christ. And it comes about that by his presence they hold out unconquerable amid the alarming
adversities, and at the same time the attractive prosperity,
of the age.

With the Lord's help I have completed an explanation of
the gospel reading, dearly beloved brothers. But it seems
to be in accord with the solemn celebration that we are observing to recall something about the building of the temple, and to search out how appropriately its adornment suits
the significance of the church. Scripture tells how Solomon
ordered that *they should take very great costly stones for the
foundation of the temple, and should square them off.*[37] These
great and costly stones that were laid as a foundation, and
that supported the entire bulk of the temple built upon
them, suggest the extraordinary teachers of holy Church:
'great' because of the outstanding quality of their merits;
'costly' because of the splendor of the signs which those
who heard the word from the Lord himself produced by
their preaching as the fabric of the growing Church.

When in the scriptures 'foundation' is used in the plural, it means either holy preachers[38] or the unshakable
thoughts of the just. Hence there is the [verse] of the psalmist, *Its foundations [are] on the holy mountains.*[39] When 'foundation' is used in the singular, it often indicates the Author
of all good things, [Christ], concerning whom the Apostle
says, *No one can lay any other foundation except that which has
already been laid, which is Christ Jesus;*[40] and again he says
to believers about it, *But you are fellow-citizens of the saints*

37. 1 K 5:17   38. var.: 'preachings of holy ones'
39. Ps 87:1 (86:1)   40. 1 Co 3:11

and members of the household of God, constructed upon the foundation of the apostles and prophets.[41] For this foundation there were laid great and costly stones to carry [the superstructure of] the entire temple. First of all the patriarchs and the prophets, and afterwards the apostles, were instructed by [Christ] in order to spread the Church throughout the whole world. The more closely they clung to their love for him, the more strongly did they support his followers in the building-up of the heavenly [temple]. The king commanded them to square these stones to signify that the teachers of the Church ought to be of settled character and unalterable mind. Just as what is squared will stand upright no matter how it is turned, so the life of those who are perfect, which has been carefully directed toward[42] the straight line of truth, cannot be overturned from its base by any pressure from temptations.

The temple was built of Parian marble, a white stone,[43] to represent the brilliance of chastity in the Church, concerning which the Lord says in the canticle of love, *Like a lily among thorns, so is my love among maidens.*[44] [The temple] was sixty cubits long, twenty cubits wide, and thirty cubits high.[45] [1]* The length of the temple designates the faith of holy Church, through which she bears with long-suffering patience in the midst of her good works the adversities brought against her by the wicked. The width designates the charity by which she expands inwardly through the essential working[46] of piety. The height designates the hope with which she awaits the rewards of the heavenly life, [which she will receive] as a result of the good deeds she performs through charity.

It was appropriate that the [temple's] length was sixty cubits, for the perfection of good works is wont to be designated by the number sixty. This is because the Lord completed the creation of the world in six days,[47] and because there are six ages of this world during which, by her pious

---

41. Eph 2:19-20
43. Joseph., *Ant. Iud.* 8, 3, 2
45. 1 K 6:2
47. Gn 2:1-2
42. 'toward' = *ad;* var. 'by' (*a*)
44. Sg 2:2
46. *uiscera*

actions, holy Church presses on toward eternal rest.[48] Its
width of twenty cubits was appropriate because the precept of charity, by which the Church is extended, even in
tribulation, is twofold, since anyone perfect is proven to love
his Maker with all his heart, all his soul, and all his strength,
and his neighbor as himself.[49] That its height was thirty
cubits is appropriate, because every hope of the elect prepares them as much as it can, by training and purifying
them, for the vision of the Holy Trinity. Therefore six,
related to the long-suffering patience of faith, three to the
eminence of hope, [and] two to the wide, all-inclusive scope
of love, indicate the three notable virtues that belong to the
full character of holy Church. That all these are multiplied
by ten, the perfect number, figuratively denotes the increase
of her perfection.

We should certainly note that the height of thirty cubits
did not extend to the top of the temple's roof, but only to
the ceiling panels; from there to the ceiling panels of the
middle upper room there rose another thirty cubits of
height; then, a third upper room, above this one, was sixty
cubits high. Thus the entire height of the house reached
one hundred and twenty cubits.[50] The first [part of the]
house rose thirty cubits in height because the Church of the
present age has dedicated all her attention to viewing the
beauty of the Holy Trinity. The middle [part of the] house
was likewise thirty cubits high because the souls of the perfect, freed from their bodies, are enjoying a direct vision
of the blessed and indivisible Trinity until the day of the
universal judgment. The highest [part of the] house was
twice thirty cubits high because when all the elect have been
raised from the dead they will rejoice in eternal immortality, both of spirit and body, in the contemplation of their
Maker, who is one God in three persons.

A dividing wall of cedar planks, twenty cubits high, was
built in the temple to separate the inner sanctuary, that is,
the Holy of Holies, from the forepart of the temple.[51] The

---

48. Bede, *Hom.* I.11 (*CC* 122: 77, 149 ff.); I.14 (*Ibid.*, 98, 103 ff.)
49. Mk 12:30-31   50. 2 Ch 3:4; Joseph., *Ant. Iud.* 8, 3, 2
51. 1 K 6:16

inner sanctuary was twenty cubits deep, twenty cubits wide, and twenty cubits high.[52] The [part of the temple] in front of the inner sanctuary was forty cubits long,[53] and in it were tables and the golden candelabrum, as well as the golden altar near the door of the inner sanctuary.[54] This was done so that when incense was offered upon it, the cloud of smoke might rise up and cover the inner sanctuary, where the Ark of the Covenant was,[55] *and above it the cherubim of glory overshadowing the mercyseat.*[56]

The first part of the house represents the character of the Church of the present time, the inner part the entrance into heavenly life. The table and the candelabrum were properly situated in the first part, because in the [present] life we need the light of the sacred scriptures and the refreshment of the heavenly sacraments, but in the future we shall have no need of such aids. According to the word of the psalmist, whoever appears there will be fully satisfied with justice when the glory of the Lord is made manifest.[57] In this life the hearts of the just, like the golden altar of incense, shine brightly by the purity of their holiness; they are covered with the fragrance of the spices of spiritual desires; they glow with the fire of continual love; and as if they were near the entrance to heaven, they send forth the sweet smoke of their prayer within the Holy of Holies on high, *where Christ is, seated at the right hand of God.*[58] The Ark of the Covenant, which was inside the veil,[59] and *in which there was a golden urn containing manna, and the staff of Aaron which had put forth leaves, and the tablets of the covenant,*[60] very suitably symbolizes the nature of [Christ's] humanity; the urn [containing] manna symbolizes the fullness of his divinity; the staff of Aaron symbolizes the indestructible power of his priesthood; [and] the tablets of the covenant symbolize that it is he who gave the law and will also give his blessing to those who fulfill the law.[61]

And it was fitting that the [part of the] temple in front of the inner sanctuary was forty cubits long, since while still

52. 1 K 6:20   53. 1 K 6:17   54. Ex 25:23-31; 30:1-6
55. Lv 16:13   56. Heb 9:5   57. Ps 17:15 (16:15)
58. Col 3:1   59. Ex 30:6   60. Heb 9:4
61. Ps 84:6-7 (83:8; but see Endnote 4 to Homily II.15)

in this life we must be chastened by fasting and self-restraint
so that we may be worthy to come to the full satisfaction
of inner sweetness. Now everyone who has wanted to understand properly [the meaning of] the forty-day fast of
Moses,[62] and Elijah,[63] and our Lord himself,[64] understands
that this number signifies voluntary penitence of the present life. It was appropriate that the inner sanctuary, in which
the Ark was overshadowed by the cherubim of glory, was
twenty feet deep and twenty feet wide and twenty feet high.
This number, as I have said, suggests that perfection of twofold love. Whatever is done for the Lord's sake in this life-
journey is brought to full perfection in the shelter of the
everlasting fatherland, where his magnificence is extolled
in the continual praise of blessed spirits, since there alone
exists the fullness of love.

There was also a porch in front of the temple, twenty cubits in
length to correspond with the width of the temple.[65] It had a door
opposite the door of the temple, and was ten cubits deep,
facing the east. This porch represents the people belonging to holy Church who preceded the time of our Lord's
incarnation, yet were not empty of faith in his incarnation.
This is [the meaning of] the door of the porch opposite the
door of the temple, facing the east—that the faith of the people in Christ before his coming was the same as that of those
who came after his arrival,[66] and that the hearts of all the
faithful are illumined by the same light of the grace of the
Orient.

Hence it is good that we are told that two bronze pillars
of excellent and marvelous work were set up in this porch,
and that capitals worked to resemble lilies were placed on
top of them.[67] The pillars stood in front of the door of the
temple because illustrious teachers, concerning whom the
Apostle says, *James and Cephas and John, who were reputed*
to be pillars,[68] preceded the coming of our Redeemer, to bear
testimony to the coming of the one who said, *'I am the door;*
if anyone enters through me, he will be saved'.[69] One of these

62. Ex 34:28   63. 1 K 19:8   64. Mt 4:2   65. 1 K 6:3
66. Bede, *Hom.* II.15 (*CC* 122: 280, 12/15)
67. 1 K 7:15-22   68. Ga 2:9   69. Jn 10:9

[pillars] stood at the right of the door and the other at the left, because they foretold to the people of Israel, then fervent with divine faith and charity, the future incarnation of their Redeemer; and proclaimed to the gentiles, still as it were facing north, numb with the cold of unbelief, that this [door] was to be opened to make way for the entry of the Redeemer. That the capitals of the pillars were made by a workman to resemble lilies signifies that the entire import of the preaching [of James, Cephas, and John] resounded with the clarity of everlasting happiness, and promised that his glory would be seen by their hearers. He who existed as God before the ages became a human being at the end of the ages, so that like the flower of the lily he might have a golden color within and be white on the outside. For what is [the significance of] the glow of gold surrounded by whiteness except the brilliance of divinity in a human being? He first revealed this human being as brilliant because of his virtues, and after his death he clothed him in the snowy white splendor of incorruptibility.

It has been pleasant, dearly beloved, for me to explain to this fraternal gathering, as part of the joy of our present festival, a few of the many details concerning the building of the temple. [I did this] so that the marvelous workmanship that went into the construction of the Lord's earthly house might delight you as you heard about it, and so that these details, spiritually understood, might arouse our minds to more ardent love of our heavenly dwelling place. Therefore, my brothers, let us love wholeheartedly the beauty of the eternal house[70] we have from God in the heavens,[71] and let us take care to think attentively about the place of the tabernacle of his glory and prompt one another [to do likewise]. Above all, let us ask one thing from him and let us seek this with unwearied intention—that we may be worthy to dwell in his house all the days of our life,[72] that is, [to be] blissful from everlasting life and light. He does not reject or scorn the prayer of the poor[73] when we entreat him for what he himself loves, but he graciously hearkens; and

70. Ps 26:8 (25:8)   71. 2 Co 5:1   72. Ps 27:4 (26:4)
73. Ps 22:24 (21:25)

he will grant us to see his good things in the land of the living,[74] Jesus Christ our Lord, who lives and reigns with the Father in the unity of the Holy Spirit, God throughout all ages of ages. Amen.

74. Ps 27:13 (26:13)

NOTE

1. The cubit is eighteen inches, in modern terms, or a foot and a half. Hence the temple at Jerusalem measured ninety feet in length, thirty feet in width, and it was forty-five feet high inside. A little further along (lines 264/70 in the Latin text), Bede says that above the central portion of what we would call the nave there was another section, also forty-five feet high, and above that a third section ninety feet high, so that the outside height of the temple was one hundred and eighty feet. This bit of information he picked up from Josephus' *Antiquities of the Jews* (8. 3. 2). 2 Ch 3:4 says that the porch in front of the temple rose to a height of one hundred and eighty feet, seemingly bearing out Josephus' statement.

inδex

Index of patristic and other ancient sources and parallels

index

Scriptural index

Psalm verses are cited according to the Hebrew enumeration.
The pericope for each homily is printed in bold face, and the page
number given is for the beginning of the homily.

CISTERCIAN PUBLICATIONS INC.
Kalamazoo, Michigan

TITLES LISTING

CISTERCIAN TEXTS

THE WORKS OF BERNARD OF CLAIRVAUX

Apologia to Abbot William
Five Books on Consideration: Advice to a
    Pope
Grace and Free Choice
Homilies in Praise of the Blessed Virgin
    Mary
The Life and Death of Saint Malachy the
    Irishman
Parables
Sermons on the Song of Songs I-IV
Steps of Humility and Pride

THE WORKS OF WILLIAM OF SAINT THIERRY

The Enigma of Faith
Exposition on the Epistle to the Romans
The Golden Epistle
The Mirror of Faith
The Nature and Dignity of Love

THE WORKS OF AELRED OF RIEVAULX

Dialogue on the Soul
The Mirror of Charity
Spiritual Friendship
Treatises I: On Jesus at the Age of Twelve,
    Rule for a Recluse, The Pastoral Prayer

THE WORKS OF JOHN OF FORD

Sermons on the Final Verses of the Song of
Songs I-VII

THE WORKS OF GILBERT OF HOYLAND

Sermons on the Songs of Songs I, II, III
Treatises, Sermons and Epistles

OTHER EARLY CISTERCIAN WRITERS

The Letters of Adam of Perseigne I
Baldwin of Ford: Spiritual Tractates
Guerric of Igny: Liturgical Sermons I-II
Idung of Prüfening: Cistercians and Cluniacs:
    The Case for Citeaux
Isaac of Stella: Sermons on the Christian Year
Serlo of Wilton & Serlo of Savigny
Stephen of Lexington: Letters from Ireland
Stephen of Sawley: Treatises

MONASTIC TEXTS

EASTERN CHRISTIAN TRADITION

Besa: The Life of Shenoute
Cyril of Scythopolis: Lives of the Monks of
Palestine
Dorotheos of Gaza: Discourses
Evagrius Ponticus: Praktikos and Chapters
    on Prayer
The Harlots of the Desert
Iosif Volotsky: Monastic Rule
The Lives of the Desert Fathers
Menas of Nikiou: Isaac of Alexandra & St
Macrobius
Pachomian Koinonia I-III
The Sayings of the Desert Fathers
Spiritual Direction in the Early Christian East
    (I. Hausherr)
The Syriac Fathers on Prayer and the Spiritual
Life

WESTERN CHRISTIAN TRADITION

Anselm of Canterbury: Letters I-[III]
Bede: Commentary on the even Catholic
Epistles
Bede: Commentary on Acts
Bede: Gospel Homilies
Gregory the Great: Forty Gospel Homilies
Guigo II the Carthusian: Ladder of Monks
    and Twelve Meditations
Peter of Celle: Selected Works
The Letters of Armand-Jean de Rancé I-II
The Rule of the Master

CHRISTIAN SPIRITUALITY

Abba: Guides to Wholeness and Holiness
East and West
Athirst for God: Spiritual Desire in Bernard
    of Clairvaux's Sermons on the Song of Songs
    (M. Casey)
Cistercian Way (A. Louf)
Fathers Talking (A. Squire)
Friendship and Community (B. McGuire)
From Cloister to Classroom
Herald of Unity: The Life of Maria Gabrielle
    Sagheddu (M. Driscoll)
Life of St Mary Magdalene... (D. Mycoff)
Rancé and the Trappist Legacy (A.J.
Krailsheimer)
Roots of the Modern Christian Tradition
Russian Mystics (S. Bolshakoff)
Spirituality of Western Christendom
Spirituality of the Christian East
(T. Spidlék)

MONASTIC STUDIES

Community and Abbot in the Rule of St
Benedict I-II (Adalbert De Vogüé)
Consider Your Call: A Theology of the
Monastic Life (Daniel Rees et al.)
The Finances of the Cistercian Order in the
Fourteenth Century (Peter King)

Fountains Abbey and Its Benefactors
(Joan Wardrop)
The Hermit Monks of Grandmont
(Carole A. Hutchison)
In the Unity of the Holy Spirit
(Sighard Kleiner)
Monastic Practices (Charles Cummings)
The Occupation of Celtic Sites in Ireland by
the Canons Regular of St Augustine and the
Cistercians (Geraldine Carville)
The Rule of St Benedict: A Doctrinal and
Spiritual Commentary (Adalbert de Vogüé)
The Rule of St Benedict (Br. Pinocchio)
St Hugh of Lincoln (D. H. Farmer)
Serving God First (Sighard Kleiner)

CISTERCIAN STUDIES

A Second Look at Saint Bernard (Jean Leclercq)
Bernard of Clairvaux and the Cistercian
Spirit (Jean Leclercq)
Bernard of Clairvaux: Studies Presented to
Dom Jean Leclercq
Christ the Way: The Christology of Guerric
of Igny (John Morson)
Cistercian Sign Language
The Cistercian Spirit
The Cistercians in Denmark (Brian McGuire)
Eleventh-century Background of Citeaux
(Bede K. Lackner)
The Golden Chain: Theological Anthropology of
Isaac of Stella (Bernard McGinn)
Image and Likeness: The Augustinian
Spirituality of William of St Thierry   (David
N. Bell)
The Mystical Theology of St Bernard
(Étienne Gilson)
Nicholas Cotheret's Annals of Citeaux
(Louis J. Lekai)
William, Abbot of St Thierry
Women and St Bernard of Clairvaux
(Jean Leclercq)

MEDIEVAL RELIGIOUS WOMEN

Distant Echoes (Shank-Nichols)
Gertrud the Great of Helfta: Spiritual Exercises
(Gertrud J. Lewis-Jack Lewis)
Peace Weavers (Nichols-Shank)

STUDIES IN CISTERCIAN ART AND ARCHITECTURE
Meredith Parsons Lillich, editor

Studies I, II, III now available
Studies IV scheduled for 1991

THOMAS MERTON

The Climate of Monastic Prayer (T. Merton)
The Legacy of Thomas Merton (Patrick Hart)
The Message of Thomas Merton (Patrick Hart)
Solitude in the Writings of Thomas Merton
(Richard Cashen)
Thomas Merton Monk (Patrick Hart)
Thomas Merton Monk and Artist
(Victor Kramer)
Thomas Merton on St Bernard
Toward an Integrated Humanity
(M.Basil Pennington et al.)

CISTERCIAN LITURGICAL DOCUMENTS SERIES
Chrysogonus Waddell, ocso, editor

Cistercian Hymnal: Text & Commentary
(2 volumes)
Hymn Collection of the Abbey of the Paraclete
Molesme Summer-Season Breviary
(4 volumes)
Institutiones nostrae: The Paraclete Statutes
Old French Ordinary and Breviary of the
Abbey of the Paraclete: Text and
Commentary (5 volumes)

STUDIA PATRISTICA

Papers of the 1983 Oxford Patristics Conference
Edited by Elizabeth A. Livingstone

XVIII/1 Historica-Gnostica-Biblica
XVIII/2 Critica-Classica-Ascetica-Liturgica
XVIII/3 Second Century-Clement & Origen-
Cappodician Fathers
XVIII/4 available from Peeters, Leuven

TEXTS AND STUDIES
IN THE
MONASTIC TRADITION

North American customers may order these books
through booksellers or directly from the warehouse:

Cistercian Publications
St Joseph's Abbey
Spencer, Massachusetts 01562
(508) 885-7011

Editorial queries and advance book information
should be directed to the Editorial Offices:

Cistercian Publications
Institute of Cistercian Studies
Western Michigan University
Kalamazoo, Michigan 49008
(616) 387-5090

A complete catalogue of texts in translation and
studies on early, medieval, and modern monasticism
is available at no cost from Cistercian Publications.